QUALITY BOOKS OF INTEREST FROM ST. LUCIE PRESS

The 90-Day ISO 9000 Manual and Implementation Guide

Deming: The Way We Knew Him

The Executive Guide to Implementing Quality Systems

Focused Quality: Managing for Results

Improving Service Quality: Achieving High Performance in the Public and Private Sectors

Introduction to Modern Statistical Quality Control and Management

ISO 9000: Implementation Guide for Small to Mid-Sized Businesses

Organization Teams: Continuous Quality Improvement

Organization Teams: Facilitator's Guide

Principles of Total Quality

Quality Improvement Handbook: Team Guide to Tools and Techniques

The Textbook of Total Quality in Healthcare

Total Quality in Organizational Development

Total Quality in Higher Education

Total Quality in Managing Human Resources

Total Quality in Marketing

Total Quality in Purchasing and Supplier Management

Total Quality in Radiology: A Guide to Implementation

Total Quality in Research and Development

Total Quality Management for Custodial Operations

Total Quality Management: Text, Cases, and Readings, 2nd Edition

Total Quality Service: Principles, Practices, and Implementation

For more information about these titles
simply call, fax or write St. Lucie Press.

St. Lucie Press
100 E. Linton Blvd., Suite 403B
Delray Beach, FL 33483
TEL (407) 274-9906
FAX (407) 274-9927

INTRODUCTION

TO

Modern Statistical

Quality Control
and
Management

J.A. Swift, Ph. D., P.E., C.Q.E.

S^{t}L

St. Lucie Press
Delray Beach, Florida

Phone: (407) 274-9906
Fax: (407) 274-9927

S_L^t

Published by
St. Lucie Press
100 E. Linton Blvd., Suite 403B
Delray Beach, FL 33483

DEDICATION

Inspired by the lessons learned from
Le Petit Prince, by Antoine De Saint-Exupery,
I dedicate this book to "matters of most importance"
—my family

CONTENTS

PART III: QUALITY TOOLS AND METHODS

PART IV: OTHER QUALITY ISSUES

PART V: APPENDICES

PREFACE

This book is intended as an introduction to the most practical and commonly used statistical quality control and management techniques. The book is written so that it can be used as an educational and training text by those just beginning and as a reference source by experienced practitioners. Enough theory and statistical development are provided so that this book can easily be used as the primary text in a statistical quality control course. In addition, many case studies are provided so that the text can also be used in a quality management course. By covering both the statistical and managerial aspects of quality in one text, a more realistic and synergistic view of quality is provided. The current integration of engineering and management is also reflected.

The book is divided into four distinct parts. The first part is a basic introduction into the concepts, principles, and people commonly associated with quality management. Shewhart, Deming, Ishikawa, and Juran are discussed so that the reader can gain a real appreciation of the importance of their contributions and the impact they have had on the world. The second part concentrates on the three major quality awards. Details on the history and content of the three most common quality awards, as well as who to contact, are provided in one place for the first time. This allows for easier comparison and serves as a reference source when deciding or preparing to pursue one of the awards. The third part provides detailed, step-by-step instructions in the implementation and use of the more commonly used quality tools and methods. This section is considered the heart of the book. It is expected that this section will provide the user with valuable and practical assistance in choosing, implementing, and using the different quality tools and methods. The fourth section provides a discussion of some of the other quality techniques being used today. Most of these discussions also include case studies for added emphasis.

This book has been compiled based on years of teaching the various quality tools and methods to a wide variety of audiences in different parts of the world. The content of this book is the result of my experience in different situations and with a variety of audiences. In most of the audiences made up of industry practitioners, requests for more practical and usable information became a common occurrence. I was never able to find all the material the audience wanted in one text. Therefore, I collected the most commonly requested topics and developed the fundamental theories into simplified presentations and have provided them in this text. The information I have assembled has greatly enhanced their understanding and appreciation of the quality imperative. I hope you also find the collection of topics informative and useful.

ACKNOWLEDGMENTS

No book is written without assistance and a great deal of encouragement and support. I would first like to thank my husband, Fred, for making me write this book after five years of talking about it. I would also like to thank him for giving me the freedom and the time to get it done. In addition to taking care of the kids and the house, Fred found time to proofread and edit my manuscript and also write the chapter on benchmarking. I thank my children, Andrew and Samantha, for trying to understand why I had to work on weekends and for giving me lots of warm hugs when I got home late and tired and for giving me love and understanding when I needed it most.

The majority of the figures in this book were prepared by Rosie Herrera. Her expertise and the speed with which she prepared the figures are greatly appreciated. I would have never met my deadline if she had not been helping me.

I would like to thank Vincent Omachonu, a colleague and a friend, for providing encouragement in finishing the book and help in finding a publisher. I am also grateful to Bill Golomski, who took the time to review my manuscript. Bill gave me many useful suggestions which have been incorporated into the text.

Since little information on Dr. Ishikawa was available in English, I appreciate the assistance of Noriko Hosoyamada of FPL and Dr. Yoshio Kondo of Kyoto University in verifying what facts I had and supplying details I did not have.

The fourteen points listed in Chapter 2 were originally published in *Out of the Crisis* by W. Edwards Deming (published by MIT Center for Advanced Engineering Study, Cambridge, MA 02139. Copyright 1986 by W. Edwards Deming. Revised by W. Edwards Deming in 1993). They are reprinted by permission of MIT and the W. Edwards Deming Institute.

The chain reaction (Figure 2.3) and the flow diagram (Figure 2.4) were originally published in *Out of the Crisis* by W. Edwards Deming (published by MIT Center for Advanced Engineering Study, Cambridge, MA 02139. Copyright 1986 by W. Edwards Deming. Revised by W. Edwards Deming in 1990). They are reprinted by permission of MIT and the W. Edwards Deming Institute.

THE AUTHOR

J.A. Swift, Ph.D., P.E., C.Q.E., is a faculty member of the Department of Industrial Engineering at the University of Miami. She received a B.S. and M.S. degree in Mechanical Engineering from Memphis State University and a Ph.D. in Industrial Engineering from Oklahoma State University.

Dr. Swift is a registered professional engineer and has been an ASQC certified quality engineer since 1988.

Dr. Swift has taught, consulted, and conducted workshops in the area of quality control and management in the United States, Europe, Central America, and the Middle East.

PART I

QUALITY MANAGEMENT

1

TOTAL QUALITY MANAGEMENT: CONCEPTS AND PRINCIPLES

INTRODUCTION

There are many definitions of total quality management (TQM). One of the most comprehensive is given by Jack Strickland in the May–June 1989 issue of *Army Research, Development & Acquisition Bulletin:*

> TQM is both a philosophy and a set of guiding principles that represent the foundation of a continuously improving organization. TQM is the application of quantitative methods and human resources to improve the material and services supplied to an organization, all the processes within an organization, and the degree to which the needs of the customer are met, now and in the future.

This definition is an operative definition in that it includes what most perceive to be the five basic tenets of TQM: (1) quality is customer driven, (2) quality improvement efforts focus on preventing problems, (3) TQM focuses on process optimization, (4) management decisions are based on facts, and (5) TQM is a never-ending process of continuous improvement.

The first tenet, **quality is customer driven**, provides the fundamental building block of any TQM effort. From this, the working definition of "quality is conformance to the customer's valid requirements" evolved. Customer means both the external (or ultimate) customer and the internal (or intermediate) customer. The *external customer* is the party that pays money for the final product. Without an external customer, a company (whether manufacturing or service oriented) cannot survive. The *internal* *customer* is considered the next process or person with which the product comes into contact. The fundamental realization is that as a product is produced, it must pass through many workstations. Each workstation has an incoming standard which must be met by the previous workstation. If this standard is not met, then the current workstation cannot perform its job. Therefore, TQM requires that all employees be educated and trained in meeting their customers' requirements.

The second tenet is **quality and process improvement through problem prevention**. It has been found that it is much easier and less costly to design quality into a product than it is to change the product after production has started. This reduces rework and scrap in addition to reducing wasted labor. It is also easier to prevent problems than it is to try and handle them as they arise (in other words, fight fires). For example, if a particular product has a problem with delivery time, it is more effective in the long run to analyze the problem and implement a solution than it is to deal with each individual late delivery. It definitely takes more time initially, but the time ultimately saved (not to mention customer goodwill) more than justifies the initial cost.

The third tenet, **process optimization**, is a direct result of the first two concepts. If rework, scrap, and downtime are reduced by designing quality into the product and if all employees have been trained to think of the next process as their customer, then the first step toward process optimization has been taken. Ultimately, all process objectives, requirements, and capabilities will be examined. The processes can then be simplified and changes can be implemented. In order to ensure that the changes are effective, the processes are standardized and all employees are trained in the new procedures. As new products or changes are introduced, process procedures are reexamined and updated if necessary.

The fourth tenet is that management makes **decisions based on facts**. In the past, management by objectives was the accepted way of managing. Now, due to intense competition in the world market, decisions must be driven by facts which are supported by data. The organization can still have objectives, but these objectives evolve from examining what the organization can realistically achieve and then setting attainable goals. More importantly, management by fact means that not only managers but all employees manage the work they do by collecting objective data and making decisions based on this information. This creates an organization where everyone is "speaking with facts."

TQM is a never-ending process of **continuous improvement**, which is the fifth tenet. Basically, this means that just making one improvement does not mean that all issues are resolved forever. It means always striving for and seeking new ways of improving processes and people. This is best illustrated through the use of the Plan-Do-Check-Act (PDCA) cycle, which is the work philosophy behind the continuous improvement process. It separates the continuous improvement process into four distinct phases, within which there are specific goals and tasks:

Plan what to do
- Determine goals and priorities
- Determine process
- Determine tracking indicators

Do it
- Apply the plan
- Train and educate workers
- Monitor tracking indicators

Check it
- Check results of the implemented plan
- Identify any problems

Act on results
- Take action to eliminate any problems found
- Standardize process if plan is successful
- Plan future improvements

Repeated use of the cycle provides for continuous process improvement. The PDCA cycle as an integral part of the continuous improvement process is illustrated in Figure 1.1.

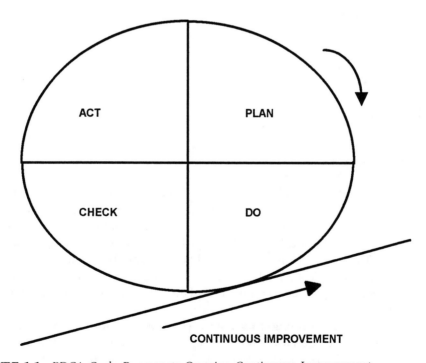

FIGURE 1.1   PDCA Cycle Represents Ongoing Continuous Improvement

An integral element of all five tenets is **respect for people**. The people are the employees, who are the key to making any TQM effort work. They know the process best and are the most capable of identifying process problems and making viable suggestions for process improvement.

Therefore, each employee needs to be listened to, supported, and encouraged by all others. By creating a supportive environment, an employee's capability for self-motivation and creative thought is enhanced. This enhanced capability is transferred to the work an employee does, thus enhancing the process.

TOOLS AND TECHNIQUES

The tools and techniques of TQM are a group of process-oriented management and technical methods which are used to accomplish specific tasks. These tools and techniques are the means for implementing TQM. They are used by everyone in the organization to identify problem areas, structure data collection efforts, analyze data, focus problem-solving efforts on areas of special concern, and disseminate information throughout the organization.

There are two primary sets of TQM tools and techniques. The first is the seven basic quality control tools. The second is the seven management and planning tools. The **seven basic quality control tools** are:

1. Check sheet

2. Pareto chart

3. Cause-and-effect diagram

4. Histogram

5. Scatter diagram

6. Graphs

7. Control charts

These tools are used primarily to collect and analyze numerical data. Therefore, they are taught at all levels within the organization. However, because first-line supervisors and line workers typically deal almost exclusively with numerical data, these tools end up being used by them the most. This does not imply that middle and upper-level managers do not use these tools. They do. It is just that these managers deal more with issues and ideas as opposed to numbers and therefore use the seven management tools more.

The **seven management and planning tools** are not new. The Japanese have been using them for years. In fact, they originated from post-World War II operations research work and are specifically geared toward planning, managing, and prioritizing processes. The seven management and planning tools are:

1. Affinity diagram

2. Interrelationship digraph

3. Tree diagram

4. Prioritization matrices

5. Matrix diagram

6. Process decision program chart

7. Activity network diagram

Other tools, such as experimental design, Taguchi methods, sampling plans, flag diagrams, quality function deployment, etc, have more specific uses. However, these special tools are typically taught on an as-needed basis. The seven basic quality control tools are taught to everyone in order to create a common language. The seven management tools are taught to all middle and upper-level managers.

TQM requires education and training for everyone. It is important to note that just giving employees one training course is not sufficient. In order for TQM to work, all employees must be trained and retrained (or refreshed) on a continuous basis. This ensures that all employees are working with the same knowledge base and are utilizing the tools effectively. When all employees have the same knowledge base, a common language evolves. When everyone speaks the common language, the goal of continuous improvement is attainable. This is one reason why quality experts say *"TQM begins and ends with training."*

IMPLEMENTATION

The hallmark of TQM is **continuous improvement**. In order to achieve continuous improvement, TQM employs a very structured and rigorous methodology. The first step is *top management orientation.* TQM demands long-term commitment, participation, and leadership. It requires that top management be aware of the need to change to a quality environment. It is easy to make top management aware of the need for change, but it is difficult to get top management commitment, because a change in commitment requires corporate behavioral changes (changes in allocation of resources, for example). This leads to the second step, *management and administrative structural changes.* This change is necessary to facilitate the flow of communication between and within levels of an organization. These first two steps are probably the most difficult to implement, but without them, TQM is doomed to failure.

The third step is *training for all employees at all levels.* Actually, training is done in conjunction with the structural changes, because training serves as the means by which the new philosophies and changes are introduced to the rest of the organization. This allows employees time to get acquainted with the new direction the company is taking and also provides a set of tools by which employees can participate in achieving the new goals. It also develops a common language for easier communication between departments, levels, groups, etc.

The fourth step is *initiating quality improvement actions,* which is a key step in ensuring success. Care must be taken in choosing the first quality improvement projects. They cannot be viewed by employees as trivial problems. They must be real problems that have a direct impact on either the employees or the overall company. In this way, employees see the benefit of using the new tools they have been taught and also see that management has a commitment to implementing TQM.

The fifth step is *system expansion.* Once the trial quality improvement projects have been successfully completed, projects throughout the organization can begin. This is where quality teams (or circles) are formed within different departments. These groups work on only those projects for which they have decision-making authority. If the problem to be addressed expands to several departments, then a team composed of members from all affected departments is formed. This increased communication between departments aids in finding a solution that satisfies all interested parties.

Implementation of these five steps is not easy, but there are several ways to facilitate successful implementation. First, a clear and specific mission statement must be established. This statement should address why the company is in business and where it would like to be in the near future. It should not be written in stone (as many mission statements have been in the past). The mission statement should be a living document that is ever-changing. Second, a transition steering committee should be formed. This committee must be made up of individuals who are respected and have the power and authority to make changes. Third, an implementation plan should be developed. This plan will expedite the transition from the former philosophy to the new one. It will also establish key measures of performance to ensure that the transition is staying on track. The implementation plan should also address the structural changes that must take place and establish a relative timetable for implementation. Finally, information on all TQM activities should regularly be dispersed throughout the organization in order to include everyone in the effort.

CONCLUSION

The Department of Defense has issued a one-page summary entitled "Total Quality Management (In a Nut Shell)" (undated). It states that TQM:

- Builds and sustains a culture committed to continuous improvement

- Focuses on satisfying service needs and expectations

- Requires dedication, commitment, and participation from all work levels

- Requires every individual to improve his/her own work processes
- Creates teamwork and constructive working relationships
- Recognizes people as the most important resources
- Achieves continuous improvement by focusing on the processes that create products

In short, TQM is not easy, but it is indeed necessary for the survival of a company.

EXERCISES

1.1 What is the working definition of quality?

1.2 What are the five basic tenets of TQM?

1.3 Discuss the importance of having a "common language."

1.4 List the seven basic quality control tools. Who typically uses these tools and why?

1.5 List the seven management and planning tools. What are they used for?

1.6 What is the hallmark of TQM?

1.7 What are the five basic steps to implementing TQM? What can be done to facilitate this implementation?

1.8 Do you agree or disagree that TQM is necessary for company survival? Justify your answer.

BIBLIOGRAPHY

Boudreaux, J.C., "Total Quality Management: A DoD Example," *Program Manager*. July–August 1988, p. 42(3).

Deming, W.E., *Out of the Crisis*. MIT Press, Cambridge, Mass., 1986.

Dockstader, S.L. and A. Houston, "A Summary from a Total Quality Management Process Improvement Model." NPRDC Tech. Rep. 89-3, Navy Personnel Research and Development Center, San Diego, 1988.

Landau, S.B., "Total Quality Management as an Organizational Change Effort: Implementation Requirements." In C.S. Greebler and J.G. Suarez (Eds.), *Total Quality Management Implementation: Selected Readings*. Navy Personnel Research and Development Center, San Diego, 1988, p. 1(10).

Strickland, Jack C., "TQM: Linking Together People and Processes for Mission Excellence," *Army Research, Development & Acquisition Bulletin*. May–June 1989, p. 9(4).

"Total Quality Management." Department of Defense, Washington, D.C. (undated).

"Total Quality Management (In a Nutshell)." Office of the Deputy Assistant Secretary for Total Quality Management, Department of Defense, Washington, D.C. (undated).

2 QUALITY INNOVATORS

INTRODUCTION

Before considering the various tools and techniques of quality, it is appropriate to introduce the men who paved the way for the quality movement in the United States, Japan, and the world. There are four quality innovators:

- Walter A. Shewhart

- W. Edwards Deming

- Kaoru Ishikawa

- Joseph M. Juran

Each man's life as well as what are considered to be his major contributions to the quality movement are briefly detailed in this chapter.

WALTER A. SHEWHART

His Life

Walter Andrew Shewhart, the son of Anton and Esta Shewhart, was born on March 18, 1891 in New Canton, Illinois. He grew up in Illinois and later attended the University of Illinois, where he received a B.A. degree in 1913 and a M.A. degree in 1914. Later that year, on August 14, 1914, Walter Shewhart married Edna Hart. He then went to study at the University of California as a Whiting Fellow where he received his Ph.D. in physics in

1917. From 1917 to 1918, he was the head of the Physics Department at Wisconsin Normal School in LaCrosse.

In 1918, Dr. Shewhart joined the Western Electric Company as an engineer in the Engineering Department. One of his initial work assignments was the development of a soundproof aviation helmet, for which he was awarded a patent in 1921. It was this work which involved a study of head sizes that sparked his interest in statistical methods. In 1925, the Engineering Department became Bell Telephone Laboratories. From 1925 to his retirement in 1956, Dr. Shewhart worked as a research engineer and statistician at Bell Labs. During his tenure at Bell Labs, he specialized in the application of statistics to engineering and in the theory and practice of the control of quality of products.

During this time, Dr. Shewhart's work was not confined to Bell Labs. He lectured on quality control and applied statistics at the Stevens Institute of Technology (1930), the University of London (1932), and the graduate school of the U.S. Department of Agriculture (1938). His lectures at the graduate school of the U.S. Department of Agriculture became the basis for his book entitled *Statistical Method from the Viewpoint of Quality Control* (published in 1939). From 1941 to 1948, Dr. Shewhart served as a member of the mathematics department advisory council at Princeton University.

In addition to lecturing, Dr. Shewhart served as a consultant on ammunition specifications for the War Department (1935–44), where he advised Captain Simon (later General Simon) on introducing quality control at Picatinny Arsenal. He was also consulting editor of the *Series in Probability and Mathematical Statistics* published by John Wiley & Sons (1943–65). He was a member of the National Research Council (1944–46), where he was made chairman of the Subcommittee on Engineering Applications of Statistics. From 1945 to 1954, he served on the joint committee of the National Research Council and the Social Science Research Council on the Measurement of Opinion, Attitudes and Consumer Wants. In 1947, he was a U.S. delegate to the World Statistical Congress. From 1947 to 1959, Dr. Shewhart visited India three times to confer with government and industry leaders and to deliver lectures on quality control. In 1952, he served as president of the Committee on Statistics in Industry and Technology for the International Statistical Institute.

His affiliations with professional societies were numerous ("Highlights in the Life of Walter A. Shewhart," 1967, p. 109). He was a member of the:

- American Mathematical Society
- Mathematical Association of America
- American Physical Society
- Psychometric Society
- American Society for Testing and Materials
- Association for Symbolic Logic
- Philosophy of Science Association

He was a Fellow of the:

- Institute of Mathematical Statistics (vice-president 1936, president 1937 and 1944)
- American Association for Advancement of Science (Council 1942–49)
- American Statistical Association (president 1945)
- Econometric Society
- International Statistical Institute
- New York Academy of Science

He was an Honorary Member of the:

- American Society for Quality Control
- Royal Statistical Society (England)
- Calcutta Statistical Association (India)

Dr. Shewhart received several distinguished honors and awards. In 1947, the American Society for Quality Control established the Shewhart Medal to recognize those individuals who have made "suitably outstanding contributions to the cause of quality control" ("The Shewhart Medal," 1967, p. 74). The first metal made was awarded to Dr. Shewhart in 1948. In 1954, the American Society of Mechanical Engineers awarded Dr. Shewhart its Holley Medal. The Holley Medal is given "for some great and unique act of genius of engineering nature that has accomplished a great and timely public benefit." The Holley Medal honored Dr. Shewhart as a "pioneer in the application of statistical methods to quality control in industrial stan-dardization, specification and inspection procedures, [who] enjoys the distinction of having almost single-handedly initiated and implemented this great contribution to scientific and engineering enterprise. He developed the statistical quality control chart and expanded the use of statistical methods in the inspection engineering and research departments" ("Holley Medal," 1955, p. 87). He was named Honorary Professor of Statistical Quality Control at Rutgers University (1954–56). In 1962, he received an Honorary Doctorate of Science from the Indian Statistical Institute in Calcutta.

On March 11, 1967, Dr. Walter A. Shewhart died in Mountain Lakes, New Jersey.

His Contributions

To list all of Dr. Shewhart's achievements and contributions would require several books. What follows is a list of what are considered to be the major achievements and contributions of Dr. Shewhart.

First and foremost is the **control chart**. On May 16, 1924, Dr. Shewhart sent a one-page memo to which the first control chart was attached (see Figure 2.1). In the memo, Dr. Shewhart stated that "the attached form of

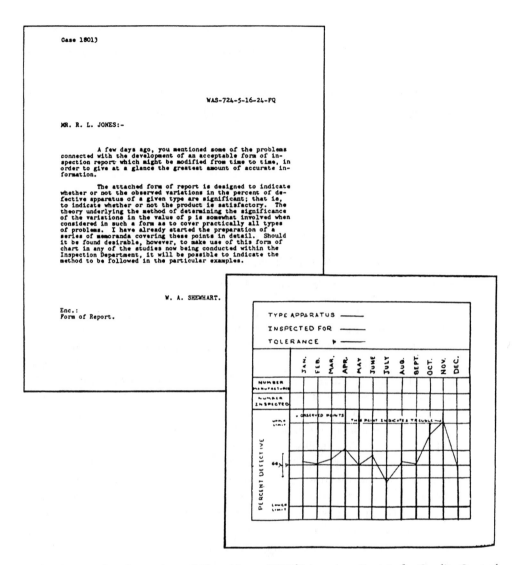

FIGURE 2.1 Shewhart's Control Chart Memo (©1967 American Society for Quality Control. Reprinted with permission.)

report [the control chart] is designed to indicated whether or not the observed variations in the percent of defective apparatus of a given type are significant; that is, to indicate whether or not the product is satisfactory" ("The First Shewhart Control Chart," 1967, p. 74). This first memo "set forth all of the essential principles and considerations which are involved in what we know today as process quality control" (Golomski, 1967, p. 83). It also provided the foundation of his first book, *Economic Control of Quality of Manufactured Product,* first published by D. Van Nostrand and Company in 1931. Many regard this book as a classic and as being influential in promoting the growth of statistics.

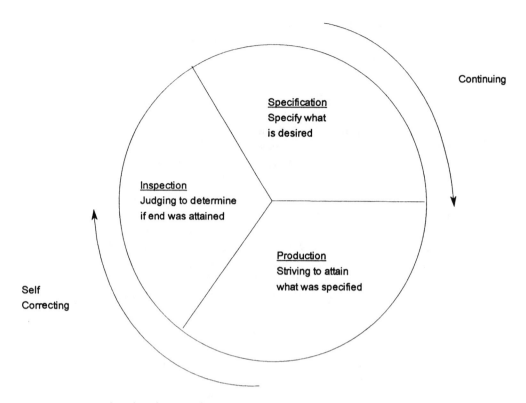

FIGURE 2.2 The Shewhart Cycle

A second major contribution was the concept of **assignable causes**. Dr. Shewhart discovered that there are two types of variation in manufacturing. The first type is chance cause variation, which is random in nature and cannot be controlled. The second type is assignable cause variation, which is variation that is controlled by some outside influence or special cause. Through the use of his control charts, Dr. Shewhart demonstrated that assignable cause variation could be identified and either eliminated from the process or controlled.

Another significant contribution was what is now commonly known as the **Plan-Do-Check-Act (PDCA) cycle**. The concept of this cycle came from lectures Dr. Shewhart gave at the graduate school of the U.S. Department of Agriculture which were later documented in his book *Statistical Methods from the Viewpoint of Quality Control*. This cycle is illustrated in Figure 2.2. Dr. Shewhart called this cycle "the act of control." The cycle is made up of three components. Component 1 is the act of specifying what end is desired. Component 2 is the act of striving to attain the end specified. Component 3 is the act of judging whether the end was attained. When applied to a manufacturing environment, the three components are easily recognized as specification, production, and inspection.

Dr. Shewhart felt that these three components corresponded to the three steps in a dynamic scientific process of acquiring knowledge:

Manufacturing	Scientific method
Specification	Hypothesis
Production	Experiment
Inspection	Test of hypothesis

By visualizing the "act of control" as scientific, Dr. Shewhart was able to introduce statistical hypothesis, statistical experimentation, and statistical tests of hypotheses into the scientific method, which led into the concept of statistical quality control. Thus, Dr. Shewhart was able to illustrate "that mass production plus statistical techniques when combined in the operation of statistical control provide a continuing, self-correcting process of making the most efficient use of raw materials and fabrication processes" (Shewhart, 1939, pp. 149–150). Dr. Shewhart further noted that "the adjectives continuing and self-correcting were also the essential characteristics of the scientific method" (Shewhart, 1939, p. 150).

Having edited Dr. Shewhart's book entitled *Statistical Method from the Viewpoint of Quality Control,* Dr. Deming was very familiar with Shewhart's cycle of control. Dr. Deming first presented this cycle in Japan in 1950 and referred to it as the Shewhart Cycle. However, upon its revision and use in Japan, it was called the Deming Cycle, which it is still known as today (Deming, 1986, p. 88).

A fourth major contribution is Dr. Shewhart's **definition of control**:

> For our present purpose a phenomenon will be said to be controlled when, through the use of past experience, we can predict, at least within limits, how the phenomenon may be expected to vary in the future. Here it is understood that prediction within limits means that we can state, at least approximately, the probability that the observed phenomenon will fall within the given limits. (Shewhart, 1931, p. 6)

From this definition, Dr. Shewhart put forth the concept of ± 3 sigma limits as the region of control in control charts.

Fifth is Dr. Shewhart's role in bringing **human factors** "into effective perspective in equipment and system design. In 1947, Dr. Shewhart was selected to head up the newly formed User Preference Department in the Research Division at Bell Telephone Laboratories. This department was charged with the responsibility of finding out whether more valid methods of determining and measuring human wants and needs could be developed as a guide in the choice of new service offerings" ("Tributes to Walter A. Shewhart," 1967, p. 116). In essence, Dr. Shewhart was the first to be interested in identifying and satisfying the customer's needs.

Sixth is the **Shewhart bowl**. Dr. Shewhart "simulated theoretical models by marking numbers on three different sets of metal-rimmed tags. Then he used an ordinary kitchen bowl—the Shewhart bowl—to hold each set of chips as different sized samples were drawn from his three different populations (normal, rectangular and right-triangular). He learned then that not only does the central limit theorem hold for large n, but even for n as small as four" ("Tributes to Walter A. Shewhart," 1967, p. 118). The Shewhart bowl experiment is still used today to demonstrate the concept of the central limit theorem.

Finally, Dr. Shewhart was the first person to successfully **integrate the disciplines of statistics, engineering, and economics**. This integration continues to have a profound impact on the way products are made, marketed, and studied.

For all of his achievements and contributions to the field of quality, Dr. Shewhart is generally regarded as the "founder of statistical quality control" and the "father of the control chart."

Special Note

To get an idea of the breadth of Dr. Shewhart's influence, read "Tributes to Walter A. Shewhart" published in the August 1967 issue of *Industrial Quality Control*. Upon reading the tributes, several impressions of the man emerge. First, Dr. Shewhart was quiet, gentle, unassuming, patient with everyone, and, above all, respected. Second, he was influenced by a book entitled *Mind and the World Order* by C.I. Lewis. He recommended this book to many of his colleagues.

W. EDWARDS DEMING

His Life

William Edwards Deming was born in Sioux City, Iowa on October 14, 1900. His family moved many times during his early life. In 1902, they moved to the Edwards farm near Polk City, Iowa. When free land became available in Wyoming, Deming's father acquired some, and the family moved to Cody, Wyoming in 1906. Later, more land opened up near Powell, Wyoming. The family secured a 40-acre homestead and moved there in 1908.

Deming's father, William Deming, earned money by doing free-lance legal work, selling insurance, and conducting various real estate deals. His mother, Pluma Irene Edwards Deming, had been educated in music in San Francisco and earned money and food by giving piano and voice lessons. (This is where Deming's love of music began.) Even Deming and his brother, Robert, and his sister, Elizabeth, took on odd jobs to earn extra money.

Deming's father was a believer in education and strongly encouraged all of his children to seek a good education. In 1917, W. Edwards Deming went to Laramie to begin his college education at the University of Wyoming. While at the university, he earned money doing odd jobs. When he wasn't studying or working, he sang in the choir and played in the band.

In 1921, Deming graduated with a bachelor of science degree in electrical engineering. He stayed at the university for another year to study mathematics and help teach engineering. During his stay at the university, he met Agnes Belle, a young schoolteacher. After a year's courtship, they were married on June 14, 1922.

He was then offered a job as a physics teacher at the Colorado School of Mines, where he worked for two years. While teaching there, Deming decided to get a master's degree in mathematics and physics at the University of Colorado in Boulder. He took courses there in the summers and correspondence courses during the school year. In 1924, Deming and his wife moved to Boulder so that he could finish work on his master's degree. After he had earned his master's degree at the end of 1924, Dr. Lester, a professor of physics at the University of Colorado, suggested that Deming go to Yale to work on his Ph.D. Dr. Lester wrote to Yale on Deming's behalf. In response, Yale offered Deming free tuition and a job as a part-time instructor at $1000 per year. From 1925 to 1927, Deming studied and taught at Yale. During the summers of 1925 and 1926, he worked for the Western Electric Company at the Hawthorne Works plant in Chicago,* where he learned of Walter A. Shewhart and the work he was doing.

In 1927, after finishing his studies,[†] Deming was offered the chance to continue his work at Western Electric Company. Instead, he chose to work for the U.S. Department of Agriculture in Washington, D.C., where he was assigned to the Fixed Nitrogen Research Laboratory. Dr. Charles Kunsman, deputy chief at the Fixed Nitrogen Laboratory, arranged the first meeting between Dr. Shewhart and Dr. Deming. The two met in the fall of 1927, and for several years thereafter, Dr. Deming made regular trips to New York to study with Dr. Shewhart. In 1930, shortly after adopting their daughter, Dorothy, Agnes died. In 1932, Deming married Lola Shupe, one of his research assistants. They had two daughters, Diana in 1934 and Linda in 1942.

In 1933, Deming was named head of the Department of Mathematics and Statistics of the Graduate School of the U.S. Department of Agriculture. In 1936, he took a year's leave of absence to study the theory of statistics with Sir Ronald A. Fisher[‡] at University College, the University of London. While at University College, Dr. Deming attended several guest lectures given by Dr. Jerzy Neyman. Dr. Neyman had been head of the Biometrics Laboratory of the Necki Institute in Warsaw, Poland. It was at one of these guest lectures that Dr. Deming heard Dr. Neyman read his paper "On the Two Different Aspects of the Representative Method: the Method of Stratified Sampling and the Method of Purposive Selection."

Upon returning home, Dr. Deming arranged for Dr. Neyman to be the

---

* The Hawthorne Works plant is where Harvard researcher Elton Mayo did his experiments on the relationship between working conditions and productivity.

[†] Deming was awarded his Ph.D. in physics in 1928.

[‡] Sir Ronald Fisher developed the Design of Experiments as a principal problem-solving technique.

principal speaker at the USDA Graduate School's conference on mathematical statistics in April of 1937. Dr. Deming went to great lengths to ensure that Dr. Neyman's lectures were well attended by U.S. government statisticians. Two things followed from this conference. First, Dr. Deming edited the book *Lectures and Conferences on Mathematical Studies,* which had a great impact on sampling theory in the years to come. Second, the participants quickly recognized that Dr. Neyman's approach could be used in many of the U.S. government's statistical programs. In fact, in November 1937, Dr. Neyman's method was tested during the Check Census of Unemployment. The success of this test changed the statistical practices of the U.S. government forever.

In 1938, Dr. Deming invited another guest speaker, Dr. Walter A. Shewhart. Dr. Deming arranged for Dr. Shewhart to deliver a series of four lectures entitled "Statistical Method from the Viewpoint of Quality Control." Again, Dr. Deming edited the lectures into book form. This book, along with Dr. Shewhart's first book, *Economic Control of Quality of Manufactured Product,* became the foundation of statistical quality control theory.

In 1939, the Bureau of the Census was working on plans for the 1940 population census. After the success of the 1937 Check Census of Unemployment, many in the bureau wanted to use sampling for the 1940 population census, but many others in the bureau were opposed. When the final decision in favor of using sampling was reached, the bureau needed an expert to help design the sampling procedure. At this time, Dr. Deming was hired as Head Mathematician and Advisor in Sampling.

In addition to helping design the sampling procedure for the 1940 census, Dr. Deming also began implementing statistical controls in non-industrial operations. The first implementation was on the clerical operations (coding and card-punching) of the 1940 population census. It was shown that during the learning period, the error rate for an individual punching cards was high. With training and experience, a good card puncher's error rate would drop significantly and could be brought under statistical control. This allowed for sample verification as opposed to 100% verification of cards punched (Mann, 1989, p. 8).

In 1942, while working at the bureau, Dr. Deming was also working as a consultant to the U.S. Secretary of War. At this time, he received a letter from W. Allen Wallis. Wallis* was on the statistics faculty at Stanford University and part of a group interested in contributing to the war effort. Wallis wrote to Dr. Deming for advice. Deming's response was to develop and teach a series of courses on statistical methods to engineers and other industrial workers involved in wartime production. In July 1942, the first course was given. By early 1943, intensive eight-day courses in statistical quality control were given at many universities throughout the country. Within two years, nearly 2000 men and women from almost 700 industrial concerns had attended the courses. Many of the students became part-time

---

* Wallis later became an undersecretary of state.

instructors for other courses which were attended by another 31,000 people. This program had a strong impact on the quality and volume of wartime production.

Whenever Dr. Deming taught during this time, he emphasized that people continue to work together and meet to exchange new ideas and methods. Out of the many people being trained and educated in quality control, some small groups followed Dr. Deming's advice and continued to meet. These small groups and the education program laid the groundwork for the establishment of the American Society for Quality Control in February 1946.*

In 1946, Dr. Deming left the Census Bureau and opened his office in Washington, D.C. as a consultant in statistical studies. At the same time, he joined the faculty of the Graduate School of Business Administration at New York University as a full professor. Before retiring from NYU in 1975, Dr. Deming regularly taught a course in survey sampling and one in quality control. Dr. Deming continued to teach at NYU as Professor Emeritus until his death.

In 1946, Dr. Deming made his first trip to Japan. He was working for the Economic and Scientific Section of the U.S. Department of War. His job was to assist the U.S. occupation forces in studying nutrition, agricultural production, housing, etc. This included working on the population census, the agriculture census, the monthly report on the labor force, and numerous other demographic studies. He stayed two months. In 1948, he returned to continue working on what he had done before, but this time for the Department of Defense. During his stay, he would buy food at the Army PX and take it back to his hotel. He would then arrange for a private dining room in the hotel and serve the food to his Japanese friends, many of whom were statisticians. During these meetings, Deming would talk to them about the future of their country and the important role that they as statisticians would play. On his many visits to Japan, he continued to hold these evening meetings.

In late 1949, Dr. Deming received a letter from Mr. Koyanagi (the founder of the Union of Japanese Scientists and Engineers [JUSE]), asking him to come to Japan and deliver a lecture course to Japanese research workers, plant managers, and engineers on quality control methods. In June 1950, under the auspices of the Supreme Commander of the Allied Powers, Deming went to Japan. His first lecture was in Tokyo, where 230 scholars and statisticians gathered to hear him. He repeated his lectures many times throughout Japan.

It was during these lectures that Deming realized that he was teaching the work force and not top management. He knew that if he did not educate top management, his efforts in Japan would be for naught (as he felt they had been in the United States). If top management was not educated, nothing would change. Therefore, he set out to talk to top

---

* Deming was a charter member.

management in Japan. Before long, he was introduced to Mr. Ichiro Ishikawa,* who had formed the Japanese association of top management known as the great *Kei-dan-ren*. Mr. Ishikawa was also president of JUSE.[†] Dr. Deming had three meetings with Mr. Ishikawa to discuss what Deming felt that top management in Japan needed to do. As a result of these meetings, Mr. Ishikawa invited 21 presidents of Japan's leading industries to listen to Dr. Deming. They all attended. Dr. Deming spoke to them about producing quality items for export. He emphasized working with vendors to improve incoming quality (which was a huge problem in Japan at the time). He specifically told them, "Don't just make it and try to sell it. Redesign it and then again bring the process under control. The cycle goes on and on continuously, with quality ever increasing" (Mann, 1989, p. 20). He also told them that "the consumer is the most important part of the production line" (Walton, 1986, p. 14). He held two more meetings with top manufactures. The first was in Tokyo with 50 manufacturers. The second was in Hakone with 45 more top industrialists. This ultimately led to Dr. Deming teaching and educating both engineers and management about the importance of quality and the use of statistical methods.

Six months later, Dr. Deming was back in Japan. Things had already started to improve. Several top managers showed Dr. Deming the things they had already accomplished. One pharmaceutical company had increased production of one product threefold without changes in the machinery. Another electric materials company had reduced rework on insulated wire by 10%.

In 1951, JUSE established the Deming Prize. The original funding for the prize came from the royalties on *Elementary Principles of the Statistical Control of Quality*. The book was assembled from the lecture notes Dr. Deming used in his 1950 lecture series. JUSE also established training courses similar to Dr. Deming's for the people of Japan. Between 1950 and 1960, nearly 20,000 workers, engineers, and managers were trained in basic statistical methods.

In 1960, Dr. Deming was decorated in the name of the Emperor[‡] of Japan with the Second Order of the Sacred Treasure.[§] The medal was pinned on Dr. Deming by Prime Minister Kishi. With the medal came a certificate signed by the Prime Minister which stated that "the Japanese people attribute the rebirth of Japanese industry, and their success in marketing their radios and parts, transistors, cameras, binoculars and sewing machines all over the world, to his work there" (Walton, 1986, pp. 15–16).

---

* Mr. Ichiro Ishikawa was the father of Dr. Kaoru Ishikawa.

[†] Dr. Deming did not know Mr. Ishikawa through JUSE because the office of president deals primarily with high-level external relations in government and industry. The managing director of JUSE, Mr. Koyanagi (who Deming knew well), was responsible for the operation of the organization.

[‡] Hirohito was Emperor of Japan in 1960.

[§] Deming was the first American to receive such an honor. Subsequently, Americans Joseph M. Juran and Larry Miles have received the same honor.

Back in the United States, Dr. Deming was still unknown. He continued to teach at NYU and did considerable consulting in the trucking industry. Not until 1980 did Dr. Deming become nationally prominent. On June 24, 1980, the NBC documentary "If Japan Can…Why Can't We?" aired. The documentary, produced by Clare Crawford-Mason, introduced the country to Dr. Deming and his work. The last part of the program was devoted to the work Dr. Deming was doing at Nashua Corporation in Nashua, New Hampshire. "Nashua President William E. Conway reported that the company was saving millions of dollars and substantially increasing productivity under Dr. Deming's guidance" (Walton, 1986, p.19). After the documentary aired, the demand for Dr. Deming's time became phenomenal. Dr. Deming had realized the mistake he had made during the wartime training classes by not including top management. Thus, he refused to work for any company that would not commit top management to the quality effort. He charged large fees for his time and efforts. (He donated a large portion of those fees to his local church and to medical charities.) He continued to consult and teach up until his death from cancer on December 20, 1993.

Dr. Deming received many awards and honors during his lifetime, including honorary doctorate degrees from fifteen universities. In 1950, the Union of Japanese Scientists and Engineers decided to name its annual quality award after him. In 1956, he was awarded the Shewhart Medal by the American Society for Quality Control (ASQC). In 1960, he received his most treasured award, the Second Order of the Sacred Treasure, for the improvement of quality and the Japanese economy through the statistical control of quality. In 1970, the ASQC made Dr. Deming an honorary member. In 1983, he was elected to the National Academy of Sciences. In 1986, he was enshrined in the Science and Technology Hall of Fame. In 1987, President Reagan awarded Dr. Deming the National Medal of Technology. In 1988, the National Academy of Sciences gave him the Distinguished Career in Science Award. In 1989, he received the Edison Award, and in 1991, Dr. Deming was inducted into the Automotive Hall of Fame.

He was a Fellow of the American Statistical Association, the Royal Statistical Society, and the Institute of Mathematical Statistics. He was an Honorary Life Member of the Union of Japanese Scientists and Engineers, the Japanese Statistical Association, the ASQC, the Biometric Society, the American Society for Testing and Materials, the Institute of Industrial Engineers, and the Deutsche Statistische Gesellschaft.

His Contributions

The contributions of Dr. Deming are too numerous to list completely here. What follows are what are generally considered to be his major contributions.

First and foremost are his **Fourteen Points to Quality**. They were originally presented in his book *Quality, Productivity, and Competitive Position*. This book was later revised into the bestseller *Out of the Crisis,* which he used in his many seminars. Recently, his Fourteen Points were expanded by Lloyd Dobyns and Clare Crawford-Mason.* Dr. Deming reviewed their expanded version. The expanded version and Dr. Deming's preface follow:

> The 14 points all have one aim: to make it possible for people to work with joy.
>
> *Deming*

1. Create constancy of purpose for the improvement of product and service, with the aim to become competitive, stay in business, and provide jobs.

2. Adopt the new philosophy of cooperation (win–win) in which everybody wins. Put it into practice and teach it to employees, customers, and suppliers.

3. Cease dependence on mass inspection to achieve quality. Improve the process and build quality into the product in the first place.

4. End the practice of awarding business on the basis of price tag alone. Instead, minimize total cost in the long run. Move toward a single supplier for any one item, on a long-term relationship of loyalty and trust.

5. Improve constantly and forever the system of production, service, planning or any activity. This will improve quality and productivity and thus constantly decrease costs.

6. Institute training for skills.

7. Adopt and institute leadership for the management of people recognizing their different abilities, capabilities, and aspirations. The aim of leadership should be to help people, machines, and gadgets do a better job. Leadership of management is in need of overhaul, as well as leadership of production workers.

8. Drive out fear and build trust so that everyone can work effectively.

9. Break down barriers between departments. Abolish competition and build a win–win system of cooperation within the organization. People in research, design, sales and production must work as a team to foresee problems of production and in use that might be encountered with the product or service.

10. Eliminate slogans, exhortations, and targets asking for zero defects or new levels of productivity. Such exhortations only create adversarial relationships, as the bulk of the causes of low quality and low productivity belong to the system and thus lie beyond the power of the work force.

---

* Dobyns was the narrator and Crawford-Mason was the producer of the NBC documentary "If Japan Can...Why Can't We?"

11. Eliminate numerical goals, numerical quotas, and management by objectives. Substitute leadership.

12. Remove barriers that rob people of joy in their work. This will mean abolishing the annual rating or merit system that ranks people and creates competition and conflict.

13. Institute a vigorous program of education and self-improvement.

14. Put everybody in the company to work to accomplish the transformation. The transformation is everybody's job. (Stratton, 1994, pp. 26–27)

Second is Dr. Deming's system of **Profound Knowledge**. Dr. Deming preached the need to have profound knowledge in order to effectively apply his Fourteen Points. His system of Profound Knowledge includes four categories:

1. Appreciation for a system

2. Theory of variation

3. Theory of knowledge

4. Psychology

The best explanation of Dr. Deming's system of Profound Knowledge can be found in Chapter 4 of his last book, *The New Economics for Industry, Government, Education.*

Third is his list of the **seven deadly diseases** that afflict most companies in the Western world (Deming, 1986, pp. 97–121):

1. Lack of constancy of purpose

2. Emphasis on short-term profits

3. Evaluation of performance, merit rating, or annual review

4. Mobility of management

5. Running a company on visible figures alone (counting money)

6. Excessive medical and health-care benefits costs

7. Excessive liability costs

A complete discussion of these seven deadly diseases can be found in Chapter 3 of his book *Out of the Crisis.*

Next is Dr. Deming's **chain reaction** and **flow diagram**, which are shown in Figures 2.3 and 2.4. Both figures were used at every meeting with top management in Japan from 1950 onward.

Sixth is the popularization of the **red bead experiment** which Dr. Deming used in his lectures and seminars. He used the experiment to demonstrate that "it is all too easy to blame workers for faults that belong to the system" (Deming, 1986, p. 346). The only way to improve a product

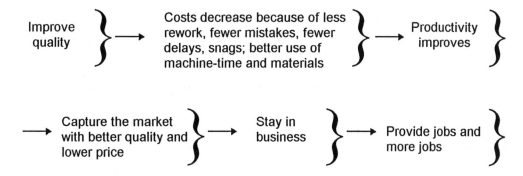

FIGURE 2.3 Deming's Chain Reaction

is for management to improve the system that creates that product. Dr. Deming discusses his red bead experiment in Chapter 3 of his book *Out of the Crisis*. An additional discussion can be found in Chapter 4 of Mary Walton's book, *The Deming Management Method*.

Seventh is Dr. Deming's **funnel experiment**.* Dr. Deming used the funnel experiment to demonstrate the need for understanding variation. Dr. Deming discusses this experiment in Chapter 11 of his book *Out of the Crisis*.

Eighth is the **Plan-Do-Check-Act (PDCA) cycle** of continuous improvement.† This cycle was adapted from Shewhart's "act of control" cycle. It has been used extensively in its present form.

His final contribution is Dr. Deming's belief in **respect for people**. He

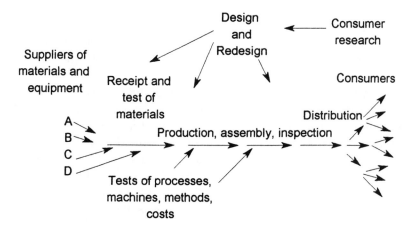

FIGURE 2.4 Deming's Flow Diagram

---

* Dr. Deming credits Dr. Lloyd S. Nelson for this experiment.
† This cycle was previously discussed in Chapter 1.

preached that management had to treat people as human beings, not as machines, and had to create the conditions in which people would be treated with respect and dignity. He believed in obtaining the willing contribution of workers to do things right the first time. In order to achieve this, management has to provide workers with the proper tools and training needed to do the job right.

Special Note

Dr. Deming loved music. He sang in his church choir until his travels kept him so busy that he could not attend rehearsals. He also studied the theory of music under Dr. James Dickinson, Mr. Russell Woollen, and others in Washington. By the time he died, Dr. Deming had composed two masses and several canticles and anthems.

KAORU ISHIKAWA

His Life

Kaoru Ishikawa, the son of Ichiro Ishikawa,* was born in 1915 in Tokyo, Japan. He was the eldest of eight sons. He studied applied chemistry at the Imperial University of Tokyo and graduated in 1939 with a bachelor's degree. Upon graduating, he joined the navy and served as a naval technical officer. He left the navy after serving for two years and joined the Nissan Liquid Fuel Company as a production engineer. During his time at Nissan, Ishikawa "obtained experience in the fields of design, construction, operations, and research" (Ishikawa, 1985, p. 2). In 1947, he left Nissan to return to the University of Tokyo as an assistant professor. When he began conducting experiments in the laboratory, he "was faced with the problem of widely scattered data, which made it impossible to reach correct conclusions" (Ishikawa, 1985, p.2). It was at this time that he began to study statistical methods.

In 1949, Ishikawa heard that JUSE had a variety of research materials on statistical methods. He requested to see them and was informed by Mr. Kenichi Koyanagi, the senior managing director of JUSE, that he could use the materials only if he joined the newly formed quality control research group and become an instructor. As Ishikawa said, "he was forced to join" (Ishikawa, 1985, p. 2). However, he soon became fascinated with statistical methods. He learned about Dr. Shewhart and his control charts and developed great respect for him. This was the start of his quest for knowledge of quality control.

In 1952, Ishikawa established a sampling study group for the mining

---

* Ichiro Ishikawa was the first president of the Federation of Economic Organization of Japan.

the Juran Trilogy can be found in his writings: "The Quality Trilogy—A Universal Approach to Managing for Quality," *Juran on Leadership for Quality—An Executive Handbook,* and *Juran's Quality Control Handbook.*

Another major contribution is his **spiral of progress in quality**, illustrated in Figure 2.6. The spiral illustrates a typical progression of activities and functions that are performed in getting a product on the market. A detailed discussion of the spiral can be found in *Juran's Quality Control Handbook.*

EXERCISES

2.1 Who is considered the founder of statistical quality control? Why?

2.2 Who was the first person to successfully integrate the disciplines of statistics, engineering, and economics?

2.3 What is Dr. Shewhart's foremost contribution to the quality movement?

2.4 While studying for his Ph.D., where did Deming get a summer job? Why is this important?

2.5 Where did the concept of the PDCA cycle originate?

2.6 How did Deming introduce sampling theory to U.S. government statisticians? Why is this important?

2.7 Where was the first non-industrial implementation of statistical controls performed? Who implemented it?

2.8 How did Dr. Deming's first trip to Japan come about? What did he do on this trip?

2.9 How did Dr. Deming's second trip to Japan come about? What did he do on this trip?

2.10 Who was Ichiro Ishikawa? How did he help Deming?

2.11 What do you consider to be Deming's major contribution to the quality movement? Why?

2.12 Who was instrumental in getting JUSE to open the Deming Prize to overseas companies?

2.13 Discuss the six categories of Ishikawa's quality transformation.

2.14 What is considered to be Dr. Ishikawa's most famous contribution?

2.15   Who is credited with forming the first quality circles?

2.16   Do you agree with Ishikawa's 14 areas of difference between Japan and the West? Discuss those with which you disagree.

2.17   How did Dr. Juran's first visit to Japan come about? What did he do there?

2.18   What is considered to be Juran's foremost contribution to the quality movement?

2.19   Do you think that Juran's "spiral of quality" is complete? If not, what additions would you make?

2.20   Research the Juran Trilogy. Do you think that the trilogy is universal? Support your answer.

2.21   Of the four quality innovators, which one do you think has contributed the most? Support your answer.

2.22   Which two of the quality innovators were most interested in the implementation of quality to improve "the human element"?

2.23   Review Dr. Deming's Fourteen Points. Which ones (if any) do you think cannot be implemented? Why?

2.24   What does Deming's red bead experiment demonstrate?

2.25   What does Deming's funnel experiment demonstrate?

BIBLIOGRAPHY

Bhote, Keki R., "Dr. W. Edwards Deming—A Prophet with Belated Honor in His Own Country," *National Productivity Review.* Spring 1994, p. 153.

Cunningham, Nina, "Deming and the Vindication of Knowledge in the Philosophy of C.I. Lewis," *Quality Management Journal.* April 1994, p. 7(9).

Deming, W. Edwards, "What Happened in Japan?" *Industrial Quality Control.* August 1967, p. 89(5).

Deming, W. Edwards, *Out of the Crisis.* Center for Advanced Engineering Study, Massachusetts Institute of Technology, Cambridge, Mass., 1986.

Deming, W. Edwards, *The New Economics for Industry, Government, Education.* Center for Advanced Engineering Study, Massachusetts Institute of Technology, Cambridge, Mass., 1993.

Dodge, Harold F., "Walter A. Shewhart," *Industrial Quality Control.* August 1967.

Golomski, William A., "Walter A. Shewhart—Man of Quality—His Work, Our Challenge," *Industrial Quality Control.* August 1967, p. 83(3).

"Highlights in the Life of Walter A. Shewhart," *Industrial Quality Control.* August 1967, p. 109(2).

"Holley Medal," *Mechanical Engineering*. January 1955, p. 87(2).

Ishikawa, Kaoru, "Quality Control Starts and Ends with Education," *Quality Progress*. August 1972, p. 18(1).

Ishikawa, Kaoru, *Guide to Quality Control*. Asian Productivity Organization, Hong Kong, 1982 (available in North America, the U.K., and Western Europe from Unipub, a division of Quality Resources).

Ishikawa, Kaoru, *What Is Total Quality Control? The Japanese Way*. Prentice-Hall, New York, 1985.

Ishikawa, Kaoru, "The Quality Control Audit," *Quality Progress*. January 1987, p. 39(3).

Ishikawa, Kaoru, "How to Apply Companywide Quality Control in Foreign Countries," *Quality Progress*. September 1989, p. 70(5).

"Joseph M. Juran Fact Sheet." Juran Institute, Wilton, Conn., 1994.

Juran, J.M., "Japanese and Western Quality—A Contrast," *Quality Progress*. December 1978, p. 10(8).

Juran, J.M., "The Quality Trilogy—A Universal Approach to Managing for Quality," *Quality Progress*. August 1986, p. 19(6).

Juran, J.M., *Juran on Planning for Quality*. The Free Press, New York, 1988.

Juran, J.M., "A Tale of the Twentieth Century," *Juran Report*. Autumn 1989a, p. 4(10).

Juran, J.M., *Juran on Leadership for Quality—An Executive Handbook*. The Free Press, New York, 1989b.

Juran, J.M., "The Century of Quality," *Manufacturing Engineering*. September 1994, p. 10(2).

Juran, J.M. and Frank M. Gryna (Eds.), *Juran's Quality Control Handbook*. 4th ed., McGraw-Hill, New York, 1988.

Karabatsos, Nancy A., "In Memoriam—Dr. Kaoru Ishikawa: Quality Organizer," *Quality Progress*. June 1989, p. 20(1).

Kilian, Cecelia S., *The World of W. Edwards Deming*. CEEPress Books, George Washington University, Washington, D.C., 1988.

Kondo, Yoshio, "Kaoru Ishikawa: What He Thought and Achieved, a Basis for Further Research," *Quality Management Journal*. July 1994, p. 86(6).

Mann, Nancy R., *The Key to Excellence: The Story of the Deming Philosophy*. Prestwick Books, Los Angeles, 1989.

Nelson, Lloyd S., "The Legacy of Walter A. Shewhart," *Quality Progress*. July 1979, p. 26(3).

Olmstead, Paul S., "Our Debt to Walter Shewhart," *Industrial Quality Control*. August 1967, p. 72(2).

"Recollections about Deming," *Quality Progress*. March 1994, p. 31(5).

"Recollections from Japan," *Quality Progress*. March 1994, p. 47(2).

Shewhart, Walter A., *Economic Control of Quality of Manufactured Product*. D. Van Nostrand, New York, 1931 (republished by ASQC Quality Press, Milwaukee, 1980).

Shewhart, Walter A., *Statistical Method From the Viewpoint of Quality Control*. Graduate School, Department of Agriculture, Washington, D.C., 1939 (republished by Dover Publications, New York, 1986).

Shewhart, Walter A., "Nature and Origin of Standards of Quality," *The Bell System Technical Journal*. January 1958, p. 1(22).

Stratton, Brad, "Gone But Never Forgotten," *Quality Progress*. March 1994, p. 25(4).

"The First Shewhart Control Chart," *Industrial Quality Control*. August 1967, p. 72(1).

"The Government Learns about Quality in Japan," *Quality Progress.* March 1994, p. 36(6).

"The Shewhart Medal," *Industrial Quality Control.* August 1967, p. 74(1).

"Tributes to Walter A. Shewhart," *Industrial Quality Control.* August 1967, p. 111(12).

"Walter A. Shewhart—Father of Statistical Quality Control," *Quality Progress.* January 1986, p. 50(2).

Walton, Mary, *The Deming Management Method.* Putnam, New York, 1986.

PART II

QUALITY AWARDS

3 MALCOLM BALDRIGE NATIONAL QUALITY AWARD

HISTORY

A 1982–83 White House study on productivity recommended that the U.S. government create a national quality award similar to the Deming Prize given in Japan. On August 20, 1987, President Reagan signed the Malcolm Baldrige National Quality Improvement Act (Public Law 100-107), which provided for the creation of the Malcolm Baldrige National Quality Award. The award was named in honor of Malcolm "Mac" Baldrige, the former Secretary of Commerce who died in a rodeo accident in July 1987. In his duties as Secretary of Commerce (1980–87), Mac Baldrige developed and carried out President Reagan's administrative trade policy. He concerned himself with problems of productivity and tried to decrease the U.S. trade deficit by increasing exports. More importantly, he actively promoted quality improvement in industry.

The award itself is made of two solid crystal prismatic forms which are held in a base of black anodized aluminum. It stands 14 inches high, and embedded in the center is an 18-karat gold-plated bronze medallion. The front of the medal bears the inscriptions "Malcolm Baldrige National Quality Award" and "The Quest for Excellence." The back of the medal bears the U.S. Presidential Seal.

OBJECTIVE AND CANDIDATE ELIGIBILITY

Objective

The purpose of the award is to promote quality awareness, recognize quality achievements of U.S. businesses, and publicize successful quality

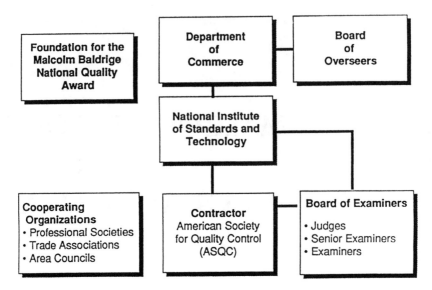

FIGURE 3.1   Malcolm Baldrige Award Organizational Structure (Source: Malcolm Baldrige National Quality Award Office.)

strategies. The award is managed by the National Institute of Standards and Technology (NIST) under the U.S. Department of Commerce. (The organizational structure of the Malcolm Baldrige National Quality Award is depicted in Figure 3.1.) NIST was chosen to manage the program based upon its "long history of helping industry to improve the quality of its products and processes" and its reputation for impartiality (Reimann, 1988, pp. 5–8). NIST is responsible for setting the award criteria and the application guidelines. It is also responsible for the selection and training of the award examiners. The examination process is administered by the Malcolm Baldrige National Quality Award Consortium formed by the American Society for Quality Control.

Candidate Eligibility

The award is only available to those businesses that are incorporated and located within the United States or its territories. All local, state, and national government organizations are ineligible for the award. Non-profit organizations, trade associations, and professional societies are also exempt from the award. The award is given in three different categories:

1. **Manufacturing:** Companies or subsidiaries that produce and sell manufactured products or manufacturing processes and those companies that produce agricultural, mining, or construction products.

2. **Service:** Companies or subsidiaries that sell services.

3. **Small businesses:** Complete businesses with not more than 500 full-time employees. Business activities may include manufacturing

and/or service (*Malcolm Baldrige National Quality Award, 1995 Award Criteria,* p. 47).

For those companies that are engaged in both service and manufacturing, classification is based on the larger percentage of sales.

Up to two awards per category are given each year. Fewer than two awards can be given in a category if it is felt the high standards of the award have not been met.

Candidate Restrictions

There are four basic restrictions to the award:

1. A company or its subsidiary is eligible only if the practices associated with all major business functions of the applicant are inspectable in the U.S. or its territories.

2. A subsidiary unit is not eligible if its parent company or other subsidiary of the parent company is the customer for more than one-half of its total products and services.

3. Individual units or groups of units or "chain" organizations (such as hotels, retail stores, or restaurants) where each unit performs a similar function, are not eligible. Similarly, a potential applicant is not eligible if the parent company or another unit of the parent company provides similar products or services for substantially the same customer base.

4. Company units performing any of the business support functions of the company are not eligible (*Malcolm Baldrige National Quality Award, 1995 Award Criteria,* pp. 47–48).

There are two multi-application restrictions:

1. A subsidiary and its parent company may not both apply for the award in the same year.

2. Only one subsidiary of a company may apply for an award in the same year in the same award category (*Malcolm Baldrige National Quality Award, 1995 Award Criteria,* p. 48).

Further restrictions include:

1. If a company receives an award, the company and all of its subsidiary units are ineligible to apply for an award for a period of five years.

2. If a subsidiary unit receives an award, it is ineligible to apply for an award for a period of five years.

3. If a subsidiary unit consisting of more than one-half of the total sales of a company receives an award, neither that company nor any of its other subsidiary units is eligible for another award for a period of five years (*Malcolm Baldrige National Quality Award, 1995 Award Criteria,* p. 48).

EXAMINATION PROCESS

Award Examination Criteria

The purpose of the criteria is "to serve as a working tool for managing performance, planning, training and assessment" (*Malcolm Baldrige National Quality Award, 1995 Award Criteria*, p. 2). The criteria are broken down into seven categories:

1. Leadership   90 points
This category examines "senior executives' personal leadership and involvement in creating and sustaining a customer focus, clear values and expectations, and a leadership system that promotes performance excellence. Also examined is how the quality values and expectations are integrated into the company's management system, including how the company addresses its public responsibilities and corporate citizenship" (*Malcolm Baldrige National Quality Award, 1995 Award Criteria*, p. 21).

2. Information and Analysis   75 points
This category examines "the management and effectiveness of the use of data and information to support customer-driven performance excellence and marketplace success" (*Malcolm Baldrige National Quality Award, 1995 Award Criteria*, p. 23).

3. Strategic Planning   55 points
This category examines "how the company sets strategic directions and how it determines key plan requirements. Also examined is how the plan requirements are translated into an effective performance management system" (*Malcolm Baldrige National Quality Award, 1995 Award Criteria*, p. 25).

4. Human Resource Development and Management   140 points
This category examines "how the work force is enabled to develop and utilize its full potential, aligned with the company's performance objectives. Also examined are the company's efforts to build and maintain an environment conducive to performance excellence, full participation, and personal and organizational growth" (*Malcolm Baldrige National Quality Award, 1995 Award Criteria*, p. 27).

5. Process Management   140 points
This category examines "the key aspects of process management, including customer-focused design, product and service delivery processes, support services and supply management involving all work units, including research and development. The category examines how key processes are assigned, effectively managed, and improved to achieve higher performance" (*Malcolm Baldrige National Quality Award, 1995 Award Criteria*, p. 30).

6. **Business Results** **250 points**

   This category examines "the company's performance and improvement in key business areas—product and service quality, productivity and operational effectiveness, supplier quality, and financial performance indicators linked to these areas. Also examined are performance levels relative to competitors" (*Malcolm Baldrige National Quality Award, 1995 Award Criteria,* p. 34).

7. **Customer Focus and Satisfaction** **250 points**

   This category examines "the company's systems for customer learning and for building and maintaining customer relationships. Also examined are levels and trends in key measures of business success—customer satisfaction and retention, market share, and satisfaction relative to competitors" (*Malcolm Baldrige National Quality Award, 1995 Award Criteria,* p. 36).

The specific examination items and their point values are listed in Table 3.1. The linkages between categories are illustrated in Figure 3.2.

Award Scoring System

The award scoring system is based on three factors: approach, deployment, and results. Each examination item is evaluated on some combination of these three factors. The approach factor refers to the methods the company uses to achieve the purposes of the examination item being reviewed. The deployment factor refers to the extent to which approaches are applied to all relevant areas and activities addressed and implied in the examination item being reviewed. The results factor refers to the outcomes and effects in achieving the purposes addressed and implied in the examination item being reviewed. The scoring guidelines using this three-dimensional framework are listed in Table 3.2.

Evaluation Process

All of the applicants are reviewed by the Board of Examiners. The Board of Examiners is a three-tiered structure with more than 270 members, of which 9 are judges and nearly 50 are senior examiners. These examiners are selected from industry, universities, and professional and trade organizations.

Each application is evaluated and scored by at least five members of the board. Those companies that score high on this first stage proceed to the second stage. Those companies that do not pass the first stage receive a feedback report highlighting the company's strengths and areas of improvement in its quality management system. The second stage is called the consensus review. Six to eight senior examiners now evaluate the application. The companies that score the highest are selected for site visits. Those not chosen for site visits are sent a feedback report. Each site visit

TABLE 3.1 Malcolm Baldrige National Quality Award

1995 examination categories/items	Point values
1.0 Leadership	**90**
1.1 Senior Executive Leadership	45
1.2 Leadership System and Organization	25
1.3 Public Responsibility and Corporate Citizenship	20
2.0 Information and Analysis	**75**
2.1 Management of Information and Data	20
2.2 Competitive Comparisons and Benchmarking	15
2.3 Analysis and Uses of Company-Level Data	40
3.0 Strategic Planning	**55**
3.1 Strategy Development	35
3.2 Strategy Deployment	20
4.0 Human Resource Development and Management	**140**
4.1 Human Resource Planning and Evaluation	20
4.2 High-Performance Work Systems	45
4.3 Employee Education, Training, and Development	50
4.4 Employee Well-Being and Satisfaction	25
5.0 Process Management	**140**
5.1 Design and Introduction of Products and Services	40
5.2 Process Management: Product and Service Production and Delivery	40
5.3 Process Management: Support Service	30
5.4 Management of Supplier Performance	30
6.0 Business Results	**250**
6.1 Product and Service Quality Results	75
6.2 Company Operational and Financial Results	130
6.3 Supplier Performance Results	45
7.0 Customer Focus and Satisfaction	**250**
7.1 Customer and Market Knowledge	30
7.2 Customer Relationship Management	30
7.3 Customer Satisfaction Determination	30
7.4 Customer Satisfaction Results	100
7.5 Customer Satisfaction Comparison	60
TOTAL POINTS	**1000**

Source: *Malcolm Baldrige National Quality Award, 1995 Award Criteria,* p. 20.

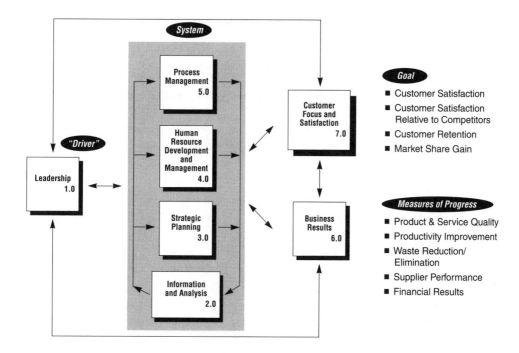

FIGURE 3.2 1994 Baldrige Award Criteria Framework: Dynamic Relationships (Source: *Malcolm Baldrige National Quality Award, 1995 Award Criteria,* p. 5.)

TABLE 3.2 1995 Scoring Guidelines for the Malcolm Baldrige National Quality Award

Score	Approach/deployment
0%	• No systematic approach evident; anecdotal information
10–30%	• Beginning of a systematic approach to the primary purposes of the item
	• Early stages of a transition from reacting to problems to a general improvement orientation
	• Major gaps exist in deployment that would inhibit progress in achieving the primary purposes of the item
40–60%	• A sound, systematic approach, responsive to the primary purposes of the item
	• A fact-based improvement process in place in key areas; more emphasis is placed on improvement than on reaction to problems
	• No major gaps in deployment, though some areas or work units may be in very early stages of deployment

TABLE 3.2   1995 Scoring Guidelines for the Malcolm Baldrige National Quality Award (continued)

Score	Approach/deployment
70–90%	• A sound, systematic approach, responsive to the overall purposes of the item • A fact-based improvement process is a key management tool; clear evidence of refinement and improved integration as a result of improvement cycles and analysis • Approach is well-deployed, with no major gaps; deployment may vary in some areas or work units
100%	• A sound, systematic approach, fully responsive to all the requirements of the item • A very strong, fact-based improvement process is a key management tool; strong refinement and integration—backed by excellent analysis • Approach is fully deployed without any significant weaknesses or gaps in any areas or work units

Score	Results
0%	• No results or poor results in areas reported
10–30%	• Early stages of developing trends; some improvements *and/or* early good performance levels in a few areas • Results not reported for many to most areas of importance to the applicant's key business requirements
40–60%	• Improvement trends *and/or* good performance levels reported for many to most areas of importance to the applicant's key business requirements • No pattern of adverse trends *and/or* poor performance levels in areas of importance to the applicant's key business requirements • Some trends *and/or* current performance levels—evaluated against relevant comparisons *and/or* benchmarks—show areas of strength *and/or* good to very good relative performance levels
70–90%	• Current performance is good to excellent in most areas of importance to the applicant's key business requirements • Most improvement trends *and/or* performance levels are sustained • Many to most trends *and/or* current performance levels—evaluated against relevant comparisons *and/or* benchmarks—show areas of leadership and very good relative performance levels
100%	• Current performance is excellent in most areas of importance to the applicant's key business requirements • Excellent improvement trends *and/or* sustained excellent performance levels in most areas • Strong evidence of industry and benchmark leadership demonstrated in many areas

Source: *Malcolm Baldrige National Quality Award, 1995 Award Criteria,* p. 41.

is performed by one senior examiner and five to eight examiners. For each site visited, a full evaluation is performed and a feedback report is written. (An effort is made to keep the same examiners for all stages.) A panel of judges reviews the site visit evaluations and recommends the winners. The winners of the award are then selected by the Secretary of Commerce. Throughout the entire evaluation process, heavy emphasis is given to quality achievement and quality improvement.

Award Process

The award process follows the general schedule given below.

January/February	Applications/guidelines available
March 3, 1995	Eligibility determination forms due
April 4, 1995	Award applications due
May–September	Application review/site visits
November	Award ceremony

Award Recipients

Manufacturing Category

1988   1. Motorola, Inc.

2. Westinghouse Electric Corporation
   Commercial Nuclear Fuel Division

1989   1. Milliken & Company

2. Xerox Corporation
   Business Products & Systems

1990   1. Cadillac Motor Car Company

2. IBM (Rochester, Minnesota)

1991   1. Solectron Corporation

2. Zytec Corporation

1992   1. AT&T Network Systems Group
   Transmission Systems Business Unit

2. Texas Instruments Incorporated
   Defense Systems & Electronics Group

1993   Eastman Chemical Company

1994   None

Service Category

1988   None

1989   None

1990   Federal Express Corporation

1991   None

1992   1. AT&T Universal Card Services

        2. Ritz-Carlton Hotel Company

1993   None

1994   1. AT&T Consumer Communications Services

        2. GTE Directories Corporation

Small Business Category

1988   Globe Metallurgical, Inc.

1989   None

1990   Wallace Company, Inc.

1991   Marlow Industries

1992   Granite Rock Company

1993   Ames Rubber Company

1994   Wainwright Industries, Inc.

USE OF THE CRITERIA

As previously stated, the purpose of the criteria is "to serve as a working tool for planning, training, assessment and other uses." The developers of the criteria intended that they be used for more than just judging companies. It is felt that the criteria can be used to provide a framework for a company's total quality management system. If such a system already exists, the award criteria can be used to modify the existing plan to address each of the seven criteria (assuming the company is interested in applying for the award). The criteria can be used for self-assessment and evaluation in order to provide actionable feedback and to measure progress over time. They can be used to identify improvement opportunities and where additional training or resources are needed. They can also aid in the communication of the level of quality of a division or the company.

HOW TO APPLY

Applications and guidelines can be obtained by contacting:

    Malcolm Baldrige National Quality Award
    NIST
    Rte. 270 and Quince Orchard Rd.
    Administration Bldg., Rm. A537
    Gaithersburg, MD 20899-0001
    Phone: (301) 975-2036
    Fax: (301) 948-3716

There is a fee associated with applying for the award. At the present time, a non-refundable eligibility determination fee of $50 is required for all potential applicants. The application fees for the different categories are as follows:

Manufacturing	$4000
Service	$4000
Small business	$1200
Supplemental section	$1500

These fees cover all expenses associated with distribution of applications, review of applications, and development of feedback reports.

EXERCISES

3.1 When was the Malcolm Baldrige award created, and what is the purpose of the award?

3.2 Who manages the award?

3.3 Who is not eligible to apply for the award?

3.4 What are the three different award categories, and how many awards per category can be given?

3.5 If a company or one of its subsidiaries wins the award, how long does it have to wait before it becomes eligible for another award?

3.6 List the seven examination criteria. Which criteria has the highest point value?

3.7 The award scoring system is based on what three factors?

3.8 Who selects the final award winner each year?

3.9 Do the award criteria have any usefulness beyond judging? If so, what else could they be used for?

BIBLIOGRAPHY

Band, William, "Use Baldrige Criteria as Guide to Improving Quality," *Marketing News*. October 1, 1990, p. 2(3).

Brown, Mark G., "The Baldrige Award: How Do You Win?" *Automation*. October 1991, p. 34(4).

Brown, Mark G., *Baldrige Award Winning Quality: How to Interpret the Malcolm Baldrige Award Criteria*. ASQC Quality Press, Milwaukee, 1992.

Crosby, Philip B. and Curt W. Reimann, "Criticism and Support for the Baldrige Award," *Quality Progress*. May 1991, p. 41(4).

DeCarlo, Neil J. and W. Kent Sterett, "History of the Malcolm Baldrige Quality Award," *Quality Progress*. March 1990, p. 21(7).

Drayton, Kevin G., "Are You Ready to Apply for the Award?" *Management Review*. November 1991, p. 40(4).

Garvin, David A., "How the Baldrige Award Really Works," *Harvard Business Review*. November/December 1991, p. 80(13).

Golomski, William A., "The American Quality Awards," talk presented at *Challenges in the 21st Century*. The International Congress and Exhibition on Quality '94, Singapore, August 25, 1994.

"Inside the Baldrige Award Guidelines" (seven-part series), published in *Quality Progress*:

Bemowski, Karen, "Introduction," June 1992, p. 24(1).

Sullivan, Rhonda L., "Category 1: Leadership," June 1992, p. 25(4).

Omdahl, Tracy, "Category 2: Information and Analysis," July 1992, p. 41(6).

Marquardt, Ingeborg A., "Category 3: Strategic Quality Planning," August 1992, p. 93(4).

Leifeld, Nicholas, "Category 4: Human Resource Development and Management," September 1992, p. 51(5).

Heaphy, Maureen S., "Category 5: Management of Process Quality," October 1992, p. 74(6).

Case, Kenneth E. and James S. Bigelow, "Category 6: Quality and Operational Results," November 1992, p. 47(6).

Desatnick, Robert L., "Category 7: Customer Focus and Satisfaction," December 1992, p. 69(6).

Main, Jeremy, "How to Win the Baldrige Award," *Fortune*. April 23, 1990, p. 101(5).

Main, Jeremy, "Is the Baldrige Overblown?" *Fortune*. July 1, 1991, p. 62(4).

Malcolm Baldrige National Quality Award, 1995 Award Criteria. National Institute of Standards and Technology, Gaithersburg, Md., 1994.

Reimann, Curt W., "National Quality Award Brings Opportunities for Industry," *Business America*. May 9, 1988, p. 5(3).

Reimann, Curt W., "The Baldrige Award: Leading the Way in Quality Initiatives," *Quality Progress*. July 1989, p. 35(5).

Smith, Jim and Mark Oliver, "The Baldrige Boondoggle," *Machine Design*. August 6, 1992, p. 25(5).

Stankard, Martin F., "Use Baldrige Criteria for Self Assessment," *Transportation and Distribution*. October 1991, p. 50(2).

Stratton, Brad, "A Different Look at the Baldrige Award," *Quality Progress*. February 1991, p. 17(4).

Sunday, John L. and Larry Liberty, "Benchmarking the Baldrige Award," *Quality Progress*. September 1992, p. 75(3).

4 GEORGE M. LOW AWARD (NASA EXCELLENCE AWARD)

HISTORY

In 1982, NASA launched its Productivity Improvement and Quality Enhancement (PIQE) program. The purpose of this program was to aid the U.S. aerospace community in preserving its competitive edge in the world marketplace. In 1985, the PIQE initiative was expanded with the creation of the NASA Excellence Award for Quality and Productivity, thus making it the first major quality award given in the United States. The purpose of the award was to recognize current NASA contractors, subcontractors, and suppliers that demonstrated "sustained excellence" in quality and productivity for three or more years and to transfer their techniques to others. In 1990, the award was renamed the George M. Low Award in recognition of the contribution of George M. Low, a former NASA deputy administrator who worked in the area of quality for 27 years. In 1990, the decision was also made to give separate awards based on company size. In 1993, the Low Award was enhanced by linking it with the Malcolm Baldrige National Quality Award. In doing so, "the new award process is more closely aligned with NASA's quality improvement policy and assists their supplier base in understanding NASA's expectations for continually improving quality" (*Application Guidelines for the George M. Low Award*, 1994, p. 1).

The award itself is a trophy on top of which a medallion in the shape of an Apollo Command Module is embedded. The medallion is alloyed with a portion of an artifact that traveled to the moon and back on the Apollo 11 voyage (the first manned lunar landing mission) (*Application Guidelines for the George M. Low Award*, 1994, inside front cover). The inscription on the award is as follows: "The Trophy is awarded in memory of George M. Low, who greatly contributed to the early development of

NASA Space Programs during his 27 years of Government Service" (*Application Guidelines for the George M. Low Award,* 1994, inside front cover).

OBJECTIVE AND CRITERIA

Objective

The award is managed by the NASA Quality and Productivity Improvement Programs Division. The objectives of the award are:

- To recognize outstanding achievements in continual improvement and quality management among members of the NASA contractor community

- To provide members of the NASA contractor community the impetus to define and assess internal quality management benchmarks from which to implement a continual improvement program

- To facilitate the transfer of superior quality management and continual improvement theory and methods within the NASA contractor community

- To provide members of the NASA contractor community a target for continual improvement initiatives (*Application Guidelines for the George M. Low Award,* 1994, p. 3)

The presentation of the George M. Low Award "signifies NASA's recognition that the award recipient has demonstrated sustained excellence and outstanding achievements in continual improvement and quality management. The Award signifies that the recipient not only meets contract requirements, but goes further: they provide products/services at such a high quality level that they set new levels of customer satisfaction and are an exemplary NASA partner in achieving excellence" (*Application Guidelines for the George M. Low Award,* 1994, p. 14).

Candidate Eligibility

The award is presented to any applicant that has "demonstrated an exceptional level of excellence in continual improvement and quality management in NASA-related contracts or subcontracts over a three-year period" (*Application Guidelines for the George M. Low Award,* 1994, p. 3). Companies that are direct contractors, subcontractors, and suppliers of NASA can apply for the award provided they or their parent company has applied for and reached the consensus stage of the Malcolm Baldrige National Quality Award. The remaining requirements are based upon which award category the company is in: manufacturing, service, or small business.

Organizations that apply in the manufacturing and service categories must be located within the United States, be self-sustaining with a majority of their resources at one location, and have aggregate sales to NASA of $1 million with at least $250,000 for each of the three previous years or at least 50% of total sales that are NASA related. A minimum of 50 full-time employees (or 100,000 labor hours) must be work done as a prime contractor to NASA or as a subcontractor to a NASA contractor.

In the small business category, aggregate sales to NASA must be at least $250,000 for the three previous years (or a minimum of 50% of a company's total sales must be NASA related). In addition, a minimum of 25 employees must be devoted to NASA projects.

Due to the restructuring of the award, all previous winners of the NASA Excellence Award for Quality and Productivity or the Low Award are eligible to apply under the revised guidelines.

Evaluation Criteria

The achievements of the applicants are evaluated using several criteria. These criteria are divided into the following five major categories:

1. NASA Contract Performance

2. NASA Schedule Performance

3. NASA Cost Performance

4. NASA Problem Prevention and Resolution

5. Innovation and Technology Achievements

The first four categories have a number of subelements. The five categories, including their subelements, and the number of points available are listed in Table 4.1.

The evaluation and scoring of each criteria element is based on the following three factors:

1. How long in place

2. Deployment

3. Performance

The actual awarding of points is based on the scoring guidelines given in Table 4.2.

Every applicant receives a written feedback report identifying specific strengths and opportunities for improvement. These reports are sent to applicants within two months of the announcement of the Low Award recipients.

TABLE 4.1   George M. Low Award Evaluation Criteria

Evaluation criteria elements	Total points
1. NASA Contract Performance	**300**
1.A. Provide evidence of how performance requirements are determined and communicated throughout the organization	50
1.B. Provide objective data demonstrating the level of performance in all areas of activity	50
1.C. Document continual improvement with objective data	50
1.D. Provide evidence of initiatives which improved the value of products, processes and services	50
1.E. Identify the processes used to determine and measure customer needs and satisfaction	100
2. NASA Schedule Performance	**250**
2.A. Provide sufficient data to demonstrate the degree to which schedule requirements have been met over the three-year period	150
2.B. Describe how schedule requirements are evaluated, documented and disseminated	25
2.C. Describe how the scheduling system is used to analyze past and anticipated schedule performance over the life of the contract	25
2.D. Provide examples demonstrating exceptional responsiveness to rescheduling, work-around and reprioritized work activities	50
3. NASA Cost Performance	**250**
3.A. Document that actual costs are at or below the estimated contract cost, taking customer-initiated changes into account	100
3.B. Demonstrate an ability to accurately and consistently forecast costs	25
3.C. Describe the system that ensures that the customer is advised of pending cost changes or cost risks in a timely manner	25
3.D. Document savings from cost reduction/avoidance programs	100
4. NASA Problem Prevention and Resolution	**125**
4.A. Describe the process used for problem resolution and provide an example	75
4.B. Demonstrate the processes used to prevent problems	50
5. Innovation and Technology Achievements	75
TOTAL POINTS	**1000**

Source: *Application Guidelines for the George M. Low Award: NASA's Quality and Excellence Award 1994,* pp. 9–10.

TABLE 4.2   George M. Low Award Scoring Guidelines

Percentage	Description	How long in place	Deployment	Performance
91–100	Excellent	3+ years	91–100%	Sustained high performance with constant improvement
81–90	Very good	3 years	81–90%	Starts moderately and improves to high performance
71–80	Good	2–3 years	61–80%	Gradual continual improvement
61–70	Average	2 years	41–60%	Starts low to moderate and improves slightly
51–60	Fair	1–2 years	21–40%	Starts low and improves to moderate
<50	Poor	<1 year	0–20%	Starts and stays low

Source: *Application Guidelines for the George M. Low Award: NASA's Quality and Excellence Award 1994,* p. 11.

Selection Process

The selection process follows a schedule similar to the one given below. Dates change, but the general timing is the same.

October 1993	Malcolm Baldrige National Quality Award Guidelines are available.
March 1994	Baldrige Award eligibility determination forms due at the National Institute of Standards and Technology (NIST).
April 1994	Baldrige Award applications due at NIST.
April–June 1994	Applications reviewed by Baldrige Award Board of Examiners.
June–Aug. 1994	Consensus review by Baldrige Award Board of Examiners. Applicants reaching the consensus stage are notified by NIST.
July–Sept. 1994	Eligible companies apply for the George M. Low Award.
Oct.–Nov. 1994	NASA Low Award Recommendation Board reviews, evaluates, and validates applications. Recommended applicants are selected for validation visits.

Jan.–Feb. 1995	NASA Low Award Recommendation Board conducts validation visits. Low Award Panel of Judges reviews validation results and recommends award recipient(s) to NASA administrator for approval.
April 1995	Formal announcement and presentation of award recipients.

AWARD RECIPIENTS

1986	Six finalists—no award recipients
1987	1. IBM Federal Systems Division Houston, Texas
	2. Martin Marietta Michoud Aerospace New Orleans, Louisiana
1988	Rocketdyne Division of Rockwell International Corporation Canoga Park, California
1989	Lockheed Engineering & Science Company (subsidiary of Lockheed Corporation) Houston, Texas
1990	1. Space Systems Division of Rockwell International Corporation Downey, California (large business category)
	2. Marotta Scientific Controls, Inc. (small business category) Montville, New Jersey
1991	1. Grumman Technical Services Division Titusville, Florida
	2. Thiokol Corp. Space Operations Brigham City, Utah
1992	1. Honeywell Space and Strategic Systems Operation Clearwater, Florida
	2. IBM Federal Sector Division Houston, Texas
1993	Due to restructuring, no awards given

HOW TO APPLY

Benchmarking and External Programs Division
Office of Continual Improvement (Code T)
NASA Headquarters
Washington, DC 20546
Phone: (202) 358-2161
Fax: (202) 358-4165

EXERCISES

4.1 When was the NASA award created?

4.2 When was the award renamed the George M. Low Award? Why was it renamed?

4.3 When was the award linked with the Malcolm Baldrige National Quality Award?

4.4 How does the new linkage with the Baldrige Award strengthen the Low Award?

4.5 What are the objectives of the award?

4.6 What three factors are considered when scoring the Low Award?

4.7 What is the primary eligibility requirement for applying for the Low Award?

BIBLIOGRAPHY

Application Guidelines for the George M. Low Award: NASA's Quality and Excellence Award 1994. NASA Headquarters, Washington, D.C.

"ASQC to Lead NASA Quality Award Effort," *Quality Progress.* June 1985.

Bemowski, Karen and Brad Stratton, "The Triumph of David and Goliath," *Quality Progress.* December 1990, p. 23(2).

Henry, Craig A., "Does the United States Need Quality Awards?" *Quality Progress.* December 1990, p. 26(2).

Jarrett, Joyce, R., "Long Term Strategy...A Commitment to Excellence," *Journal for Quality and Participation.* July/August 1990, p. 28(6).

Rodney, George A., "Epilogue to NASA Excellence Award," *Quality Progress.* September 1987, p. 23(1).

Ryan, John, "High Tech, High Touch," *Quality Progress.* September 1987, p. 19(5).

Ryan, John, "This Company Hates Surprises," *Quality Progress.* September 1987, p. 12(6).

Young, Robert B., "Building the Foundation for Quality Culture," *Journal for Quality and Participation.* March 1991, p. 92(7).

5

THE DEMING PRIZE

HISTORY

In the years following World War II, Japan's primary focus was on raising the standard of living through revitalizing its economy. Due to scarce natural resources, Japan decided to do this by becoming a vigorous trading nation. In order to become a successful trading nation, the image of Japanese-made product had to be greatly improved. The approach the Japanese chose to accomplish this was to improve the quality of their products by adopting and practicing statistical quality control. As one of the first steps, the Union of Japanese Scientists and Engineers (JUSE) invited Dr. W. Edwards Deming to give a series of lectures, which he presented in July 1950. His lectures provided the stimulus needed for Japan's early efforts in the use of statistical quality control.

In 1951, the JUSE Board of Directors established the Deming Prize "to commemorate the achievements of Dr. Deming, the friendship between Dr. Deming and JUSE cultivated through Dr. Deming's visits to Japan, and Dr. Deming's contribution to Japanese industry through his introduction and guidance in the application of the statistical method of quality control to industries" (*The Deming Prize Guide: For Overseas Companies*, 1986, p. 30). Initially, funding for the award came from Dr. Deming, who donated the royalties from the sale of the Japanese edition of his works used or published in Japan. Today, funding for the prize comes from JUSE.

Since the early 1950s, quality control and its techniques have been adopted by virtually every sector of Japanese industry. In Japan, it has become customary for companies that want to improve their performance in products or services to vie for the Deming Prize. They do so not only for the prestige, but also to benefit from the internal improvements that result from the implementation of company-wide quality control, which is required to qualify for the prize.

The prize itself is in the form of a medal. On the front is a profile of Dr. Deming. Across the top of the medal is the inscription "Deming Prize Committee, JUSE." Below the profile of Dr. Deming is the inscription "The right quality and uniformity are foundations of commerce, prosperity and peace...W. Edwards Deming."

PURPOSE AND CATEGORIES

The purpose of the Deming Prize is "to award prizes to those companies which are recognized as having successfully applied company-wide quality control (CWQC) based on statistical quality control and which are likely to keep up with it in the future" (*The Deming Prize Guide: For Overseas Companies,* 1986, p. 4).

There are three categories of the Deming Prize:

1. Deming Prize for Individuals

2. Deming Application Prize

3. Deming Application Prize for Overseas Companies

The Deming Prize for Individuals is given to a person who has demonstrated excellent achievement in the theory or application of statistical quality control. It also is given to a person who makes an outstanding contribution to the dissemination of statistical quality control.

The Deming Application Prize is given to organizations (including public institutions) that achieve the most distinctive improvement of performance through the application of statistical quality control. This category includes the following four subcategories:

1. Large enterprises

2. Small or medium enterprises

3. Corporate divisions

4. Factories

The Deming Application Prize for Overseas Companies is a relatively new category. Because the initial purpose of the prize was to encourage the development of quality control in Japan, the prize was restricted to Japanese companies. However, in recent years, non-Japanese companies have shown strong interest in the Deming Prize. Therefore, in 1984, the Deming Prize Committee revised the basic regulations to allow overseas companies to apply as candidates. In 1987, the first non-Japanese companies were allowed to apply for the prize. To date, Florida Power and Light (1989), headquartered in Miami, Florida, and Phillips Taiwan Ltd. (1991) are the only overseas companies to apply for and win the Deming Prize.

These prizes are the highest awards in Japan relating to statistical quality control and company-wide quality control. By insisting on the highest performance, the prize has brought about organizational overhauls in Japanese industries by practicing statistical quality control and company-wide quality control.

EVALUATION

There is no limit to the number of winners in each category. However, a limiting factor is the examination capacity of the Deming Prize Committee and on-site examiners. Because these two groups are made up of university professors and quality control experts in government and other non-profit institutions in Japan, availability of time is limited.

Examination Objective

The objective of the Deming Prize examination is to ensure that "good results are being comprehensively achieved through the implementation of company-wide quality control, particularly in regard to the potential for the future advancement of the company's CWQC effort" (*The Deming Prize Guide: For Overseas Companies,* 1986, p. 12). Special emphasis is given to how well statistical quality control techniques are used to achieve customer satisfaction. All aspects of an organization are evaluated, including re-search, development, design, purchasing, manufacturing, inspection, sales, marketing, etc.

Examination Criteria

The examination criteria are separated into ten categories. A description of each category follows:

1. **Company policy and planning:** How the policy for man-agement, quality and quality control is determined and transmit-ted throughout all sectors of the company will be examined together with the results being achieved. Whether the contents of the policy are appropriate and clearly presented will also be examined.

2. **Organization and its management:** Whether the scope of responsibility and authority is clearly defined, how cooperation is promoted among all departments, and how the organization is managed to carry out quality control will be examined.

3. **Quality control education and dissemination:** How quality control is taught and how employees are trained through training courses and routine work in the company concerned and the related companies will be examined. To what extent the concept of quality control and statistical techniques are understood and

utilized and the activeness of quality control circles will be examined.

4. **Collection, transmission and utilization of information on quality:** How the collection and dissemination of information on quality from within and outside the company are conducted by and among the head office, factories, branches, sales offices, and the organizational units will be examined, together with the evaluation of the organization and the systems used, and how fast information is transmitted, sorted, analyzed and utilized.

5. **Analysis:** Whether or not critical problems regarding quality are properly grasped and analyzed with respect to overall quality and the existing production process, and whether the results are being interpreted in the frame of the available technology will be subject to scrutiny, while a check will be made on whether proper statistical methods are being used.

6. **Standardization:** The establishment, revision and rescission of standards and the manner of their control and systematization will be examined, together with the use of standards for the enhancement of company technology.

7. **Control (*kanri*):** How the procedures used for the maintenance and improvement of quality are reviewed from time to time when necessary will be examined. Also scrutinized will be how the responsibility for and the authority over these matters are defined, while a check will be made on the use of control charts and other related statistical techniques.

8. **Quality assurance:** New product development, quality analysis, design, production, inspection, equipment maintenance, purchasing, sales, services and other activities at each stage of the operation, which are essential for quality assurance, including reliability, will be closely examined, together with overall quality assurance management system.

9. **Effects:** What effects were produced or are being produced on the quality of products and services through the implementation of quality control will be examined. Whether products of sufficiently good quality are being manufactured and sold will be examined. Whether products have been improved from the viewpoint of quality, quantity, and cost, and whether the whole company has been improved not only in the numerical effect of quality and profit, but also in the scientific way of thinking of employers and employees and their heightened will to work will be examined.

10. **Future plans:** Whether the strong and weak points in the present situation are properly recognized and whether the promotion of quality control is planned in the future and is likely to continue will be examined. (*The Deming Prize Guide: For Overseas Companies,* 1986, pp. 7–9)

Each of these items is evaluated with regard to the method used to maintain effective control. Also, the term "quality control" denotes company-wide quality control based on statistical quality control techniques. A checklist for each of the ten categories is provided in Table 5.1.

Scoring Method

The Deming Prize Committee evaluates the results reported by the on-site examination teams. All examination team members' scores are treated equally, on the basis of 100 possible points. The passing points are (*The Deming Prize Guide: For Overseas Companies,* 1986, p. 16):

1. The CEO   70 points or more

2. Whole company average, excluding the CEO   70 points or more

3. Minimum for any examined unit   50 points or more

The above scores are not disclosed. Only a written opinion on the examination of the applicant's company and its respective work sites is provided.

Schedule of Examination

The examination process follows the general schedule given below (*The Deming Prize Guide: For Overseas Companies,* 1986, pp. 17–18):

Preceding year

November 20	Closing date for filing of applications
December 20	Final date for the decision of acceptance

Examination and award year

January 20	Closing date for the submission of the Description of QC Practices
January 21–30	Decision of the exam schedule Appointment of committee members Notification to the applicant of the exam schedule
February 18–28	Decision on results of documentary examination
March 20–Sept. 30	On-site examinations
October 10–20	Selection of prize awardees; public announcements and notifications
November	Deming Prize awards ceremony and reporting sessions

TABLE 5.1   Checklist for Deming Prize Examination Categories

Item	Particulars
1. Policy	1. Policies pursued for management, quality, and quality control 2. Method of establishing policies 3. Justifiability and consistency of policies 4. Utilization of statistical methods 5. Transmission and diffusion of policies 6. Review of policies and the results achieved 7. Relationship between policies and long- and short-term planning
2. Organization and its management	1. Explicitness of the scopes of authority and responsibility 2. Appropriateness of delegations of authority 3. Interdivisional cooperation 4. Committees and their activities 5. Utilization of staff 6. Utilization of QC circle activities 7. Quality control diagnosis
3. Education and dissemination	1. Education programs and results 2. Quality and control consciousness, degrees of understanding of quality control 3. Teaching of statistical concepts and methods, and the extent of their dissemination 4. Grasp of the effectiveness of quality control 5. Education of related company (particularly those in the same group, subcontractors, consignees, and distributors) 6. QC circle activities 7. System of suggesting ways of improvements and its actual conditions
4. Collection, dissemination, and use of information on quality	1. Collection of external information 2. Transmission of information between divisions 3. Speed of information transmission (use of computers) 4. Data processing, statistical analysis of information, and utilization of the results
5. Analysis	1. Selection of key problems and themes 2. Propriety of the analytical approach 3. Utilization of statistical methods 4. Linkage with proper technology 5. Quality analysis, process analysis 6. Utilization of analytical results 7. Assertiveness of improvement suggestions

TABLE 5.1   Checklist for Deming Prize Examination Categories (continued)

Item	Particulars
6. Standardization	1. Systematization of standards 2. Method of establishing, revising, and abolishing standards 3. Outcome of the establishment, revision, or abolishing of standards 4. Contents of the standards 5. Utilization of statistical methods 6. Accumulation of technology 7. Utilization of standards
7. Control	1. Systems for the control of quality and such related matters as cost and quantity 2. Control items and control points 3. Utilization of such statistical control methods as control charts and other statistical concepts 4. Contribution to performance of QC circle activities 5. Actual conditions of control activities 6. State of matters under control
8. Quality assurance	1. Procedures for the development of new products and services (analysis and upgrading of quality, checking of design, reliability, and other properties) 2. Safety and immunity from product liability 3. Process design, process analysis, and process control and improvement 4. Process capability 5. Instrumentation, gauging, testing, and inspecting 6. Equipment maintenance and control of subcontracting, purchasing, and services 7. Quality assurance system and its audit 8. Utilization of statistical methods 9. Evaluation and audit of quality 10. Actual state of quality assurance
9. Results	1. Measurement of results 2. Substantive results in quality, services, delivery time, cost, profits, safety, environment, etc. 3. Intangible results 4. Measures for overcoming defects
10. Planning for the future	1. Grasp of the present state of affairs and the concreteness of the plan 2. Measures for overcoming defects 3. Plans for further advances 4. Linkage with the long-term plans

Source: *The Deming Prize Guide: For Overseas Companies,* 1986, pp. 24–26.

Examination Costs

The following is a list of the examination costs for which overseas applicants are responsible:

1. Examination fee of approximately $2500 to $4000 per person* per day (add one day to the actual number of days to be used for the examination)

2. Per diem compensation for each examiner

3. Travel expenses for each examiner (first-class air fare)

4. Hotel expenses for each examiner (first-class hotel)

5. Cost of preparing a written opinion

6. Interpreter/translator fees

7. Other costs: registration fee, correspondence charges, etc. (*The Deming Prize Guide: For Overseas Companies,* 1986, p. 5).

All costs except item 4 are to be paid on demand in a lump sum.

HOW TO APPLY

Information on how to apply for the Deming Prize can be obtained by writing to:

Union of Japanese Scientists and Engineers (JUSE)
5-10-11
Sendagaya
Shibuya-ku, Tokyo
151
Japan

EXERCISES

5.1 Who established the Deming Prize and why?

5.2 Discuss the three categories of the Deming Prize.

5.3 How does the Deming Prize differ from the Malcolm Baldrige National Quality Award with regard to candidate eligibility?

---

* The number of persons forming the examination team is based on the business size of the applicant, the number of sites to be examined, and other requirements.

6

DATA AND SAMPLING

INTRODUCTION

Successful use of many of the quality tools is dependent on the input of some type of data. However, seldom does the tool indicate what type of data is needed or how the data should be collected. Before going out and collecting measurements, counts, etc., one needs to know what type of data is required and how it can be used to solve quality problems. It is also helpful to have a little knowledge about sampling.

DATA

Webster's defines data as "figures from which conclusions can be drawn, a basis for reasoning, discussion or calculation." Data is merely a group of numbers which can represent the measurement of something, such as temperature (degrees), or the count of something, such as the number of rotten apples. Data are transformed into information through analysis. This information influences decision making and the types of actions that result from these decisions.

Purpose

A purpose or reason should be established before setting out to collect data. There are many uses or reasons for collecting data, including:

1. Answer questions

2. Identify problems

3. Control processes

4. Accept/reject products

5. Present current situation

The purpose or reason for collecting data should be driven by the type of problem or improvement the team is studying. Since a carefully thought out problem statement defines the boundary and population of the process or service to be studied, the purpose for collecting data is usually clear.

Once the purpose for collecting data has been established, the types of comparisons that need to be made can be determined. This in turn identifies the type of data to collect and where in the process one needs to collect the data.

One type of comparison looks at the performance of one particular machine/line/employee over some time period. The comparison is made hourly, daily, weekly, etc. Another type of comparison is the performance of multiple machines/lines/employees. A third type of comparison studies the relationship between things, like how does increasing x affect y. The type of comparison needed is driven by the original purpose for collecting data.

Types of Data

There are two main types of data: subjective and objective. **Subjective data** are based on experiences, opinions, or observations. Subjective data are typically used when making personal decisions like what to order for lunch, what to wear to work, etc. Subjective data can be difficult to quantify and should be used carefully when making decisions that affect many people. In the past, many managerial decisions were based on subjective data. Unfortunately, these decisions were often wrong, which cost the organization time and money. In today's competitive environment and with limited resources, decisions need to be based on facts that come from objective data.

Objective data are typically expressed in numerical form. There are two types of objective data: variable and attribute. If the data being collected can be measured and expressed as a number on some continuous scale, then the data are considered **variable data**. Often, it is not possible to obtain data that can be directly measured. For example, the taste of soup, the feel of carpet, and the ease of driving cannot be measured in numerical terms and would therefore be classified as subjective. However, they can be compared and given a quantitative score, or they can be classified, like good taste versus bad taste, and the number of occurrences for each classification can be counted. This type of data is called discrete or **attribute data**.

Attribute data are typically easier to collect than variable data. Attribute data usually require that an item can be categorized or that an item can be tested using a go/no-go gauge. Because the actual collection of attribute data does not require any special skills or extensive training, additional manpower or training is seldom needed. Therefore, the collection of attribute data is less expensive. Variable data, on the other hand, require the use of measurement instruments, which does require special skills and training. The skills may be simple, like telling time or using a ruler, or more complex, like determining hardness or measuring viscosity. It is important in all cases that the person collecting the data is trained with regard to data collection techniques and that all measuring devices used are calibrated. Both training and calibration increase the manpower and collection time needed. This also increases the cost.

If a team has a choice as to which type of data to collect, then the collection of variable data should be chosen. Because variable data provide more information (measurements always provide more detail than counts), the collection of variable data is usually worth the extra effort.

Data Reliability

Even if the correct data are collected, a wrong decision or action can occur if the data are unreliable. There are many causes of unreliable data. One cause is improperly calibrated instruments. Another is improper use of measuring instruments. To minimize potential problems with unreliable data, it is important to check the calibration of measurement equipment before and after the collection of data. Similarly, the people collecting the data should be trained in the use of data collection instruments before and after data collection.

For attribute data, classification and counting are based on sight, feel, taste, etc. For example, the counting of defects per item is based mainly on sight. The evaluation of wine is based on color, odor, and taste. Since these are individual interpretations, the differences in individual inspectors need to be noted and accounted for when appropriate.

Sometimes data may be reliable but unusable. This usually occurs when the origins of data are not recorded properly. Exactly when, where, who, what, and how the data were collected must be recorded. *When* includes the exact days, the time of day, etc. *Where* includes the plant/line/machine/ employee location and where in the plant or on the line the data were collected. *Who* includes who collected the data and who was working on the line/machine when the data were collected. *What* includes the data type and the model number or type of item being produced. *How* includes the instruments (identification number and storage location are helpful if calibration becomes a question) and any other special instructions given for the data collection. All of this information can be easily collected if proper care is taken when designing a check sheet. Without this information, even good data has little meaning.

Stratification

When deciding on what data to collect, it is always a good idea to think about the possibility of data stratification. Stratification is merely taking the original set of data and breaking it down into smaller, related subgroups.

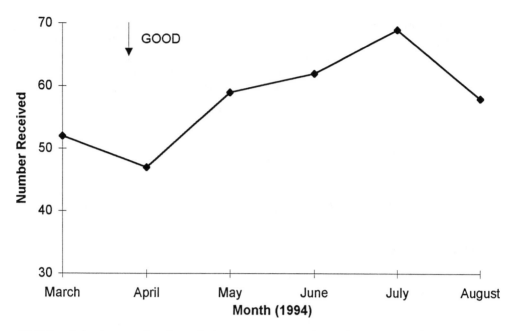

FIGURE 6.1   Damaged and Spoiled Oranges Received March–August 1994

By allowing the team to determine what effect each subgroup has on the total population, stratification enables a more precise analysis of the data. It is extremely helpful when doing root cause analysis. How stratification is used when doing root cause analysis with graphs is illustrated in Figures 6.1 and 6.2. The total number of damaged and spoiled oranges received for the last six months is charted in Figure 6.1. The number of damaged and spoiled oranges received for the last six months is graphed by orange type in Figure 6.2. Clearly, there are more damaged and spoiled mandarin oranges per month than any other type. Even further stratification is provided in Figure 6.3 by graphing the number of damaged and spoiled mandarin oranges per month by vendor. This figure indicates that a problem exists with vendor b. These three figures illustrate the power of stratification and the value of collecting all of the data. This can only be accomplished if the data collection is first carefully planned.

Summary

Remember that data provides the basis for all decisions and actions. It is important to know why it is needed and what it will be used for. Therefore, careful planning should precede every data collection effort. Be sure to collect only the data needed, and be sure that all information associated with the data itself and the data collection process is accurately recorded. When collecting the data, measure as accurately as possible within the

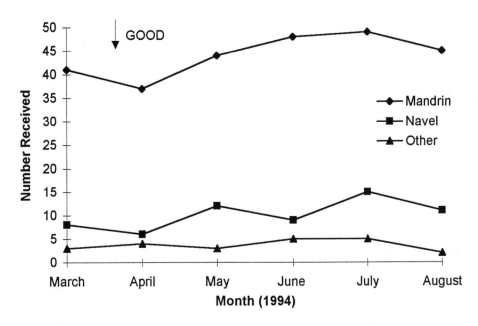

FIGURE 6.2   Damaged and Spoiled Oranges Received by Type March–August 1994

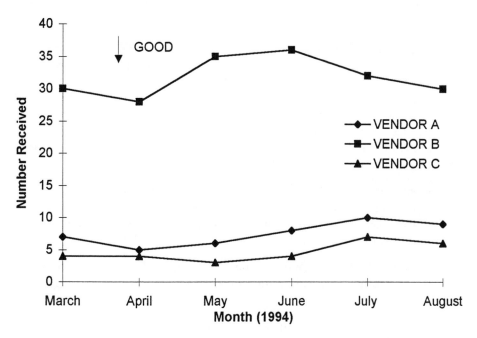

FIGURE 6.3   Damaged and Spoiled Mandarin Oranges Received by Vendor March–August 1994

given time and cost constraints. Also, all data collection should be done in such a way that the data can be easily used and understood.

SAMPLING

Because data provide the basis for all decisions and actions, it is important that the data collected accurately represent the situation, process, lot, etc. being studied. It would be ideal if every item in the population of items could be measured or tested. However, because most lots, processes, customer interactions, etc. that are typically studied contain large numbers of items, sampling is required.

Basic Definitions

Some basic terms needs to be defined before sampling can be discussed further:

Population.   A population is the totality of items being studied. This could be a single lot, output from one machine or person, or even a process line. Due to time, personnel, and money constraints, collecting population data is often impossible or impractical.

Sample.   A sample is one or more items taken from a population and used to reflect the distribution of the population and to estimate the parameters of the distribution.

Population distribution.   Because every item cannot be produced exactly the same each time, variability about the expected mean occurs. This variability has a pattern associated with it, which is referred to as the population distribution. In natural events, such as weights, heights, etc., the population distribution is usually the normal distribution. However, in the workplace, the distribution could be normal, exponential, Poisson, etc. By knowing the population distribution of the process being studied, proper corrections or improvements to the process can be made.

Parameters of a distribution.   Distribution parameters are the characteristics that describe the position and the variability of the population distribution. For a normal distribution, the parameters of interest are the mean and the variance.

Symbols.   The distribution parameters are represented by symbols. The symbols used to represent the normal distribution parameters are shown in Table 6.1.

From Table 6.1, it can be seen that two types of parameters for the population exist, known or estimated (unknown). If perfect knowledge exists about a population or if you can sample every item in the population, the parameters of the population distribution are said to be known. If the parameters are known, then Greek letters are used to represent this

TABLE 6.1   Parameter Symbols Representing the Normal Distribution

Parameter	Population Known	Population Estimated	Sample
Mean	μ	$\hat{\mu}$	$\overline{X}$
Variance	σ^2	$\hat{\mu}^2$	S^2

fact. However, perfect knowledge seldom exists, and it is usually impossible to sample every item in the population. Therefore, the parameters must be estimated. Estimated parameters are represented by Greek letters with a caret (^). Alphabetic characters are used to represent the sample parameters. Whenever the sample is used to estimate population parameters, the estimated population parameters will be the same as the sample parameters.

Types of Sampling

The purpose of sampling is to acquire accurate knowledge about a given population and to take appropriate action for improvement. Therefore, it is very important that the sample be truly representative of the population. In order to be truly representative of the population, the sample must be random.

Random sampling is taking a sample in such a way that every item in the population has an equal and independent chance of being included in the sample. **Simple random sampling** is random sampling without replacement. It is primarily used when the population being studied is felt to be homogeneous (the variance is due to chance causes instead of assignable causes). The steps for collecting a simple random sample are as follows:

Step 1   Determine the size of the population being studied and assign sequential numbers to the items. For example, if the population is 75 items, the items would be numbered from 1 to 75.

Step 2   Determine what the sample size will be. For this example, the sample size will be 10.

Step 3   Enter a random numbers table. This is typically done by closing your eyes and putting your finger on the table. (Many books provide a single random numbers table. If there is more than one page to the tables being used, then a die can be rolled to determine which page of the tables to start on.) The number your finger points to is where you start.*

---

* There are a multitude of ways to use a random numbers table. This is just one of them.

Step 4   Determine the number of each item that will be in the sample. In this case, 10 numbers with values less than 75 have to be obtained. If the table being used provides numbers in groups of four, take either the first two, the last two, or the middle two. It doesn't matter. The table being used for this example provides numbers in groups of five. The first 15 numbers in the table (starting with the number my finger landed on and moving across the row*) are given below. Fifteen numbers are taken to ensure that there will be 10 usable numbers.

14346	09172	30168	90229	04734
59193	54164	58492	22421	74103
47072	25306	76468	26384	58151

The last two digits were used. The numbers then become:

46	72	68	29	34	93	64	92	21	03
72	06	68	84	51					

Because there are only 75 items being studied, any number greater than 75 was eliminated. Similarly, any number that appeared twice was eliminated because the sampling was being done without replacement. The numbers then left were:

46	72	68	29	34	64	21	03	06	51

These 10 numbers represent the number of the item within the population that will be included in the sample. If there had been fewer than the required 10 numbers left, then the procedure would be to return to the random numbers table at the point where the last number was obtained and collect additional random numbers. This is done until the number required has been obtained.

Step 5   Collect the sample. In this example, a random numbers table was used. This is the most convenient means of generating a set of random numbers since these tables are easily available. However, there are other ways of obtaining random numbers, such as rolling dice, tossing coins, and spinning a roulette-type wheel. These methods obviously have limitations and are not really practical on the job. One method that can be used on the job is to have a computer generate a set of random numbers.

Stratified random sampling is done by dividing the population into several mutually exclusive and exhaustive strata or regions. The division of the population into the different strata is done in such a way that the units are as similar as possible within each stratum. For example, the strata could

---

* Moving down the column is also acceptable.

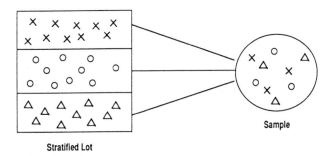

Stratified Lot

FIGURE 6.4 Stratified Sampling

be the top, middle, and bottom portions of a lot or they could be groupings by like items (see Figure 6.4). Once stratified, simple random samples are then taken from each strata (use Steps 1 to 5 to take each sample). This sampling is done independently within each stratum.

Clustered sampling is done by subdividing the population into groups or clusters and taking a sample of these clusters. Clustered sampling is performed when it is not feasible (and perhaps not possible) to exhaustively define a sampling region. For example, a survey of individual expenditures is to be done in Dade County, Florida. It is not possible to exhaustively define a sampling region due to daily births, deaths, etc. Therefore, the population is divided into several groups from which samples can be defined. In this example, Dade County has 27 incorporated cites within it. Therefore, the clusters would be the 27 incorporated cities and the remaining unincorporated portion of the county. Individuals within each cluster are chosen randomly and studied.

Selected sampling is done by taking the sample from only one special part of the population. For example, one form of selected sampling is to take the samples from the end of the roll or edge of the plate. Other types of selected sampling include sampling at specific times or sampling only one of the ingredients in a mixture (e.g., sampling only the milk in cake batter).

Systematic sampling is done by sampling at fixed intervals (e.g., every 25th transaction or every 10th item produced). The specific interval is determined by dividing the population by the sample size. Items are then selected at this interval throughout the population until the specified sample size has been reached. For example, let the population be 150 items and the sample size be 10:

$$sample\ interval = 150/10 = 15$$

Therefore the fixed interval is every 15th item or items 15, 30, 45, 60, 75, 90, 105, 120, 135, and 150. A degree of randomness is added to this method by selecting the starting point at random. This is done by randomly selecting a number from the interval range. In this example, the interval range is 15. Therefore, a number from 1 to 15 is chosen at random. If 5 is the number chosen, the items included in the sample become 5, 20, 35, 50, 65, 80, 95, 110, 125, and 140.

The collection of data using selected sampling and systematic sampling is more precise than simple random samples. It is also easier and more economical. However, there is always some bias. Also, because the sample is not truly random, the sample may not accurately represent the population.

Acceptance sampling is primarily done during incoming inspection for the purpose of accepting or rejecting a lot. Acceptance sampling plans consist of tables that are indexed according to different criteria. There are many standard acceptance sampling plans in use today. The most common is the MIL-STD 105D (or ANSI/ASQC Z1.4) acceptance sampling plan for attributes (U.S. Department of Defense, 1963) and the MIL-STD 414 (ANSI/ASQC Z1.9) acceptance sampling plan for variables (U.S. Department of Defense, 1957). Both of these plans are designed to protect the producer against having lots with a quality level as good or better than the specified acceptable quality level (AQL).

Sampling Error

Sampling error occurs when the sample statistics differ from the population statistics after the entire population has been examined. There are two types of sampling error: bias and dispersion. **Bias** or "lack of accuracy" occurs when the sample mean is different than the population mean. Bias can result from factors such as:

1. Sampling only from the surface of a liquid at rest

2. Sampling only from one edge of rolls or sheets

3. Sampling from only one segment of the lot

4. Instruments out of calibration

The result of a bias error is illustrated in Figure 6.5. Dispersion or "lack of precision" occurs when the measurements taken and recorded vary around the true measurement. **Dispersion error** is the result of variability in the sample standard deviation (see Figure 6.6). This type of error is typically due to improper reading or use of an instrument or an instrument that cannot read to the specified precision. The key to eliminating dispersion error is to choose the proper measuring instruments and make sure that the people using them are sufficiently trained in their use. The key to eliminating bias error is to make sure the instruments are calibrated and that the sample chosen accurately represents the population.

Summary

Data used to make decisions are collected from samples. Therefore, it is critical that the sample be carefully chosen. When choosing a sampling

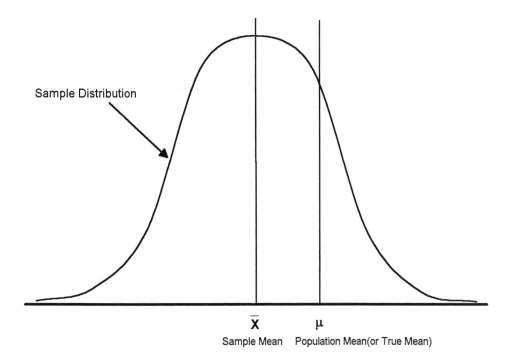

FIGURE 6.5 Bias Error

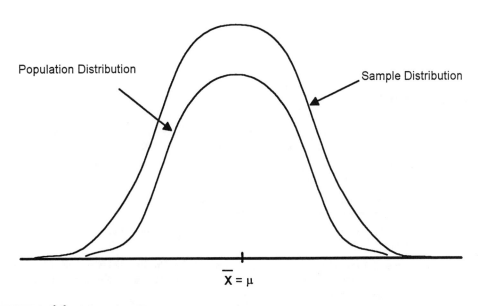

FIGURE 6.6 Dispersion Error

scheme, several aspects should be considered: (1) the accuracy and reliability the scheme provides, (2) the additional cost in time and personnel that will be incurred, and (3) the timeliness with which the sample can be taken. If sampling is done properly, the data will accurately represent the population, and correct decisions can be made and appropriate actions taken. If sampling is not done properly, the data will not truly represent the population and the decisions made and actions taken may be the wrong ones. Therefore, whatever sampling method is used, it should be carefully designed.

EXERCISES

6.1 List several possible reasons why you might need to collect data in your job.

6.2 What are the two main types of data? Give an example of each.

6.3 What is the difference between attribute data and variable data? Give several examples of each.

6.4 What is stratification?

6.5 What is the purpose of sampling?

6.6 What is sampling error?

6.7 What is dispersion error and bias error?

6.8 What factors should be considered when choosing a sampling scheme?

BIBLIOGRAPHY

Cohen, Ruben D., "Why Do Random Samples Represent Populations So Accurately?" *Journal of Chemical Education.* November 1991, p. 902(2).

Dallal, Gerard E., "The 17/10 Rule for Sample-Size Determinations," *The American Statistician.* February 1992, p. 70(1).

Dietz, E. Jacquelin, "A Cooperative Learning Activity on Methods of Selecting a Sample," *The American Statistician.* May 1993, p. 104(5).

Eckblad, James W., "How Many Samples Should Be Taken?" *BioScience.* May 1991, p. 346(2).

Ishikawa, Kaoru, *Guide to Quality Control.* Asian Productivity Organization, Hong Kong, 1982 (available in North America, the U.K., and Western Europe from Unipub, a division of Quality Resources).

Levy, Paul S. and Stanley Lemeshow, *Sampling of Populations—Methods and Applications.* John Wiley & Sons, New York, 1991.

Taylor, John Keenan, *Statistical Techniques for Data Analysis.* Lewis Publishers, Chelsea, Mich., 1990.

Thompson, Steven K., *Sampling.* John Wiley & Sons, New York, 1992.

U.S. Department of Defense, "Sampling Procedures for Inspection by Variables for Percent Defective, MIL-STD 414." U.S. Government Printing Office, Washington, D.C., 1957.

U.S. Department of Defense, "Sampling Procedures and Tables for Inspection by Attributes, MIL-STD 105D." U.S. Government Printing Office, Washington, D.C., 1963.

7

PROBLEM IDENTIFICATION TOOLS

INTRODUCTION

Throughout any problem-solving or improvement process, team members have to generate and evaluate a lot of ideas. Several methods are used to generate and evaluate ideas. The most commonly used methods are brainstorming, nominal group technique, and multivoting.

BRAINSTORMING

Brainstorming was developed by Alex F. Osborn in the 1930s. At the time, Osborn had just become executive vice-president of Batten, Barton, Durstine and Osborn (one of the world's largest advertising agencies). Osborn had discovered that during conferences in which new advertising ideas were supposed to be generated and discussed, there was always a negative atmosphere among the group. Comments like "it won't work," "we've never done it that way before," or "it's not in the budget" were constantly being expressed. This type of response suffocated original or creative ideas from being generated. As a result, progress was slow. Because survival in the advertising business depends on original and creative ideas being developed and implemented quickly, Osborn developed brainstorming as a means of countering negative conference thinking.

Brainstorming is used to generate a large quantity of ideas without criticism in a short period of time. Use of brainstorming is not limited to the advertising industry. In fact, this technique is used by many groups that try to generate ideas. It can also be used to (1) identify problems for the team to work on, (2) identify possible causes of a problem, (3) perform root cause analysis, (4) identify possible solutions to a problem, and (5) identify ways of implementing problem solutions. The focus is initially on quantity of ideas, instead of quality, since the ideas are evaluated later. It documents what the team knows. It stimulates creative thinking. It gets everyone on the team involved. Finally, because everyone is contributing, it brings the group together to work and think as a team.

Methodology

Preliminary Stage

Step 1: Determine the purpose of the brainstorming session. Has a problem been handed down from upper management? Is the problem the result of customer complaints? Is the purpose to identify opportunities for improvement? The brainstorming session must have a purpose.

Step 2: Identify the team members. The purpose will direct the selection of team members. If the problem is handed down by management or if it is the result of customer complaints, the team may need to include people from many different departments. In such cases, team members are often assigned. If the purpose is to identify improvement opportunities, the team usually comes from a single work unit. This type of team is made up mostly of volunteers.

Step 3: Distribute all data related to the purpose of the meeting. This ensures that all the team members are aware of the purpose of the meeting and are well-informed about the current situation.

Step 4: Select an appropriate location and time for the meeting. The location needs to be a place that is comfortable and free of interruptions. The meeting place should have adequate seating and provide a casual atmosphere. The time should be as convenient for all team members as possible.

Step 5: Make sure the proper tools will be in the meeting room on the day of the meeting. Brainstorming requires that all the ideas generated be recorded in such a way that all of the team members can see them. This can be done by using a flip chart. A flip chart provides a hard copy of all ideas generated. Typically, many sheets of flip chart paper are needed to record all of the ideas generated. As soon as one sheet of the flip chart is filled, it can be torn off of the chart and taped to the wall for continued viewing by the group. A chalkboard can also be used, but should be avoided if possible. If a chalkboard is used, someone in the group will have to copy the ideas down before the group leaves, whereas if a flip chart is used, a hard copy will already exist. An overhead projector can also be used. However, as soon as one transparency is filled and a new one is placed on the projector, there is no easy way for the group to continue viewing it. Therefore, a flip chart is a most effective means of recording the ideas generated. If a flip chart is used, remember to bring markers to write with, tape or thumbtacks (if a corkboard is available) for display purposes, and an easel to rest the flip chart on for easier use.

Idea Generation Stage

Step 1:   Choose a brainstorming session leader. During the first brainstorming session, the leader typically will be the individual who coordinates the meeting, but this does not have to be the case. The session leader should be someone who can keep the group focused on the topic and stimulate the flow of ideas. Because the team will meet for several brainstorming sessions throughout the life of the project, it is a good idea to let different team members lead different sessions.

Step 2:   Choose a recorder. The recorder is responsible for transferring the verbalized ideas onto the flip chart. In small groups, the recorder and the session leader are usually the same person.

Step 3:   The session leader writes out the purpose of the brainstorming session.

Step 4:   One way the session leader can coordinate the collection of ideas is to use the "round robin" approach.

4.a: One member in the group is asked for **one** idea related to the purpose. It is helpful if the team members can word their ideas as concisely as possible (try for five words or less).

4.b: The recorder documents the idea. The speaker's intent should be accurately documented. No debate is allowed at this time. However, the session leader may want to ask for clarification to ensure that the speaker's intent is accurately reflected.

4.c: The next team member is asked for his or her idea. This continues until everyone in the group has had the opportunity to contribute an idea. Then the process starts over.

4.d: When all ideas have been exhausted, the generation stage is concluded. Ideally, the session leader will go around the group many times before all ideas have been exhausted.

Special Notes

1. The session leader and the recorder are also queried for their ideas.

2. A team member may choose to pass when his or her turn comes but should be encouraged to contribute something.

3. Write down **all** ideas, even the silly or wild ones. They may inspire ideas in others.

4. The generation of ideas should be done quickly (10 to 20 minutes).

Review Stage

Step 1: Go over the list to ensure that everyone understands what has been recorded. There is no discussion or criticism at this point. The review is done purely for team clarification and understanding.

Evaluation Stage

Step 1: Combine duplicate items. Identify and exclude items that appear irrelevant to the topic. Also excluded are items related to personnel, such as salaries, promotions, discipline, etc. (Personnel items are dealt with by special teams. The problem or improvement opportunity solution should be found in the process.)

Step 2: Discuss and evaluate the ideas. Discussion and evaluation typically is done using an open-floor format. Each individual item is discussed. Any items that are closely related are combined. If the discussion generates additional ideas, they are added to the list.

Step 3: The session is concluded. The purpose of the brainstorming session was to generate a multitude of ideas. With that accomplished, the session is ended so that the team members can have time to reflect on the ideas generated.

Follow-Up Stage

Step 1: The session leader collects the list of ideas generated and has them typed up and distributed to the rest of the team.

Step 2: Another team meeting is scheduled so that the ideas generated can be reduced and prioritized. Prioritizing is usually done by using the nominal group technique or the multivoting technique.

Guidelines

Certain guidelines need to be followed to ensure that the brainstorming session is successful and that individual participation is not inhibited. It is helpful to review the guidelines with the group prior to beginning the brainstorming session. It is also helpful to post the seven guidelines where everyone can see them during the session.

1. Never criticize or judge ideas. This is one of the most important guidelines. Criticism or judgment (by action or words) inhibits participation and cannot be allowed. If someone in the group laughs, groans, grunts, or in any other way expresses an opinion on the quality of an idea, other people in the group become reluctant to participate, which severely handicaps the team effort. (It also violates one of the basic tenets of total quality management, respect for people.) If criticism does

occur, the session leader must remind everyone that the reason for the brainstorming session is to generate a large quantity of ideas. The quality of the idea will be discussed later. By postponing the discussion until a later time, the ownership of the idea no longer belongs to an individual but rather to the group.

2. Do not discuss ideas during the round robin.

3. Present one idea at a time.

4. It is okay to piggy-back or build on the ideas of others.

5. It is okay to pass.

6. Encourage everyone to participate.

7. Say whatever comes to mind, even if it seems silly or wild.

Special Notes for the Session Leader

1. Make sure every idea presented is written down.

2. Do not let the brainstorming session become a gripe session. The ideas generated need to be focused on the solution of the problem, not the justification of why it exists.

3. Do not allow the session to be dominated by one or two people.

4. Perform the round robin quickly (10 to 20 minutes).

Summary

Brainstorming is a very valuable technique for generating ideas and forming a working team. It can and should be used throughout the entire problem-solving process.

NOMINAL GROUP TECHNIQUE

The nominal group technique is used to generate ideas and then evaluate and prioritize them. The idea generation portion of the nominal group technique is very similar to brainstorming. The primary difference is that in the nominal group technique, each member of the group is asked to silently come up with as many ideas as possible by writing down his or her ideas on a sheet of paper. After a sufficient amount of time has elapsed (usually 15 to 20 minutes), the group leader asks each member to share one idea he or she has written down using the round robin technique. Everything else, including the evaluation stage, is essentially the same as in brainstorming.

One variation on the nominal group technique works quite well. After everyone has written down their ideas, the papers are collected, shuffled, and then redistributed for the round robin stage. This variation eliminates ownership of ideas and, more importantly, eliminates any embarrassment over suggesting silly or wild ideas. In order for this variation to work, the papers used by the group members to record their ideas cannot have any marks that might identify a particular person. An easy means of doing this is for the session leader to pass out index cards. If index cards are used, the session leader can request that only one idea be recorded per card (everyone can have as many blank cards as they wish). One idea per card allows for easier shuffling of ideas, which allows for the anonymous contribution of ideas.

In brainstorming, once the ideas have been generated and evaluated, the process is finished. In the nominal group technique, the team is now ready to prioritize the ideas. Prioritization of ideas does not have to be done during the same meeting as the idea generation and evaluation. It can easily be done at a later time. Typically, some time is allowed for the team to think about the ideas generated.

Prioritizing Methodology

Step 1: The group recorder writes out (so everyone in the group can see) and numbers all of the ideas that are being considered for prioritization. For example, a team is investigating a problem with the quality of a cookie they are making. At the end of the brainstorming evaluation stage, eight ideas on the possible cause of the problem remain. The eight ideas are written and numbered on a flip chart as follows:

1. Temperature

2. Pressure

3. Humidity

4. Baking time

5. Cooling time

6. Ingredients

7. Packaging

8. Mixing

Step 2: Each member copies the list or a copy is handed out to each member (to make individual voting easier). This list becomes each member's worksheet.

Step 3: Each member ranks all of the items on his or her worksheet. Each member must rank the items in the same way. The method for ranking is agreed upon at the beginning of the session. There are many appropriate means of ranking. One of the more common means of ranking is to give the highest priority item the highest number. In our cookie example, there are eight items. Therefore, the highest priority item would get an 8. (The highest number corresponds to the total number of items being considered.)

Step 4: In round robin fashion, the team leader has each member call out his or her ranking. Each member's ranking is recorded. When everyone's ranking (including the team leader's and the recorder's) has been recorded, the rankings for each item are totaled.

In the cookie example, the team consists of five members and the individual ranking is as follows:

1. Temperature	7, 6, 8, 7, 5	=	33
2. Pressure	2, 1, 1, 2, 4	=	10
3. Humidity	1, 3, 2, 1, 1	=	8
4. Baking time	8, 4, 7, 6, 2	=	27
5. Cooling time	3, 2, 6, 4, 3	=	18
6. Ingredients	5, 8, 5, 8, 7	=	33
7. Packaging	4, 7, 3, 5, 6	=	25
8. Mixing	6, 5, 4, 3, 8	=	26

Step 5: The total scores are reviewed. The higher the score, the higher the priority of that item. Because the team is trying to identify the item with the highest priority, the item with the lowest score (which indicates the lowest priority) is eliminated from the list. In this example, humidity is eliminated.

Step 6: Steps 2 to 5 are repeated until only one item remains. This is the item that the team has decided is the most important and is the one that the team will begin to work on.

Summary

The nominal group technique is very useful for both generating ideas and prioritizing ideas through team consensus.

MULTIVOTING

Multivoting is a technique used to reduce a list of ideas or problems down to the "vital few." It is very similar to the prioritizing stage of the nominal group technique. The main difference is that a team never multivotes down to one item.

Methodology

Step 1:   Similar to the nominal group technique, the group recorder writes down (so everyone in the group can see) and numbers all of the ideas that are being considered for prioritization. In the cookie example, the eight ideas are written on a flip chart as follows:

1. Temperature

2. Pressure

3. Humidity

4. Baking time

5. Cooling time

6. Ingredients

7. Packaging

8. Mixing

Step 2:   This step is called the first vote. Each member of the group votes on the items that he or she feels are of highest priority. Each group member can vote for as many as desired. The voting is coordinated by the team leader.

In the cookie example, the voting is as follows:

1. Temperature =   5 member votes

2. Pressure   =   1 member vote

3. Humidity   =   0 votes

4. Baking time   =   4 member votes

5. Cooling time =   2 member votes

6. Ingredients   =   5 member votes

7. Packaging   =   4 member votes

8. Mixing   =   4 member votes

Step 3:   Eliminate those items that received a relatively low number of votes. In our example, pressure, humidity, and cooling time are eliminated because they received less that three votes.

Step 4:   List and number the remaining items. In our example, the following five items remain:

1. Temperature

2. Baking time

3. Ingredients

4. Packaging

5. Mixing

Step 5:   This step is call the second vote. Each team member is given a specific number of votes. The number of votes each member gets is equal to half of the number of items remaining. If an odd number of items remains, round up. In our example, five items remain, so each team member gets three votes. The voting goes as follows:

1. Temperature   =   5 member votes

2. Baking time   =   3 member votes

3. Ingredients   =   4 member votes

4. Packaging   =   2 member votes

5. Mixing   =   1 member votes

Step 6:   Eliminate those items that received relatively few votes. In our example, mixing and packaging are eliminated.

Step 7:   Continue multivoting until three to five items remain. These are the items that the team will study further. In the cookie example, only three items are left (temperature, baking time, and ingredients), which are the three items the team will study further.

Summary

Multivoting is a very valuable tool when trying to reduce a large number of items down to just a few. The main advantage in using multivoting is that it is quick and easy to use.

CONCLUSION

Brainstorming, nominal group technique, and multivoting are three of the most commonly used problem identification tools. The common element among them is that they allow every member of the team to have a say. This promotes team involvement and reduces the risk of individuals not participating because they feel left out.

It is important to note that the decisions made by using these techniques are team decisions rather than individual decisions. As in any group decision, the decision is seldom made based on a unanimous vote. By using the nominal group technique and multivoting, neither is a decision made based on a majority vote. Instead, a decision is made based on team consensus. In this way, the decision made is acceptable to all team members and unacceptable to no one.

EXERCISES

7.1 Who developed the technique of brainstorming, and why did he develop it?

7.2 What is brainstorming?

7.3 What is the most important guideline to remember when brainstorming?

7.4 List the seven guidelines for effective brainstorming. Can you think of any additional guidelines?

7.5 What is the recommended means of recording a brainstorming session? Why?

7.6 What is the difference between the idea generation portion of the nominal group technique and brainstorming?

7.7 What is multivoting?

7.8 What is the difference between multivoting and the nominal group technique?

7.9 What is the common element among the three techniques?

BIBLIOGRAPHY

Clark, Charles H., *Brainstorming*. Doubleday, New York, 1958.

FPL Quality Improvement Program. QI Story and Techniques. Florida Power and Light Company, Miami, 1987.

Hawkins, Katherine W., "Team Development and Management," *Library Administration and Management.* Winter 1990, p. 11(16).

Hetzel, Robert W., "Solving Complex Problems Requires Good People, Good Processes," *NASSP Bulletin.* June 1992, p. 49(7).

Osborn, Alex F., *Applied Imagination.* Charles Scribner and Sons, New York, 1957.

Pokorny, Lois J., "Introducing a Modified Nominal Group Technique for Issue Identification," *Evaluation Practice.* May 1988, p. 40(5).

Rawlinson, J. Geoffrey, *Creative Thinking and Brainstorming.* John Wiley & Sons, New York, 1981.

The Memory Jogger: A Pocket Guide of Tools for Continuous Improvement. GOAL/QPC, Methuen, Mass., 1988.

Zemke, Ron, "In Search of...Good Ideas," *Training.* January 1993, p. 46(7).

8
THE SEVEN BASIC QUALITY CONTROL TOOLS

BACKGROUND

In 1968, Dr. Kaoru Ishikawa wrote a book entitled *Gemba no QC Shuho* to introduce quality control techniques and practices to the workers of Japan. It was designed to be "used for self-study; training of employees by foremen; or in QC reading groups" (Ishikawa, 1982, p. iii) in the Japanese workplace. It is in this book that the seven basic quality control tools were first presented. (Dr. Ishikawa did not call them the seven basic quality control tools. This descriptor came later.) In 1971, an English translation of Dr. Ishikawa's book entitled *Guide to Quality Control* was published by the Asian Productivity Organization (Ishikawa, 1982, p. i). This book has been widely used and is still a valuable resource when using the seven basic tools.

The seven basic quality control tools as originally identified by Dr. Ishikawa are:

- Check sheets

- Graphs

- Histograms

- Pareto charts

- Cause-and-effect diagrams

- Scatter diagrams

- Control charts

These seven are considered the traditional tools because they are the ones presented in Dr. Ishikawa's book. However, another basic tool, the flow-chart, is considered to be just as valuable. Because the flowchart is such a valuable tool, it sometimes replaces a lesser used tool (like scatter diagrams) in the list of seven. Depending on what book or article you read, a listing of the seven basic tools may exclude one or more of those listed above and include a personal favorite of the particular author. Regardless of which tools are listed, the fundamental criterion is that the tool be a structured technique for collecting and analyzing data.

The remainder of this chapter provides an introduction to and the basics of how to use the traditional seven tools. A section on flowcharts is also included because they are so popular. For better understanding, these tools can be divided into three distinct categories: tools for identifying, tools for prioritizing and communicating, and tools for analyzing. The identifying tools are the check sheet and the flowchart. Both are used to help identify and quantify where and what problems exist. Once a problem area has been identified, the prioritizing tools can be used. The prioritizing tools consist of histograms, Pareto charts, and graphs. These tools help the user organize, understand, interpret, and present the data gathered. With this information, the user can now prioritize which problems to work on and in what order they should be addressed. Because these tools provide charts and graphs that are very easy to understand, they can also be considered the major communication tools of the group. With a specific problem identified, the analyzing tools can be used. The analyzing tools are the cause-and-effect diagram, the scatter diagram, and control charts (histo-grams can also be considered an analyzing tool). These tools are used to examine and investigate the causes of the problem. They can also suggest possible corrective actions. It should be noted that 70 to 80% of all problems can be solved by using check sheets, Pareto diagrams, and cause-and-effect diagrams.

CHECK SHEETS

Check sheets are forms that are used to systematically collect data. They give the user a "place to start" (a major stumbling block for some) and provide a structure for collecting the data. They also aid the user in organizing the data for use later. (The data gathered in a check sheet can be used in building histograms, Pareto charts, control charts, etc.) The primary benefits of check sheets are that they are very easy to use and understand and can provide a clear picture of the situation. Check sheets essentially allow the user to speak with facts (a fundamental tenet of total quality management).

There are many types of check sheets that can be and are being used. Three major types are discussed here: defect-location check sheets, tally check sheets, and defect-cause check sheets.

ABC MOTOR COMPANY
SOUTH PLANT

Defect location check sheet for examining paint blemishes occurring on passenger and
driver front door on 1991 Model 480si

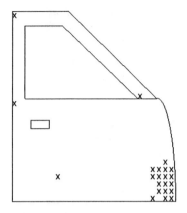

Data collected by: S.J. (Shift Supervisor)
Period of study: Shift 1, February 11, 1991

FIGURE 8.1   Defect-Location Check Sheet

Defect-Location Check Sheets

The defect-location check sheet is usually a sketch, drawing, or picture of the product being made. The location and nature of problems or defects are marked on the diagram. An example is provided in Figure 8.1, which is a sketch of an automobile door. It should be noted that the sketch is not to scale. The important thing is that it represents the part being studied and the defects can be easily stratified. This check sheet was used to examine paint blemishes on a car door. From this check sheet, it was found that the majority of paint blemishes occurred on the lower right corner. Upon investigation, it was discovered that the shape of this door differed from the shape of the door on the previous model and the programming for the spray guns had not been properly changed. This type of check sheet typically leads to fast corrective action.

Tally Check Sheet

The tally check sheet is used to count the number of occurrences of different types of defects. By knowing which type of defect occurs most frequently, appropriate action can be taken to reduce the total number of defects. Figure 8.2 is an example of a tally check sheet to collect data on the reasons for customer complaints about a particular brand of bread. The check sheet suggests that the main cause of complaints was due to packaging. The team felt that this was not an accurate representation of the problem, because the data were collected over a limited time span. To

COMPLAINT ANALYSIS
XYZ BREAD
DECEMBER 1992

COMPLAINT TYPE	TALLY	TOTAL
QUALITY	~~IIII~~ ~~IIII~~ ~~IIII~~ ~~IIII~~ ~~IIII~~ ~~IIII~~ ~~IIII~~ ~~IIII~~	39
PACKAGING	~~IIII~~ ~~IIII~~ ~~IIII~~ ~~IIII~~ ~~IIII~~ ~~IIII~~ ~~IIII~~ ~~IIII~~ ~~IIII~~ II	47
INFESTATION	~~IIII~~ ~~IIII~~ I ~~IIII~~ ~~IIII~~	21
FOREIGN MATERIAL	~~IIII~~ ~~IIII~~ ~~IIII~~ ~~IIII~~	19
OTHER	~~IIII~~ I ~~IIII~~	11

137 Total
Complaints

Data tabulated by Andrew Thomas   January 27, 1993

Data tabulated from records collected by customer service department for
the month of December 1992

FIGURE 8.2   Tally Check Sheet

verify the main cause, the team decided to collect data for the previous six months. (This was relatively easy since the customer service department had been keeping very accurate records on all complaints received during the past year.) Figure 8.3 is a summary tally sheet for this six-month time frame and indicates that the main problem was really the quality of the bread.

Defect-Cause Check Sheet

The previous check sheets are used to determine certain aspects of defects, such as location or general cause. However, when more information about the cause of a defect is required, a defect-cause check sheet is used. A defect-cause check sheet that was used to determine the reasons for poor quality bread is illustrated in Figure 8.4. The check sheet indicates that the highest percentage of poor quality bread was being produced by operator 2 in oven C. Because operator 2 also used oven D, which had the lowest percentage of poor quality bread, operator error was ruled out as the main cause. Further study showed that proper maintenance had not been done

COMPLAINT ANALYSIS
XYZ BREAD
JULY 1992 - DECEMBER 1992

COMPLAINT TYPE	TOTAL
Quality	1309
Packaging	498
Infestation	261
Foreign Material	192
Other	112

2372 Total Complaints

Data tabulated by Andrew Thomas   February 18, 1993

Data tabulated from records collected by customer service department for the   months
July - December 1992

FIGURE 8.3   Summary Check Sheet

DEFECT CAUSE ANAYLSIS
XYZ BREAD

Purpose: Investigate occurrances of poor quality bread
Location: Oven center
Study period: March 15 - 19, 1993
Data collected by: F.W. (Supervisor)

Operator	Oven	Monday 3/15/93	Tuesday 3/16/93	Wednesday 3/17/93	Thursday 3/18/93	Friday 3/19/93
1	A	xxxx	xx o	oo	x	
	B	xxx oo	x	xxx o	xx o	xxx oo
2	C	xxxxxx xxx ooooo o	xxxxxxx x ooooo	xxxxxxxx xxxx oooooo oo	xxxxxx xx ooooo	xxxxxxx ooo
	D	xxx o	x	xx	o	x

x   burned   **o**   undercooked

FIGURE 8.4   Defect-Cause Check Sheet

on oven C because this oven was older than the other three ovens and
replacement parts were difficult to get.

Constructing a Check Sheet

Rigid steps have not been developed for constructing check sheets.
Therefore, a set of guidelines has been developed:

1. Identify the problem area. This should direct the user to the type of check sheet to be used.

2. Determine the categories or types of defects possible. This is done by asking the standard questions who, what, when, where, why, and how either individually or in a group. Typically, the best results come from brainstorming. It is not necessary to define all of the categories before collecting data. If other categories are found after data collection starts, inform all personnel involved in the data gathering, add the category, and note when the category was added so that analysis will be done properly.

3. Design the form. There are many appropriate formats for the check sheet, but it is important that it be understandable and easy to use. All rows and columns should be properly labeled and enough space should be provided for easy data entry. (Leave space for unexpected extra categories.) The form should include who, where, when, why, and how the data were collected.

4. Set a schedule for collecting the data. The schedule should include who, where, and when.

5. Collect the data.

6. Summarize and analyze the check sheet.

7. Most importantly, remember the KISS principle: **keep it simple**. The simpler it is, the less likely that mistakes will be made.

Special Note

If categories are incomplete, the information in the check sheet may be misinterpreted.

FLOWCHARTS

Flowcharts are graphical representations of a process which detail the sequencing of the materials, machinery, and operations that make up that process. They are an excellent means of documenting what is going on in a process and communicating that information to everyone.

There are many benefits to using a flowchart. First, it clearly identifies the components of a process. This helps the people who work in the process understand where they fit in and what the overall objective is. Second, it also can be used as a training tool for new workers who are brought into the process or for existing workers who change location within the process. Third, it can serve as a guide for identifying problems or areas of improvement within the process. It also helps identify where and when in the process measurements can be made. Fourth, it can be used to document a simple operation such as a cash sales transaction, as

Special Note

Steps 4 and 5 can be done easily using any number of computer packages.

Bar Graphs

A bar graph, better known as a bar chart, is a visual illustration of data in which rectangular bars are used to represent the quantity of the variable being studied. This chart is used primarily for comparison purposes. There are special types of bar charts available for use. The two most common are the histogram and the Pareto chart. Each has a specific purpose and will be discussed later.

A bar chart is displayed in Figure 8.9, which illustrates the serving speed of the top ten fastest servers in the IBM/ATP tennis tour.

Constructing a Bar Chart

Step 1: Determine the variable to be measured. This will be represented by vertical bars of equal width.

Step 2: Determine the factors that are being compared, such as days of the week, different workers (see Figure 8.9), different locations, etc.

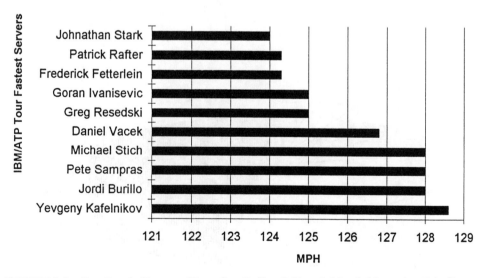

FIGURE 8.9   Bar Graph (Source: "Speeding Bullets," *Tennis Match Magazine*. July/August 1994, p. 56.)

Step 3: Collect the data.

Step 4: Label (and where appropriate scale) the x and y axes.

Step 5: Draw the vertical bars. Remember that the height of the bar is proportional to the number being represented.

Step 6: The bar chart is ready for use.

Special Note

Steps 4 and 5 can also be done using the computer.

Circle Graph

Circle graphs are more commonly known as pie charts. Pie charts represent data as slices of a pie. The larger the slice, the larger the percentage that item is of the whole. Figure 8.10 illustrates how a particular four-year-old spends his day. The whole pie represents 24 hours. Other than sleeping, this four-year-old spends most of his time playing, which is to be expected.

The pie chart is a very effective tool for comparing relative magnitude or frequency and how it contributes to the whole. This is true only if the number of categories being compared is kept low. If there are too many categories, the user spends most of his or her time trying to determine what the categories are and misses the whole point of the chart.

ACTIVITIES OF A FOUR YEAR OLD

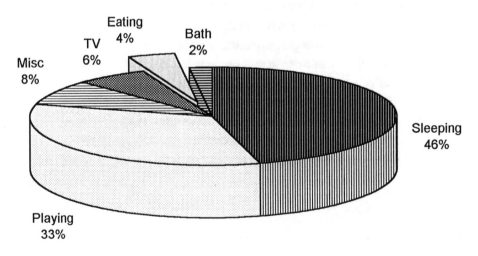

FIGURE 8.10 Pie Chart

Constructing a Pie Chart

Step 1: Determine the items to be compared.

Step 2: Collect the data.

Step 3: Draw the circle (pie).

Step 4: Divide the circle by several radii. Each wedge of the pie should represent one item. The size of each wedge should be proportional to the percentage that item contributes to the whole. An easy way to determine the size of the wedge is to take the value of the item and divide it by the total value of all of the items. Then multiply this number by 360 (the total number of degrees in a circle). The resulting number represents the number of degrees that pie wedge should encompass. A protractor should be used to accurately plot the degrees.

Step 5: Label the chart. This includes the overall subject of the chart as well as each wedge. Be sure to include the percentage of each wedge. Also make sure that everything is easily readable and understandable. If it is not, another type of chart may be more appropriate.

Step 6: The pie chart is ready for use.

HISTOGRAMS

The histogram is a type of bar chart that visually displays the variability of a product or process. It shows the various measures of central tendency (mean, mode, and average). It can be used to illustrate whether product specifications are being met by drawing the specifications on the histogram. A histogram can also be used to study and identify the underlying distribution of the variable being studied. (The histogram merely illustrates the nature of distribution. It does not, by itself, provide statistical proof of a particular distribution.)

Constructing a Histogram

Because the construction of a histogram is more complex than the previous tools discussed, a sample histogram will be created as an example.

Step 1: Determine the product, process, or parameter to be studied and the measurement of interest. For example, suppose a veterinarian is interested in studying the distribution associated with the weight of newborn German shepherd puppies. The parameter to be studied is weight (ounces) of newborn German shepherd puppies. All of the puppies sampled are less than five days old. A total of 100 newborn German shepherd puppies are randomly sampled.

Step 2:   Collect the data. The following data were collected over a two-week time period.

13.0	13.3	13.6	13.2	14.0	12.9	14.2	12.9	14.5	13.5
14.1	14.0	13.7	13.4	14.4	14.3	14.8	13.9	13.5	14.3
14.2	14.1	14.0	13.9	13.9	14.0	14.5	13.6	13.3	12.9
12.8	13.1	13.6	14.5	14.6	12.9	13.1	14.4	14.0	14.4
13.1	14.1	14.2	12.9	13.3	14.0	14.1	13.1	13.6	13.7
14.0	13.6	13.2	13.4	13.9	14.5	14.0	14.4	13.9	14.6
12.9	14.3	14.0	12.9	14.2	14.8	14.5	13.1	12.7	13.9
13.6	14.4	13.1	14.5	13.5	13.3	14.0	13.6	13.5	14.3
13.2	13.8	13.7	12.8	13.4	13.8	13.3	13.7	14.1	13.7
13.7	13.8	13.4	13.7	14.1	12.8	13.7	13.8	14.1	14.3

Step 3:   Count the data:

$$N = 100$$

Step 4:   Record the largest value and the smallest value. Calculate the range (R).

Largest value = 14.8

Smallest value = 12.7

Range = largest value − smallest value

= 14.8 − 12.7 = 2.1

Step 5:   Determine the number of cells (vertical bars) desired. Dr. Ishikawa suggests using the following as a guide when selecting the number of cells (Ishikawa, 1982, p. 8):

Number of data points	Number of cells (K)
Under 50	5–7
50–100	6–10
100–250	7–12
Over 250	10–20

When $N = 100$, the recommended number of cells (K) is 10.

Step 6:   Determine the cell width (H). This value is found by dividing the range value (determined in step 4) by the recommended number of cells (determined in step 5).

$$H = R/K = 2.1/10 = 0.21$$

This number should have the same number of decimal places as the data. In this case, it is necessary to round off H. (Sometimes, because of rounding, more cells may be needed.)

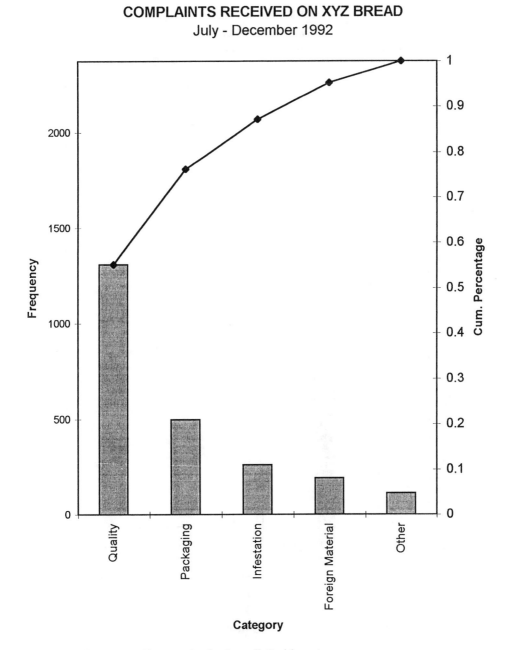

COMPLAINTS RECEIVED ON XYZ BREAD
July - December 1992

FIGURE 8.12 Pareto Chart to Study Overall Problem Area

As can be seen from Figures 8.12 to 8.14, Pareto charts can be used to study an overall problem area (Figure 8.12), study one specific cause of the overall problem area (Figure 8.13), and to provide a means of measuring the impact of any changes made (Figure 8.14).

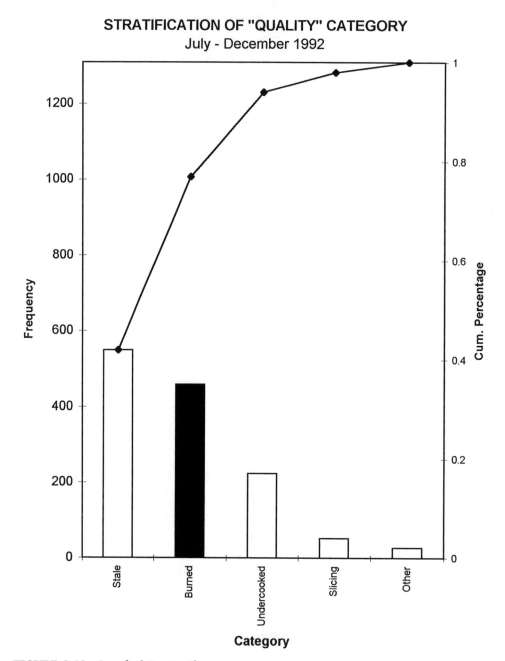

FIGURE 8.13 Stratified Pareto Chart

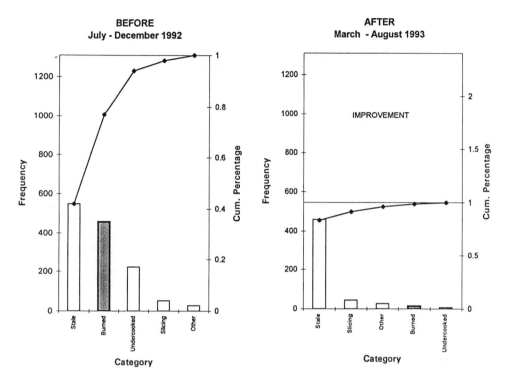

FIGURE 8.14   Before and After Pareto Charts

Constructing a Pareto Chart

It will be helpful to refer to Figures 8.12 to 8.14 when implementing the following steps.

Step 1:   Determine the problem or improvement area to be studied. This can be mandated from management, suggested by an employee, or come from an improvement team.

Step 2:   Identify the data to be used or collected and the basis of comparison. The data can already exist as inspection records, maintenance logs, time cards, etc. The basis of comparison could be frequency, cost, time, etc.

Step 3:   Identify the categories that will be used on the chart. Check sheets should be designed or revised to aid in organizing or collecting the data once the categories have been specified.

Step 4:   Identify the time period for the study. This will depend on the problem being studied. The time period can range anywhere from one hour to several years. The selected time period should be convenient, such as one day, one week, one month, quarterly, etc. If more than one Pareto chart or other charts will be used in the study, the time periods should be the same to allow proper comparison.

Step 5:   Gather the data.

Step 6:   Total the frequency of occurrences in each category. This will be the height of the bar on the Pareto chart.

Step 7:   Order the categories in descending order with respect to the totals in Step 6 and calculate the percentage that each category contributes to the whole. For example, the data from Figure 8.3 can be organized via a summary table similar to the following one:

Category	Frequency	Percentage	Cumulative Percentage
Quality	1309	55.2	55.2
Packaging	498	21.0	76.2
Infestation	261	11.0	87.2
Foreign material	192	8.1	95.3
Other	112	4.7	100.0
TOTAL	2372	100.0	

Step 8:   Draw and label the x and y axes. The categories of the problem are placed along the x axis. They are ordered in descending order starting at the left. The basis of comparison (dollars, number, time, etc.) is placed along the left y axis. A practice that is coming into wider use is to place the cumulative percentage of occurrence along the right y axis (provided the sum of percentages does not exceed 100%; the percentage will exceed 100% if the categories overlap or are not mutually exclusive). If the percentage axis is used, care should be taken to ensure that the scale on this axis directly corresponds to the scale on the left y axis. For example, the 50% point on the right side is directly opposite the halfway point on the left side.

Step 9:   Draw in the bars for each category beginning at the left. The height of each bar should correspond to a value on the left y axis. The bars should be equal in width. If there are several categories with relatively few occurrences, they can be grouped into one category labeled "other." The "other" category is always the farthest to the right. (The "other" category should never be the largest bar in the diagram.)

Step 10:   Plot the cumulative percentage line on the chart. This line starts at the lower left-hand corner, and this point represents zero. Draw a straight line from this point to the top right-hand corner of the first bar and label it with its respective percentage. Next, draw an imaginary vertical line from the right-hand corner of the adjacent bar. Locate the cumulative percentage point on this imaginary line. Then draw a straight line from the previous cumulative percentage point to this point. This is repeated until all of the cumulative percentage points have been plotted. (The last point

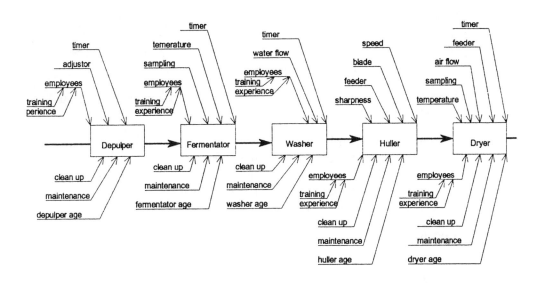

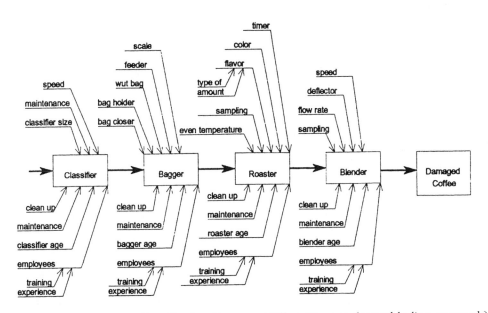

FIGURE 8.17 Process Classification Cause-and-Effect Diagram (assembly line approach) (Source: CAFENSA [Cafetaleros del Norte S.A.] Managua, Nicaragua.)

Step 3: Identify the major causes of the effect (problem). These will be the major "bones" of the diagram. The causes can be generated through brainstorming, or they can be the standard six (or five) listed previously, or they can be the different process stages.

Step 4: Draw and label the major "bones" as diagonal lines projecting off the backbone.

Step 5: Brainstorm for the reasons of these major causes by continually asking "Why does this cause produce this effect?" Each time an answer is given, a small bone, representing this subcause, is drawn extending from the cause bone. Be sure to label this subcause. This is repeated until no more answers are forthcoming.

Step 6: At this point, the diagram is complete and ready for use.

Using a Cause-and-Effect Diagram

Step 1: Identify the most likely root cause of the effect (problem) being studied and circle it.

Step 2: Verify that the most likely root cause has a significant impact on the effect. This can be done using a Pareto chart or scatter diagram (explained in the next section). Because data must be gathered and analyzed to complete this step, adequate time should be allowed. Remember that the purpose of a CE diagram is just to show the relationship between a given effect and all possible causes of that effect. At this point, the actual analysis has started.

If it is found that the root cause being studied does not have a significant impact on the effect, then the team returns to Step 1. If it is found that the root cause does have a significant impact, then the improvement process can continue.

Special Notes

1. A CE diagram does not by itself identify the major root cause(s) of a problem.

2. Be sure to test the logic of the diagram. In other words, make sure that every subcause is properly placed.

3. If one cause on the diagram appears to have many complicated subcauses, then construct a separate diagram for that cause.

4. Don't be afraid to make corrections or deletions.

5. The more a CE diagram is used, the more effective it becomes—so use it.

6. CE diagrams are also used for positive investigations. For example, Dr. Ishikawa developed a CE diagram to determine how to make perfect rice.

SCATTER DIAGRAMS

A scatter diagram is a graph of point plots that is used to compare two variables. The distribution of the points indicates the cause-and-effect relationship (or lack thereof) between two variables. In order to use a scatter diagram, paired data must be available for the two variables being studied.

Scatter diagrams are very useful in that they (1) can clearly indicate whether or not a cause-and-effect relationship exists and (2) give an idea of the strength of that relationship. Five different scatter diagrams are displayed in Figure 8.18. Figure 8.18a shows that there is a strong positive relationship between x_1 and y_1 and indicates that an increase in y_1 depends on increases in x_1. Figure 8.18b shows that there is a positive relationship between x_2 and y_2. However, other factors seem to be influencing y_2. Figure 8.18c shows that there is no relationship between x_3 and y_3. Figure 8.18d shows a negative relationship between x_4 and y_4, but that other factors are affecting y_4. Figure 8.18e shows a strong negative relationship between x_5 and y_5.

A scatter diagram by itself does not imply statistical significance of the observed relationship. Additional analysis, in the form of probability plotting or calculation of the correlation coefficient, is required for statistical correlation. It should also be noted that the conclusion drawn from a given scatter diagram is only valid over the range of values that were actually observed.

Constructing a Scatter Diagram

Step 1: Determine which two variables are to be paired and studied.

Step 2: Collect 50 to 100 paired samples and enter them on the data sheet. Make sure to document who, what, when, where, and how the data were collected.

Step 3: Draw the x and y axes of the diagram. Typically the x axis is used for the controlled, or "cause," variable and the y axis is used for the predicted, or "effect," variable.

Step 4: Plot the data. If data are repeated and fall on the same point, circle that point every time it is repeated.

Step 5: The scatter diagram is now ready for use.

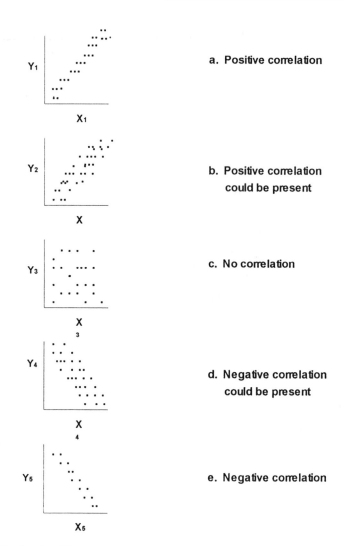

FIGURE 8.18 Scatter Diagrams

Special Notes

1. Negative relationships are just as important as positive relationships.

2. The diagram does not guarantee that a relationship really exists. For example, if food prices were plotted against clothing prices, the conclusion might be that as food prices increase, clothing prices also increase. However, what is really happening is that other factors such as inflation, availability, and production costs make it seem like a relationship exists when in fact there is none.

3. The only conclusion that can be drawn from a scatter diagram is that x and y are related, but not that one causes the other.

4. Scatter diagrams are very useful and powerful, but they can easily be misused. Be sure you understand your data.

CONTROL CHARTS

A control chart is a special type of run chart with limits. It shows the amount and nature of variation in the process over time. It also enables pattern interpretation and detection of changes in the process.

There are three main reasons for using a control chart. First, it is used to monitor a process in order to determine if the process is operating with only chance causes of variation. If it is, then the process is said to be in statistical control. If it is not, then the process is said to be out-of-control. If the process is out-of-control, then the control chart can be used to help identify the assignable causes of variation and correct the process. Second, control charts are used to estimate the parameters of a process. Third, control charts are used in reducing the variability of a process.

The type of control chart depends on the type of data used in its construction. If the data are based on measurements (such as pounds, inches, etc.), then the data are said to be **continuous** and a variables control chart is used. If the data are based on counting (such as the number of defects in a product), then the data are said to be **discrete** and an attributes control chart is used. There are two types of variables control charts. One, based on averages, is called the X bar, ($\overline{X}$), chart. An $\overline{X}$ chart is accompanied by either a range (R) chart or a standard deviation (S) chart. The second type of variables control chart is based on the individual measurements and is called an X chart. It is accompanied by a moving range (MR) chart. There are four types of control charts for attributes: the p chart, np chart, c chart, and u chart. The p chart plots the fraction non-conforming. The np chart plots the number non-conforming. The c chart plots the number of non-conformities. The u chart plots the number of non-conformitites per unit.

Because there are so many different types of control charts, separate chapters are devoted to control charts for variables and control charts for attributes.

EXERCISES

8.1 a. Design a location check sheet that can be used by the local volleyball team to help them identify in what areas of the court most of their mistakes are occurring. Mistakes include out-of-bounds spikes, spikes not returned, serves not returned, blocks out of bounds, etc.

b. Design a tally check sheet that summarizes the errors per game that the volleyball team makes during a specific match. Errors include out-of-bounds serves, spikes, blocks, double hits, foot faults, etc.

c. Design a defect-cause check sheet that summarizes the errors made by each player. This check sheet will help the coach identify specific areas that each player needs to work on during practice. Errors include out-of-bounds serves, spikes, blocks, foot faults, out of position, etc.

Note: (A) You may need to attend a volleyball match in order to develop a complete list of possible errors for parts a, b, and c. (B) Parts a, b, and c can be used for any team sport.

8.2 Given the following data, create a bar chart that shows the estimated revenues from sales, property, and income taxes paid by undocumented aliens for the states given:

State	Estimated revenue
California	$732 million
Florida	$277 million
Nevada	$175 million
New York	$422 million
Texas	$202 million

8.3 Given the following data, create a pie chart indicating the percentage distribution of substance abuse:

Distribution of substance abuse among regular users	
Beer	40
Wine	7
Liquor	17
Marijuana	49
Hashish	9
Hard drugs	22
TOTAL	144

Note: Hard drugs include speed, acid, cocaine, valium, Quaaludes, inhalants, mescaline, opium, codeine, heroin, darvon, and peyote.

8.4 Tony has been on a special diet for the past 15 weeks. His goal is to lose 40 pounds. At the end of each week, Tony weighed himself. The following table gives his weight for each week. Draw a line graph that shows Tony's progress.

Week	Weight (lbs.)	Week	Weight (lbs.)
0	245 (starting weight)	8	217
1	241	9	219

2	236	10	216
3	233	11	214
4	231	12	215
5	227	13	212
6	220	14	210
7	218	15	207

8.5 Two operators in a machine shop use the same two machines to produce a specialty item. The critical quality characteristic of this item is length. A sample of size four was taken at random from each machine every day for 18 days. The length of each item sampled was recorded and the data are given in Table 8.1.

a. Draw the following histograms:

1. An overall histogram
2. A histogram of operator A
3. A histogram of operator B
4. A histogram of machine 1
5. A histogram of machine 2

b. If the specs of the item are 112 ± 12, what conclusions can you make from the histograms drawn in part a?

TABLE 8.1   Histogram Data

Day	Operator	Machine 1				Machine 2			
1	A	109.2	109.5	100.2	112.0	114.3	121.8	114.6	114.4
2	A	108.5	108.7	106.2	107.8	115.3	116.7	112.3	112.0
3	A	104.2	110.2	110.5	105.9	115.7	113.8	115.2	102.7
4	B	104.0	103.3	98.2	99.9	112.5	110.2	111.3	110.4
5	B	109.6	103.7	113.2	109.6	108.4	114.9	112.8	114.8
6	B	99.0	97.7	102.0	113.1	107.5	109.9	110.6	112.3
7	A	108.1	107.9	111.0	106.2	112.3	116.2	108.4	110.8
8	A	105.2	104.8	98.7	105.8	108.1	111.9	112.9	109.0
9	A	104.6	107.0	100.8	104.6	112.2	109.8	107.6	112.6
10	B	97.2	110.6	99.5	115.3	106.9	107.1	113.6	112.2
11	B	99.1	107.2	100.8	101.2	109.6	109.5	106.8	114.2
12	B	114.7	107.5	105.8	100.9	111.4	111.2	114.4	112.6
13	A	100.2	105.5	108.0	102.7	103.5	106.9	110.6	112.3
14	A	101.1	109.2	105.5	100.0	109.1	106.3	109.8	111.4
15	A	101.3	103.1	96.3	105.5	108.0	107.9	105.3	103.6
16	B	104.1	96.6	104.6	99.4	109.6	109.2	106.1	107.1
17	B	102.2	104.4	102.1	106.6	110.0	109.4	109.1	107.0
18	B	94.1	111.0	108.4	102.6	115.6	111.8	105.4	109.0

TABLE 8.2 Pareto Chart Data

OPERATOR	MACHINE	MONDAY	TUESDAY	WEDNESDAY	THURSDAY	FRIDAY
1	A	◆◆◆◆ ■■ ●● ○○ □	◆◆◆◆◆ ■ ●●● ○	◆◆◆◆◆ ■■■■■ ●●●● ○○ □	◆◆◆◆ ■ ●●● ○○	◆◆◆◆◆ ■ ●●●● ○○○
	B	◆◆ ■■ ●	◆◆◆ ■■ ●● □	◆◆◆ ■■■■■ ●● ○	◆◆ ■ ● ○	◆◆ ■ ● ○
2	C	◆◆ ■■ ● ○	◆◆◆◆ ■ ●	◆◆◆ ■■■■■ ● ○	◆◆◆ ■ ● ○ □	◆◆◆◆ ■ ●● ○
	D	◆◆ ■ ●● □	◆◆◆ ■ ● ○	◆◆◆ ■■■■ ●● ○	◆◆◆ ■ ○	◆◆ ■ ●● ○

◆ SCRATCH
■ DENT
● CRACK
○ PEELING
□ OTHER

8.6 Analyze the data in Table 8.2 by drawing appropriate Pareto diagrams. (Hint: You will need several diagrams to fully analyze the data.)

8.7 In 1992, over 20 million cars traveled Interstate 10 between Pensacola and Tallahassee. That year there were 112 accidents which resulted in death. The police classified each accident into one of the five categories listed below. Draw a Pareto chart using the five categories. Further stratify the data using the additional information provided.

Cause of accident	Accidents
Excessive speed	24
Improper lane change	6
Mechanical failure	47
Incapable driver	22
Weather conditions	13
TOTAL	112

Type of mechanical failure	Accidents
Blown tire	32
Lost brakes	9
Lost steering control	5
Other	1
TOTAL	47

8.8 Half of Marion's Bridal Boutique's business consists of creating bridal gowns from a catalog of patterns. The latest gown was returned by the bride-to-be as being defective. Because it could not be fixed or altered in time, the customer went to a competitor and bought a ready-made gown. Since Marion's has a very low production rate, this one dress is a major concern. Use a cause-and-effect diagram to outline the possible causes for this problem. Use each of the three types of cause-and-effect diagrams to present your answer.

8.9 Using a cause-and-effect diagram, analyze the factors that might cause a surfboard to break.

8.10 Durgest Woods manufactures a low production volume of chairs. The wood they receive is cut, sanded, painted, and then assembled. At the end of the line, the chairs are inspected. Lately, the number of rejected chairs has increased and the company would like to know why. Analyze the situation using the three types of cause-and-effect diagrams.

8.11 Using a cause-and-effect diagram, analyze the factors that might cause a house to catch on fire.

8.12 Use a flowchart to describe the operation of pumping gas into your car at a self-service pump. To simplify the process, make the following assumptions:

- There are no power outages
- No waiting in line for a vacant pump
- No waiting in line at the cashier
- Credit cards and ATM cards are accepted
- There is no shortage of gas

8.13 Use a flowchart to describe the process involved in checking out a book at the public library. To simplify the process, make the following assumptions:

- There are no power outages
- The customer has a valid library card

- No waiting for a reference computer
- No waiting for access to the card catalog
- No waiting at the reference desk
- No overdue fees owed by the customer

BIBLIOGRAPHY

Benjamin, Marti and James G. Shaw, "Harnessing the Power of the Pareto Principle," *Quality Progress*. September 1993, p. 103(5).

FPL Quality Improvement Program. QI Story and Techniques. Florida Power and Light Company, Miami, 1987.

Ishikawa, Kaoru, *Guide to Quality Control*. Asian Productivity Organization, Hong Kong, 1982 (available in North America, the U.K., and Western Europe from Unipub, a division of Quality Resources).

Juran, Joseph M., "Pareto, Lorenz, Cournot, Bernoulli, Juran and Others," *Industrial Quality Control*. October 1950, p. 25(6).

Juran, Joseph M., "The Non-Pareto Principle; Mea Culpa," *Quality Progress*. May 1975, p. 8(2).

Juran, Joseph M., *Juran on Leadership for Quality*. 4th ed., McGraw-Hill, New York, 1989.

Kume, Hitoshi, *Statistical Methods for Quality Improvement*. The Association for Overseas Technical Scholarship, Japan, 1985.

Quality Improvement Tools Workbooks. Juran Institute, Wilton, Conn., 1989.

Seven-Part Series on "The Tools of Quality," *Quality Progress*. June–December, 1990:

> Burr, John T., "Part I: Going with the Flow(chart)," *Quality Progress*. June 1990, p. 64(4).
>
> Sarazen, J. Stephen, "Part II: Cause-and-Effect Diagrams," *Quality Progress*. July 1990, p. 59(4).
>
> Shainin, Peter D., "Part III: Control Chart," *Quality Progress*. August 1990, p. 79(4).
>
> "Part IV: Histograms," *Quality Progress*. September 1990, p. 75(4).
>
> "Part V: Check Sheets," *Quality Progress*. October 1990, p. 51(6).
>
> Burr, John T., "Part VI: Pareto Charts," *Quality Progress*. November 1990, p. 59(3).
>
> Burr, John T., "Part VII: Scatter Diagrams," *Quality Progress*. December 1990, p. 87(3).

The Memory Jogger: A Pocket Guide of Tools for Continuous Improvement. GOAL/QPC, Methuen, Mass., 1988.

9

CONTROL CHARTS FOR VARIABLES

BACKGROUND

It was Dr. Shewhart who first suggested the use of control charts. In the late 1920s, Dr. Shewhart suggested that every process exhibits some degree of variation. Since no two things can be produced exactly alike, variation is natural and should be expected. However, Dr. Shewhart discovered that there were two types of variation, chance cause variation and assignable cause variation. Chance cause variation is variation that is inherent in the process. It is random in nature and cannot be controlled. Any process that operates with only chance cause variation is said to be in a state of statistical control. Once a process is in statistical control, adjustments can be made to minimize the random variation, which will improve the process. Assignable cause variation is variation that is controlled by some outside influence or special cause, such as change in material, change in operator, change in tool setting, or other phenomena. Any process that operates with assignable cause variation is said to be out-of-control. By using Dr. Shewhart's control charts, outside influence can usually be identified and controlled.

USES OF CONTROL CHARTS

There are three basic uses of control charts. First, they are used to monitor a given process. Because a control chart shows the degree and nature of variation over time, it can be used to determine whether a process is in a state of statistical control or is out-of-control. If it is out-of-control, the chart aids in quickly finding the assignable causes of the out-of-control condition, which enables taking corrective action before too many bad products can be produced. If a process is in-control, continued monitoring allows for quicker detection of process changes. It also allows for process improvement.

Second, control charts are used to estimate the parameters (mean, variation) of a process. By knowing the parameters of a process, the output and variability of the output can be predicted.

Third, control charts are used to improve a process. Once a process is in a state of statistical control, efforts to reduce process variability can begin. By reducing the variability of the process, the overall quality of the final product increases, which reduces scrap and rework and increases profits.

In short, the emphasis in using control charts is on the early detection and prevention of problems. By preventing problems from occurring in the first place, productivity and profits increase.

VARIABLES CONTROL CHARTS

Variables control charts are the more classical type of control chart. They are used to monitor measurable quality characteristics of a process, such as weight, temperature, viscosity, etc. Anything that can be measured can be monitored using a variables control chart. The main restriction is that a variables control chart can monitor only one quality characteristic at a time. If more than one quality characteristic needs to be monitored, then a chart for each characteristic must be created.

A variables control chart monitors the mean value and the variability of the quality characteristic being studied. The mean value is monitored via an X bar ($\overline{X}$) chart or an individuals (X) chart. Variability is measured via a range (R) or moving range (MR) chart or a standard deviation (S) chart.

Because both the mean and standard deviation must be monitored, variables control charts are used in pairs. Thus an $\overline{X}$ and R chart, $\overline{X}$ and S chart, or X and MR chart would be used.

Normal Distribution

The statistical development of variables control charts assumes that the underlying distribution of the points plotted on the control chart is normally distributed. Graphically speaking, the plotted points would appear similar to the bell-shaped curve shown in Figure 9.1. The notation $x \sim N(\mu, \sigma^2)$, as shown in Figure 9.1, is a special notation used specifically to denote the normal distribution. The notation is interpreted as x is normally distributed with a mean μ and a variance σ^2. Typically, the notation would appear as $x \sim N(10, 3^2)$. This is interpreted as x is distributed with a mean of 10 and a variance of 3^2. The mean and variance are

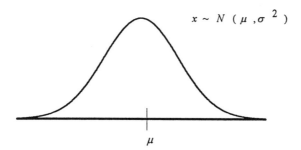

FIGURE 9.1   Normal Distribution

known as the parameters of the distribution. The **mean**, μ, represents the central tendency, or average value, of the distribution. The mean of a distribution (or population) can be estimated from a sample. This estimated mean is represented as $\hat{\mu}$ or $\overline{X}$ and can be estimated from:

$$\hat{\mu} = \overline{X} = \frac{\sum_{i=1}^{n} x_i}{n} \qquad 9.1$$

where n = the total number of items in the sample.

The **variance**, σ^2, represents the variability of the distribution about the mean. The variance can be estimated from:

$$\hat{\sigma}^2 = S^2 = \frac{\sum_{i=1}^{n} (x_i - \overline{x})^2}{n - 1} \qquad 9.2$$

The **standard deviation**, σ, is another representation of the variability, or spread, about the mean. The standard deviation is found by taking the square root of the variance. Figure 9.2 is a basic interpretation of the mean and standard deviation of a normal distribution. Note that the distribution is symmetrical about the mean. Also note that 68.26% of the population is accounted for within $\pm 1\sigma$ of the mean. Within $\pm 2\sigma$ of the mean, 95.46% of the population is accounted for, and within $\pm 3\sigma$ of the mean, 99.73% of the population is accounted for.

The normal distribution is considered to be a continuous distribution. This means that the random variable, x, can assume an infinite number of values. The range of possible values is often from $-\infty$ to $+\infty$.

Every distribution can be represented by a mathematical model that relates the value of the variable with the probability of occurrence at a given value in the population. This is known as the **probability distribution**. Therefore, if x is a normal random variable, then the probability distribution of x is

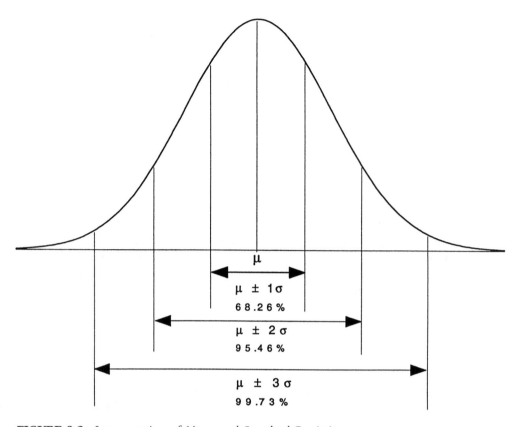

FIGURE 9.2   Interpretation of Mean and Standard Deviation

$$f(x) = \frac{1}{\sigma\sqrt{2\pi}}\, e^{-\frac{1}{2}\left(\frac{x-\mu}{\sigma}\right)^2} \text{ for } -\infty < x < +\infty \qquad 9.3$$

where $\pi = 3.14159...$ and $e = 2.71828...$

The probability that the normal variable x is less than or equal to some value j is expressed by the following cumulative normal distribution:

$$P(x \le j) = F(j) = \int_{-\infty}^{j} \frac{1}{\sigma\sqrt{2\pi}}\, e^{-\frac{1}{2}\left(\frac{x-\mu}{\sigma}\right)^2} dx \qquad 9.4$$

This integral cannot be evaluated in closed form. However, the evaluation can be made if the variable is changed using the **z-transform** or

$$z = \frac{(x-u)}{\sigma} \qquad 9.5$$

By using the z-transform, the evaluation is made independent of μ and σ^2 or

$$P(x \leq j) = P\left(z \leq \frac{j - u}{\sigma}\right) \equiv \Phi\left(\frac{j - u}{\sigma}\right)$$ 9.6

where $\Phi(\ )$ is the cumulative distribution function of the standard normal distribution. In other words, if x is normally distributed with a mean of μ and a standard deviation of σ, then z is distributed according to the standard normal distribution, where $\mu = 0$ and $\sigma = 1$. This transformation is usually called standardization, because it converts a $N(\mu, \sigma^2)$ random variable into a $N(0, 1)$ random variable.

Example 1

Suppose we have a random variable, x, that is normally distributed with a mean of 100 and a standard deviation of 5. We want to determine the probability that x is less 98.5.

Solution

$$P(x \leq 98.5) = P\left(z \leq \frac{98.5 - 100}{5}\right) \equiv \Phi(-0.30)$$

A table for the cumulative standard normal distribution is given in Appendix B. Using this table, we find that a z of –0.30 has a value of 0.38209. This means that there is a 38.209% probability that x will be less than or equal to 98.5 given the mean is 100 and the standard deviation is 5.

Example 2

For the situation described in Example 1, suppose we want to determine the probability that x will be greater than 101.

Solution

We want to find $P(x \geq 101)$. However, by examining the descriptive figure at the top of Appendix B, we see that the table only gives the probability of having a value less than or equal to the corresponding value of z. This means that if we want to determine the probability of having a value greater than a certain value of z, then we must subtract that value from 1.0. In other words,

$$P(x \geq 101) = 1 - P\left(z \leq \frac{101 - 100}{5}\right) = 1 - \Phi(-0.20)$$

$$= 1 - 0.57926 = 0.42074$$

Therefore, there is a 42.074% probability that $x \geq 101$.

Example 3

Suppose we want to find what value of x would give a probability of 15%.

Solution

The 15% is known as the α value. Therefore, what we are looking for is the z value that corresponds to an α of 0.15. Again, examine the figure at the top of Appendix B. It shows that α represents the area under the curve at a point that is less than some z_α. In this example, we are looking for $z_\alpha \geq 0.1500$. Now we look for a value of 0.1500 in the heart of the table and see what z value corresponds to that value. We find that $z_{.15} = -1.035$. To find our value of x, we use the z-transformation equation:

$$z = \frac{x - \mu}{\sigma}$$

Substituting the values we know, we get

$$-1.035 = \frac{x - 100}{5}$$

Solving for x, we get

$$x = 94.825$$

Therefore, a value of 94.825 would give the requested α of 15%.

Statistical Development of Control Charts

Distribution of x Is Normal and μ and σ Are Known

Suppose that the quality characteristic being studied (x) is normally distributed with a known mean (μ) and known standard deviation (σ). There are two charts that can be used to monitor the process mean and two charts that can be used to monitor the process variability.

Charts to Monitor the Process Mean

X bar or $\overline{X}$ Chart

An $\overline{X}$ chart is the most common type of control chart. When using an $\overline{X}$ chart, a sample of size n is taken from the population. The average of this sample is

$$\overline{x} = \frac{x_1 + x_2 + x_3 + \cdots + x_n}{n}$$

Since x is normally distributed, we know that $\overline{x}$ is normally distributed with a mean μ and a standard deviation $\sigma_{\overline{x}}$. We know that

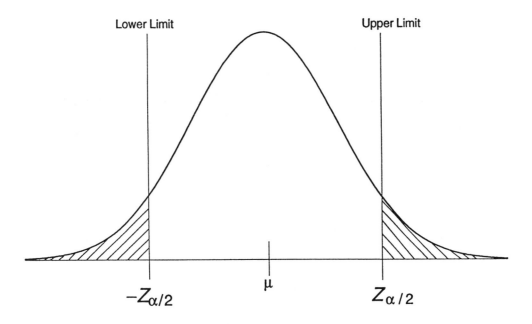

1 − α is the probability that the mean will fall between these limits.

FIGURE 9.3 $\alpha/2$ Limits for $\overline{X}$ Chart

$$\sigma_{\overline{x}} = \frac{\sigma}{\sqrt{n}}$$

Since the normal distribution is symmetric about the mean, limits for the $\overline{X}$ chart can be set by specifying an $\alpha/2$ value (see Figure 9.3). This gives an

$$\text{upper limit} = \mu + z_{\alpha/2}\,\sigma_{\overline{x}} = \mu + z_{\alpha/2}\left(\frac{\sigma}{\sqrt{n}}\right) \qquad 9.7a$$

and a

$$\text{lower limit} = \mu - z_{\alpha/2}\,\sigma_{\overline{x}} = \mu - z_{\alpha/2}\left(\frac{\sigma}{\sqrt{n}}\right) \qquad 9.7b$$

Since ± 3 standard deviations accounts for 99.73% of the population under the curve (see Figure 9.2), $z_{\alpha/2}$ is typically replaced by 3. This gives an

$$\text{upper limit} = \mu + 3\sigma_{\overline{x}} = \mu + 3\left(\frac{\sigma}{\sqrt{n}}\right) \qquad 9.8a$$

and a

$$\text{lower limit } = \mu - 3\sigma_{\bar{x}} = \mu - 3\left(\frac{\sigma}{\sqrt{n}}\right) \qquad 9.8b$$

Since n is a constant value, $\frac{3}{\sqrt{n}}$ is usually replaced by A. Since the value of this factor A is a function of the sample size, n, a table can be developed (see Appendix C).* Substituting A into the above equations gives

$$\text{upper limit } = \mu + A\sigma \qquad 9.9a$$

$$\text{lower limit } = \mu - A\sigma \qquad 9.9b$$

$$\text{center line } = \mu \qquad 9.9c$$

These equations are used to determine the control limits for an $\bar{X}$ chart when the mean and standard deviation are known.

Individuals Chart or X Chart

An individuals chart is used when the sample size is 1. A sample size of 1 typically occurs when:

1. Automated inspection is being used and every unit produced is inspected.

2. It is uneconomical to take multiple measurements.

3. Destructive testing is being used.

The individuals chart directly represents the process. Therefore, the parameters of the X chart can be found from:

$$\text{UCL} = \mu + 3\sigma \qquad 9.10a$$

$$\text{LCL} = \mu - 3\sigma \qquad 9.10b$$

$$\text{center line } = \mu \qquad 9.10c$$

Since the $\bar{X}$ and X charts only monitor the mean of the process, either an R chart or S chart is needed to monitor the process variability. Which to use is based on the size of the sample taken.

Charts to Monitor Process Variability

R Chart

An R chart is typically used when the sample size is less than or equal to 10. Each sample taken has a range, R. This range can be found by

---

* Appendix C gives all the factors needed to construct the different variables control chart limits.

subtracting the smallest value in the sample from the largest value in the sample, or

$$R = x_{max} - x_{min} \qquad \text{9.11}$$

The relationship between the range of a sample taken from a normal distribution and the standard deviation of that distribution is known and can be represented via the relative range, W. The parameters of the distribution of the random variable W are known to be a function of the sample size n. It is known that $W = \frac{R}{\sigma}$ and that the mean of $W = d_2$. Therefore,

$$\text{mean of } W = d_2 = \frac{\overline{R}}{\sigma} \qquad \text{9.12}$$

Solving for σ,

$$\sigma = \frac{\overline{R}}{d_2} \qquad \text{9.13}$$

From this equation, the center of the range chart, $\overline{R}$, equals σd_2.

It is known that the standard deviation of $W = d_3$. It is also known that

$$\sigma_R = d_3 \sigma \qquad \text{9.14}$$

To construct an R chart with μ and σ known, the control limits are set as follows:

$$\text{center line} = \overline{R} = \sigma d_2 \qquad \text{9.15a}$$

$$\text{upper limit} = \overline{R} + 3\sigma_R = \sigma d_2 + 3d_3\sigma \qquad \text{9.15b}$$

$$\text{lower limit} = \overline{R} - 3\sigma_R = \sigma d_2 - 3d_3\sigma \qquad \text{9.15c}$$

Since d_2 and d_3 are functions of the sample size, n, the constants D_1 and D_2 are typically defined as follows:

$$D_1 = d_2 - 3d_3 \qquad \text{9.16}$$

$$D_2 = d_2 + 3d_3 \qquad \text{9.17}$$

(The values of these constants are tabulated in Appendix C.) Thus, the limits for the R chart are

$$\text{center line} = \sigma d_2 \qquad \text{9.18a}$$

$$\text{upper control limit (UCL)} = D_2\sigma \qquad \text{9.18b}$$

$$\text{lower control limit (LCL)} = D_1\sigma \qquad \text{9.18c}$$

S Chart

An S (or standard deviation) chart is set up similar to the R chart. It is known that if the underlying distribution of x's is normal, then

$$\bar{S} = c_4 \sigma \qquad\qquad 9.19$$

and the standard deviation of S is

$$\sigma_s = \sigma\sqrt{1 - c_4^2} \qquad\qquad 9.20$$

Therefore, the limits on the S chart are

$$\text{UCL} = \bar{S} + 3\sigma_s = c_4\sigma + 3\sigma\sqrt{1 - c_4^2} \qquad\qquad 9.21a$$

$$\text{LCL} = \bar{S} - 3\sigma_s = c_4\sigma - 3\sigma\sqrt{1 - c_4^2} \qquad\qquad 9.21b$$

With c_4 a function of the sample size, it is common to define

$$B_5 = c_4 - 3\sqrt{1 - c_4^2} \qquad\qquad 9.22$$

and

$$B_6 = c_4 + 3\sqrt{1 - c_4^2} \qquad\qquad 9.23$$

Using these two constants gives the following parameters for an S chart when σ is known:

$$\text{center line} = c_4\sigma \qquad\qquad 9.24a$$

$$\text{UCL} = B_6\sigma \qquad\qquad 9.24b$$

$$\text{LCL} = B_5\sigma \qquad\qquad 9.24c$$

Values for B_5, B_6, and c_4 are tabulated in Appendix C.

Distribution of x Is Not Normal and μ and σ Are Unknown

Suppose that the quality characteristic being studied (x) is **not** normally distributed. It is known that irrespective of the shape of the underlying distribution, the distribution of the average values ($\bar{x}$'s) of subgroup size n will tend toward a normal distribution as the subgroup size n grows without bound. This is known as the **central limit theorem**. In simpler terms, the distribution of the $\bar{X}$ values tends to approximate the normal distribution, regardless of the distribution of the individual x values. Therefore, the control chart limits can be developed similar to the development in the preceding section.

Estimating μ and σ

Since μ and σ are not known, they must be estimated from the samples taken. The best estimator of μ is the average of the sample averages or the grand average, $\overline{\overline{X}}$. If m samples of size n are taken, the grand average is found:

$$\overline{\overline{X}} = \frac{\sum\limits_{i=1}^{m} \overline{x}_i}{m} \qquad 9.25$$

To estimate σ, either the range method or the standard deviation method can be used.

Range Method

Recall from Equation 9.13 that $\sigma = \dfrac{\overline{R}}{d_2}$. If R_1, R_2, R_3, ..., R_m are the ranges of m samples, then the average range is

$$\overline{R} = \frac{(R_1 + R_2 + R_3 + \cdots + R_m)}{m} \qquad 9.26$$

The standard deviation, σ, can be estimated by

$$\hat{\sigma} = \frac{\overline{R}}{d_2} \qquad 9.27$$

This equation is a good estimator of the standard deviation as long as $n \leq 10$. If $n > 10$, the range method loses its statistical efficiency for estimating the standard deviation.

Standard Deviation Method

When $n > 10$, the process standard deviation, σ, can be estimated from the sample standard deviation, S. Recall from Equation 9.2 that

$$\hat{\sigma}^2 = S^2 = \frac{\sum\limits_{i-1}^{n} (x_i - \overline{x})^2}{n - 1}$$

Also recall from Equation 9.19 that

$$\overline{S} = c_4 \sigma$$

By manipulating this equation, an estimate for σ becomes

$$\hat{\sigma} = \frac{\overline{S}}{c_4} \qquad 9.28$$

This equation is used to estimate the process standard deviation if the sample size is greater than 10.

$\overline{X}$ and R Chart

The development of the control chart parameters now depends on the sample size since the size of the sample directs how to properly estimate the process standard deviation. For the development of $\overline{X}$ and R charts, the sample size must be less than or equal to 10.

$\overline{X}$ Chart

Recall from Equations 9.8a and 9.8b that the upper and lower limits for the $\overline{X}$ chart can be determined by

$$\text{upper limit} = \mu + 3\sigma_{\overline{x}} = \mu + 3\left(\frac{\sigma}{\sqrt{n}}\right)$$

and

$$\text{lower limit} = \mu - 3\sigma_{\overline{x}} = \mu - 3\left(\frac{\sigma}{\sqrt{n}}\right)$$

Because μ and σ are not known, their estimates must be used. Equation 9.25 is used to estimate the mean. Since the sample size is less than or equal to 10, Equation 9.27 is used to estimate the standard deviation. This gives a

$$\text{UCL} = \overline{\overline{X}} + \frac{3\overline{R}}{d_2\sqrt{n}} \qquad \text{9.29a}$$

and a

$$\text{LCL} = \overline{\overline{X}} - \frac{3\overline{R}}{d_2\sqrt{n}} \qquad \text{9.29b}$$

To simplify further, let

$$A_2 = \frac{3}{d_2\sqrt{n}} \qquad \text{9.30}$$

Since d_2 is a function of the sample size n, then A_2 is also a function of the sample size. (The values for A_2 are tabulated in Appendix C.) This gives a

$$\text{UCL} = \overline{\overline{X}} + A_2\overline{R} \qquad \text{9.31a}$$

and a

$$\text{LCL} = \overline{\overline{X}} - A_2\overline{R} \qquad \text{9.31b}$$

with the

$$\text{center line} = \overline{\overline{X}} \qquad \text{9.31c}$$

These equations are used when the underlying distribution of the process is not known and $n \leq 10$.

R Chart

Recall from Equations 9.15b and 9.15c that the parameters for the R chart are determined by

$$UCL = \bar{R} + 3\sigma_R$$

$$LCL = \bar{R} - 3\sigma_R$$

From Equation 9.14 it is known that $\sigma_R = d_3\sigma$. Since σ is unknown, it must be estimated using $\hat{\sigma} = \dfrac{\bar{R}}{d_2}$. This gives

$$UCL = \bar{R} + 3d_3\sigma = \bar{R} + \frac{3\bar{R}d_3}{d_2}$$

$$LCL = \bar{R} - 3d_3\sigma = \bar{R} - \frac{3\bar{R}d_3}{d_2}$$

R can be factored out of the equations, leaving

$$UCL = \bar{R}\left(\frac{1 + 3d_3}{d_2}\right)$$

$$LCL = \bar{R}\left(\frac{1 - 3d_3}{d_2}\right)$$

With d_3 and d_2 as functions of the sample size, the following constants are typically defined:

$$D_3 = \left(\frac{1 - 3d_3}{d_2}\right) \qquad 9.32$$

$$D_4 = \left(\frac{1 + 3d_3}{d_2}\right) \qquad 9.33$$

This gives

$$UCL = \bar{R}D_4 \qquad 9.34a$$

$$LCL = \bar{R}D_3 \qquad 9.34b$$

$$\text{centerline} = \bar{R} \qquad 9.34c$$

These equations are used to calculate the parameters of the R chart when the underlying distribution is not known and $n \leq 10$.

$\overline{X}$ and S Chart

For the development of the $\overline{X}$ and S charts, the sample size is typically greater than 10.

$\overline{X}$ Chart

The control limits for the $\overline{X}$ chart are developed from Equations 9.8a and 9.8b as follows:

$$\text{UCL} = \mu + 3\sigma_{\overline{x}} = \mu + 3\left(\frac{\sigma}{\sqrt{n}}\right)$$

$$\text{LCL} = \mu - 3\sigma_{\overline{x}} = \mu - 3\left(\frac{\sigma}{\sqrt{n}}\right)$$

The estimate for μ is still $\overline{\overline{X}}$. Since $n > 10$, the estimate for σ is found from Equation 9.28 or $\hat{\sigma} = \frac{\overline{S}}{c_4}$.

The control limits now become

$$\text{UCL} = \overline{\overline{X}} + \frac{3\overline{S}}{c_4\sqrt{n}} \qquad \text{9.35a}$$

$$\text{LCL} = \overline{\overline{X}} - \frac{3\overline{S}}{c_4\sqrt{n}} \qquad \text{9.35b}$$

Simplify by letting

$$A_3 = \frac{3}{c_4\sqrt{n}} \qquad \text{9.36}$$

This gives

$$\text{UCL} = \overline{\overline{X}} + A_3\overline{S} \qquad \text{9.37a}$$

$$\text{LCL} = \overline{\overline{X}} - A_3\overline{S} \qquad \text{9.37b}$$

$$\text{center line} = \overline{\overline{X}} \qquad \text{9.37c}$$

These equations are used when the underlying distribution of the process is not known and $n > 10$.

S Chart

Recall from Equations 9.21a and 9.21b that the control limits for the S chart are determined by

$$\text{UCL} = \bar{S} + 3\sigma_s = \bar{S} + 3\sigma\sqrt{1 - c_4^2}$$

$$\text{LCL} = \bar{S} - 3\sigma_s = \bar{S} - 3\sigma\sqrt{1 - c_4^2}$$

From Equation 9.28, the process standard deviation can be estimated by $\hat{\sigma} = \frac{\bar{S}}{c_4}$. This substitution gives

$$\text{UCL} = \bar{S} + \frac{3\bar{S}\sqrt{1 - c_4^2}}{c_4} = \bar{S}\left(1 + \frac{3\sqrt{1 - c_4^2}}{c_4}\right) \qquad \text{9.38a}$$

$$\text{LCL} = \bar{S} - \frac{3\bar{S}\sqrt{1 - c_4^2}}{c_4} = \bar{S}\left(1 - \frac{3\sqrt{1 - c_4^2}}{c_4}\right) \qquad \text{9.38b}$$

Since c_4 is a function of the sample size, two new constants can be defined:

$$B_3 = 1 - \frac{3\sqrt{1 - c_4^2}}{c_4} \qquad \text{9.39}$$

$$B_4 = 1 + \frac{3\sqrt{1 - c_4^2}}{c_4} \qquad \text{9.40}$$

This gives

$$\text{UCL} = \bar{S}B_4 \qquad \text{9.41a}$$

$$\text{LCL} = \bar{S}B_3 \qquad \text{9.41b}$$

$$\text{center line} = \bar{S} \qquad \text{9.41c}$$

These equations are used to calculate the parameters of the S chart when the underlying distribution is not known.

X and MR Chart

X Chart

The use of the X chart when the underlying distribution is known to be not normal typically requires that the original variable be transformed to a new variable that is approximately normally distributed. This is beyond the scope of this book. The situation that usually occurs in the use of X charts is that the underlying distribution is not known but can be assumed to be normal. In this case, the control limits for the X chart can be developed directly from Equations 9.10a and 9.10b:

$$UCL = \mu + 3\sigma$$

$$LCL = \mu - 3\sigma$$

The mean μ is estimated from $\overline{\overline{X}}$ and the standard deviation is estimated from $\hat{\sigma} = \frac{\overline{R}}{d_2}$. Since the sample size is 1, a range does not exist. Therefore, a **moving range**, MR, must be established. The moving range is found by determining the range within a set of successive numbers. If the moving range size is 2, then the moving ranges would be found by taking the difference between the first and second numbers, then between the second and third numbers, then between the third and fourth numbers, etc. If the moving range size is 3, the moving ranges would be found by determining the range between the first, second, and third numbers, then between the second, third, and fourth numbers, etc. The American Society for Testing Materials (ASTM) recommends that a subgroup size of 2 be used for determining moving ranges. If moving ranges are used, then the process standard deviation can be estimated by

$$\hat{\sigma} = \frac{\overline{MR}}{d_2} \qquad\qquad 9.42$$

Substituting, the control limits become

$$UCL = \overline{X} + 3\,\frac{\overline{MR}}{d_2} \qquad\qquad 9.43a$$

$$LCL = \overline{X} - 3\,\frac{\overline{MR}}{d_2} \qquad\qquad 9.43b$$

$$\text{center line} = \overline{MR} \qquad\qquad 9.43c$$

Remember that these equations should be used only if the underlying distribution can safely be assumed to be normal.

MR Chart

The development of the parameters for the MR chart is exactly the same as the development of the parameters for the R chart. The only difference is that instead of $\overline{R}$, $\overline{MR}$ must be used. If this is done, the control limits for the MR chart are

$$UCL = D_4\,\overline{MR} \qquad\qquad 9.44a$$

$$LCL = D_3\,\overline{MR} \qquad\qquad 9.44b$$

$$\text{center line} = \overline{MR} \qquad\qquad 9.44c$$

TABLE 9.1   Control Chart Formula Summary

Chart	3σ control limits	Center line
μ and σ known		
X	$\mu \pm 3\sigma$	μ
$\overline{X}$	$\mu \pm A\sigma$	μ
R	UCL = $D_2\sigma$ LCL = $D_1\sigma$	$d_2\sigma$
S	UCL = $B_6\sigma$ UCL = $B_5\sigma$	$c_4\sigma$
μ and σ unknown		
X	$\overline{X} \pm \dfrac{3\,\overline{MR}}{d_2}$	$\overline{X}$
$\overline{X}$ (using R)	$\overline{\overline{X}} \pm A_2\overline{R}$	$\overline{\overline{X}}$
$\overline{X}$ (using S)	$\overline{\overline{X}} \pm A_3\overline{R}$	$\overline{\overline{X}}$
R	UCL = $D_4\overline{R}$ LCL = $D_3\overline{R}$	$\overline{R}$
MR	UCL = $D_4\overline{MR}$ LCL = $D_3\overline{MR}$	$\overline{MR}$
S	UCL = $B_4\overline{S}$ LCL = $B_3\overline{S}$	$\overline{S}$

Summary

Remember that variables control charts are used to monitor both the process mean and process variability. Therefore, for every quality characteristic being studied, two control charts must be done. A summary of the control chart formulas developed in this section is provided in Table 9.1.

Now that the underlying theory has been explained, the application and use of variables control charts can be discussed.

APPLICATION OF VARIABLES CONTROL CHARTS

Preparing to Use Variables Control Charts

When preparing to use variables control charts, several factors need to be decided:

1. Choice of quality characteristic
2. Size and number of samples
3. Sampling frequency
4. Rational subgroups
5. Choice of control limits

Choice of Quality Characteristic

The choice of quality characteristic is based mainly on two criteria. First, the quality characteristic to be examined must be measurable (e.g., weight, temperature, viscosity, tensile strength, etc.). The second consideration is whether studying a particular quality characteristic will lead to reduced costs. Typically, quality characteristics that are currently exhibiting high scrap or rework rates are ideal candidates for study.

Size and Number of Samples

Several factors affect the decision of the sample size. Since a variables chart is being used, the units within each sample must be measured. The measurement taken can be as simple as weighing the item or as complex as reading a vernier caliper. The time to perform each measurement is different. Therefore, when deciding on sample size, the amount of time needed to take each sample must be considered. The larger the sample, the longer it takes to gather and measure it, and the longer it takes, the higher the cost. This would seem to imply that a small sample size should always be chosen. However, the trade-off that must be considered is that by collecting smaller sample sizes, the ability of the variables control charts to accurately monitor the process is decreased. This implies that larger sample sizes are preferred. The decision must be made in light of both aspects and making trade-offs. In industry, the typical sample size is 4 or 5. Also, the sample size must remain constant.

When first setting up a control chart, enough samples need to be collected to accurately estimate the process mean and standard deviation. Also, enough samples should be collected so that any unusual source of variation has an opportunity to appear. A good rule-of-thumb is to collect 20 to 25 samples.

Sampling Frequency

The main purpose of using a control chart is to detect changes in a process over time. Therefore, how often to take a sample is of real concern. Taking small samples at short intervals provides quicker feedback. However, it costs more and the process may not produce enough in a short interval to gather a random sample. Taking large samples at longer intervals provides better feedback. However, if the interval is too long, problems can occur, causing unnecessary losses. Because every process is different, there are no guidelines; there are only trade-offs.

Rational Subgroups

The data should be collected in rational subgroups. This means that the subgroups should be selected so that each subgroup is as homogeneous as possible. It also means that samples are selected so that if a problem does exist, the chance for differences between subgroups is maximized and the chance for differences within subgroups is minimized.

Choice of Control Limits

The standard practice of choosing the width of the control limits is to choose a multiple of the standard deviation, typically $\pm 3\sigma$. All of the formulas developed so far have control limits set at $\pm 3\sigma$.

Collecting the Samples

Once all the preparations have been made, collection of the samples begins. Collection of the samples is simplified if a standardized form is used. The form can have any appearance. The key point is that all pertinent information is recorded on the form. Pertinent information includes:

1. Housekeeping items such as department, operation, specs, part number, machine number, etc.

2. A place for recording the data

3. A place for graphing the charts

4. Action instructions

5. A place for process information

A typical form is provided in Appendix D. This form has a place for all the pertinent information. The most important information that must be recorded is the process information. This information is recorded on the back of most forms (including the one in Appendix D). This allows more room for the data and graphs. The process information is a record of any changes that occur in the process while it is being monitored. This includes changes in people, material, environment, methods, or machines. These changes and the exact times they occur are recorded. If the control chart indicates that a problem exists with the process, it is the process information that will aid in identifying and correcting the problem. If the process information is not taken properly, then the control chart cannot be evaluated properly. In other words, the control chart is only usable if the process information is recorded. This underscores the need for and the value of collecting the process information.

Examples

Example 4: $\overline{X}$ and R Charts

A line foreman wants to establish statistical control on shaft lengths being cut. He decides to use $\overline{X}$ and R charts. The foreman collects 25 samples, each of size 5. The data collected are shown in Table 9.2.

When setting up the $\overline{X}$ and R charts, begin with the R chart to ensure that the variability within samples is in-control. Using the data in Table 9.2, we find that the center line for the R chart is

$$\overline{R} = \frac{27.70}{25} = 1.11$$

For samples of size 5, the values for D_3 and D_4 are found from Appendix C to be 0.00 and 2.114, respectively. Therefore, the control limits for the R chart can be determined from Equations 9.34a and 9.34b:

$$UCL = \overline{R}D_4 = (1.11)(2.114) = 2.35$$

$$LCL = \overline{R}D_3 = (1.11)(0.00) = 0.00$$

The R chart is shown in Figure 9.4. As can be seen, there is no indication of any out-of-control conditions. Since the within-sample variability is in control, the $\overline{X}$ chart can now be constructed. From Table 9.2, the center line for the $\overline{X}$ chart is

$$\overline{\overline{X}} = \frac{249.35}{25} = 9.97$$

From Appendix C, the value of A_2 is found to be 0.577 for a sample size of 5. Using Equations 9.31a and 9.31b, the control limits can be determined:

$$UCL = \overline{\overline{X}} + A_2\overline{R} = 9.97 + (0.577)(1.11) = 10.61$$

$$LCL = \overline{\overline{X}} - A_2\overline{R} = 9.97 - (0.577)(1.11) = 9.33$$

The $\overline{X}$ chart is shown in Figure 9.5. The chart shows no indication of an out-of-control condition. Therefore, both the R chart and the $\overline{X}$ chart indicate that the process is in-control.

TABLE 9.2   Shaft Length Measurements (Inches)

Sample #	Sample observations					$\overline{X}$	R
1	9.26	10.44	10.39	9.87	10.26	10.04	1.18
2	10.92	10.08	9.97	10.16	9.30	10.09	1.62
3	10.10	10.61	8.62	10.24	10.17	9.95	1.99
4	10.17	9.24	10.60	10.08	10.51	10.12	1.35
5	10.29	10.36	10.39	10.58	9.96	10.32	0.63
6	9.84	9.52	10.11	9.65	10.18	9.86	0.66
7	9.84	9.77	10.47	10.25	10.28	10.12	0.70
8	9.94	9.35	9.61	9.09	10.09	9.62	0.99
9	10.18	11.18	10.16	10.68	10.80	10.60	1.02
10	9.46	10.15	10.80	9.57	9.20	9.84	1.61
11	9.64	9.71	10.38	10.23	9.92	9.98	0.74
12	10.54	10.76	10.83	9.97	9.91	10.40	0.92
13	10.41	9.67	9.88	10.28	9.77	10.00	0.75
14	9.72	8.70	9.81	9.39	9.68	9.46	1.12
15	9.35	10.28	10.86	11.11	10.05	10.33	1.76
16	9.11	10.22	9.50	9.82	9.65	9.66	1.11
17	9.53	10.12	10.03	9.71	9.72	9.82	0.60
18	10.14	8.98	9.84	9.74	9.68	9.68	1.16
19	9.81	10.18	9.95	10.40	9.71	10.01	0.69
20	10.12	10.01	10.01	9.75	9.25	9.83	0.87
21	10.30	9.95	9.55	9.84	10.46	10.02	0.91
22	10.73	9.78	9.27	11.03	9.99	10.16	1.76
23	9.89	9.82	9.40	10.67	9.43	9.84	1.27
24	9.99	10.20	9.37	9.05	10.27	9.78	1.21
25	10.10	10.25	9.51	9.16	10.17	9.84	1.09
					TOTAL	249.35	27.70

$$\overline{\overline{X}} = 9.97 \quad \overline{R} = 1.11$$

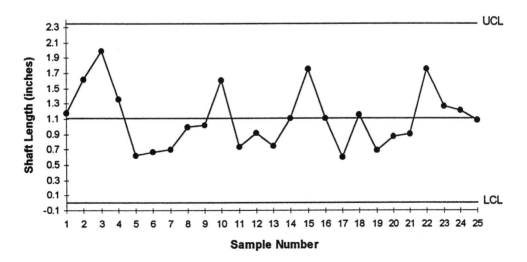

FIGURE 9.4   R Chart for Example 4

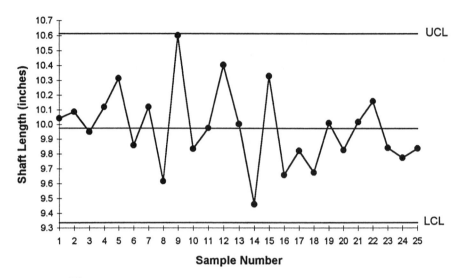

FIGURE 9.5 $\overline{X}$ Chart for Example 4

Example 5: $\overline{X}$ and S Charts

The construction of the $\overline{X}$ and S charts will be illustrated using the shaft length measurements from the previous example. The data for the $\overline{X}$ and S charts are summarized in Table 9.3.

The parameters for the S chart are determined from Equations 9.41a to 9.41c:

$$\text{center line} = \overline{S} = \frac{11.23}{25} = 0.45$$

$$\text{UCL} = \overline{S}B_4 = (0.45)(2.089) = 0.94$$

$$\text{LCL} = \overline{S}_3 = (0.45)(0.00) = 0.00$$

The S chart is shown in Figure 9.6. As can be seen, the S chart is in-control. Therefore, the $\overline{X}$ chart can be developed using Equations 9.37a to 9.37c:

$$\text{center line} = \overline{\overline{X}} = \frac{249.35}{25} = 9.97$$

$$\text{UCL} = \overline{\overline{X}} + A_3\overline{S} = 0.97 + (1.427)(0.45) = 10.61$$

$$\text{LCL} = \overline{\overline{X}} - A_3\overline{S} = 0.97 - (1.427)(0.45) = 9.33$$

The $\overline{X}$ chart is shown in Figure 9.7. Both the $\overline{X}$ chart and the S chart indicate that the process is operating in-control.

Notice that the control limits for the $\overline{X}$ chart in Example 4 are identical to the $\overline{X}$ chart control limits for this example. This will not always be the case. Many times, the $\overline{X}$ chart control limits based on $\overline{R}$ will differ slightly from those based on $\overline{S}$.

TABLE 9.3   Shaft Length Measurements (Inches)

Sample #	Sample observations					$\overline{X}$	S
1	9.26	10.44	10.39	9.87	10.26	10.04	0.49
2	10.92	10.08	9.97	10.16	9.30	10.09	0.58
3	10.10	10.61	8.62	10.24	10.17	9.95	0.77
4	10.17	9.24	10.60	10.08	10.51	10.12	0.54
5	10.29	10.36	10.39	10.58	9.96	10.32	0.23
6	9.84	9.52	10.11	9.65	10.18	9.86	0.29
7	9.84	9.77	10.47	10.25	10.28	10.12	0.30
8	9.94	9.35	9.61	9.09	10.09	9.62	0.41
9	10.18	11.18	10.16	10.68	10.80	10.60	0.43
10	9.46	10.15	10.80	9.57	9.20	9.84	0.64
11	9.64	9.71	10.38	10.23	9.92	9.98	0.32
12	10.54	10.76	10.83	9.97	9.91	10.40	0.44
13	10.41	9.67	9.88	10.28	9.77	10.00	0.33
14	9.72	8.70	9.81	9.39	9.68	9.46	0.45
15	9.35	10.28	10.86	11.11	10.05	10.33	0.69
16	9.11	10.22	9.50	9.82	9.65	9.66	0.41
17	9.53	10.12	10.03	9.71	9.72	9.82	0.25
18	10.14	8.98	9.84	9.74	9.68	9.68	0.43
19	9.81	10.18	9.95	10.40	9.71	10.01	0.28
20	10.12	10.01	10.01	9.75	9.25	9.83	0.35
21	10.30	9.95	9.55	9.84	10.46	10.02	0.36
22	10.73	9.78	9.27	11.03	9.99	10.16	0.72
23	9.89	9.82	9.40	10.67	9.43	9.84	0.51
24	9.99	10.20	9.37	9.05	10.27	9.78	0.54
25	10.10	10.25	9.51	9.16	10.17	9.84	0.48
					TOTAL	249.35	11.23

$$\overline{\overline{X}} = 9.97 \quad \overline{S} = 0.45$$

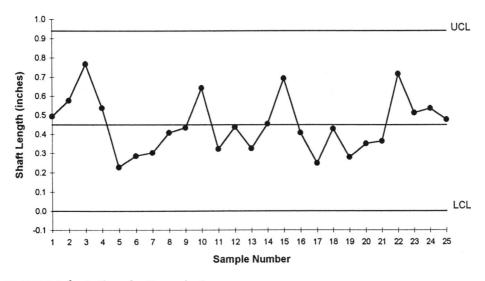

FIGURE 9.6   S Chart for Example 5

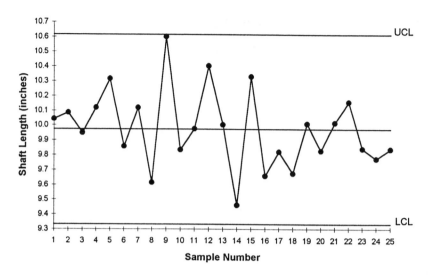

FIGURE 9.7 $\overline{X}$ Chart for Example 5

Example 6: X and MR Charts

Tensile strength is an important quality characteristic for bridge bolts. The bolts are made of a mild steel (ASTM A36). Because a tensile strength test destroys the bolt and each bolt is expensive, a sample of size 1 was decided upon. Twenty-five bolts were tested. The results are given in Table 9.4.

The moving range chart can be constructed using Equations 9.44a to 9.44c:

$$\text{center line} = \overline{MR} = \frac{275.23}{24} = 11.47$$

$$\text{UCL} = D_4\,\overline{MR} = (3.267)(11.47) = 37.47$$

$$\text{LCL} = D_3\,\overline{MR} = (0.00)(11.47) = 0.00$$

The moving range chart is shown in Figure 9.8. The moving range chart appears to be in-control. Therefore, the X chart can be constructed using Equations 9.43a to 9.43b:

$$\text{center line} = \overline{X} = \frac{1729.34}{25} = 69.17$$

$$\text{UCL} = \overline{X} + 3\,\frac{\overline{MR}}{d_2} = 69.17 + \frac{3(11.47)}{1.128} = 99.68$$

$$\text{LCL} = \overline{X} + 3\,\frac{\overline{MR}}{d_2} = 69.17 - \frac{3(11.47)}{1.128} = 38.66$$

TABLE 9.4 Tensile Strength of Bridge Bolts (ksi)

Bolt	Tensile strength	Moving range
1	70.87	—
2	60.27	10.60
3	69.51	9.24
4	66.84	2.67
5	63.94	2.90
6	70.01	6.07
7	58.73	11.28
8	80.23	21.50
9	63.26	16.97
10	77.29	14.03
11	77.01	0.28
12	62.32	14.69
13	69.54	7.23
14	63.62	5.92
15	74.95	11.33
16	73.37	1.58
17	74.13	0.76
18	76.66	2.52
19	52.95	23.71
20	64.95	12.00
21	73.93	8.99
22	53.26	20.67
23	74.19	20.93
24	93.69	19.50
25	63.82	29.87
TOTAL	1729.34	275.23
	$\overline{X}$ = 69.17	$\overline{MR}$ = 11.47

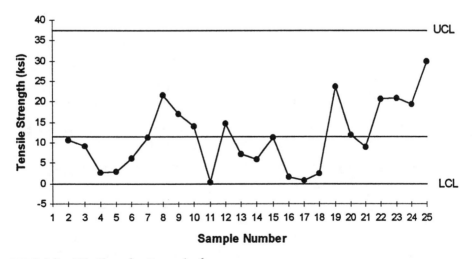

FIGURE 9.8 MR Chart for Example 6

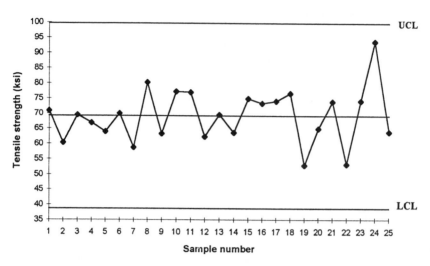

FIGURE 9.9   X Chart for Example 6

Figure 9.9 gives the X chart for the bridge bolts. Since there are no apparent out-of-control conditions present in either chart, the process producing the bridge bolts is considered to be operating in-control.

INTERPRETING THE CHARTS

Once a control chart has been set up, it needs to be interpreted. The first thing that needs to be determined is whether the process is in-control or out-of-control. Two primary characteristics of an in-control process are that the points on the chart fluctuate at random and obey the laws of chance. This implies that there are no extraneous causes working on the process. It also implies that points on the control chart exhibit the following characteristics:

1. Most of the points are near the center line. Recall from Figure 9.2 that 68% of the points should be within $\pm 1\sigma$ of the center line.

2. A few of the points approach the control limits. Again, Figure 9.2 illustrates that only 4.27% of the points should be between $\pm 2\sigma$ and $\pm 3\sigma$.

3. Rarely should a point exceed the control limits. Figure 9.2 indicates that only 0.27% of all points should exceed $\pm 3\sigma$.

The charts for a process that is in-control should exhibit all three of these characteristics simultaneously.

The most common means of determining if the process is out-of-control is to check for instability. One of the first and most widely used methods for determining if instability exists is the use of the AT&T run rules. The AT&T run rules were developed based upon the three expected control chart characteristics listed above.

UPPER CONTROL LIMIT

ZONE A

ZONE B

ZONE C

CENTER LINE

ZONE C

ZONE B

ZONE A

LOWER CONTROL LIMIT

FIGURE 9.10   AT&T Run Rule Test Zones

When applying the AT&T run rules, only one-half of the control band (area between the center line and one of the control limits) is considered at a time. This band is divided into three equal segments labeled zone A, zone B, and zone C (see Figure 9.10). Each zone is 1σ wide because the control limits being used are ±3σ.

Next, x's are marked according to the following four rules:

Rule 1:   A single point falls outside of the 3σ limit. This point is marked with an "x" (see Figure 9.11).

Rule 2:   Two out of three successive points fall in zone A or beyond. The second of the two points in or beyond zone A is marked with an "x". The other point may fall anywhere on the chart (see Figure 9.12).

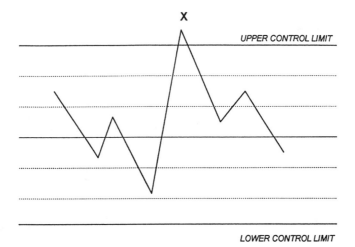

FIGURE 9.11   AT&T Run Rule 1

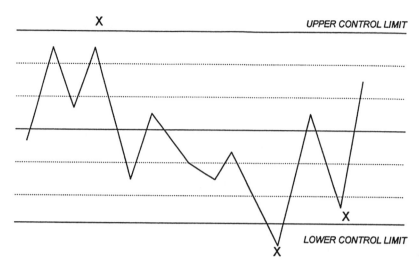

FIGURE 9.12   AT&T Run Rule 2

Rule 3:   Four out of five successive points fall in zone B or beyond. Only the fourth point in or beyond zone B is marked with an "x". As in Rule 2, the remaining point may fall anywhere (see Figure 9.13).

Rule 4:   Eight successive points fall in zone C or beyond. Only the eighth point is marked and all eight must be on the same side of the center line (see Figure 9.14) (AT&T, 1985, pp. 25–27).

These rules are applied to both sides of the center line. The more x's that have been marked, the greater the instability in the system. This method indicates two things: first, whether there is instability present in a process,

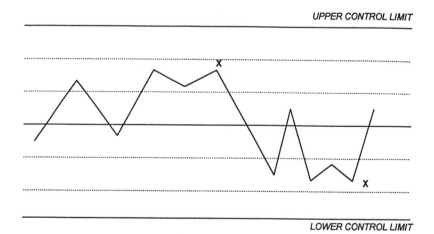

FIGURE 9.13   AT&T Run Rule 3

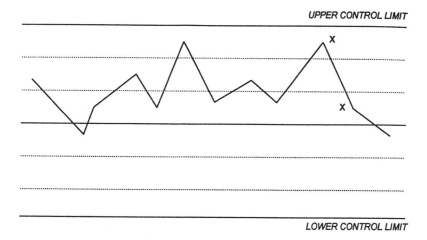

FIGURE 9.14   AT&T Run Rule 4

and second (if care was taken when plotting the control chart), the specific time of occurrence and operator present at the time of instability. (It must be remembered that the cause of the instability has usually affected more points than the ones actually marked. Therefore, when the data are being collected, any changes made to the process need to be recorded, as well as the time of occurrence and applicable operation.)

In addition to testing for instability, unusual patterns in the control charts can be looked for. An unusual pattern is basically any pattern that does not appear random. Fifteen control chart patterns that can be encountered are described in the *AT&T Statistical Quality Control Handbook* (AT&T, 1985, p. 161). Six of the most common patterns are trends, cycles, mixtures, shifts, stratification, and systematic variables.

Trends

A trend is defined as "continuous movement up or down; x's on one side of the chart followed by x's on the other; or a long series of points without a change of direction" (AT&T, 1985, p. 177). Two examples of trends are illustrated in Figure 9.15.

Trends usually result from any cause that gradually works on the process. In other words, the mean of the process shifts its location gradually in one direction over a period of time. Trends are relatively easy to identify and associate with the process. The nature of the cause can be determined by the type of chart it appears upon. If the trend appears on the $\overline{X}$ chart, the cause is one that moves the center of the distribution rather steadily from high to low or vice versa. If the trend appears on the R chart, the cause is one in which the spread is gradually increasing or decreasing. Some of the more common causes of trends as identified in the *AT&T Statistical Quality Control Handbook* (AT&T, 1985, p. 178) are:

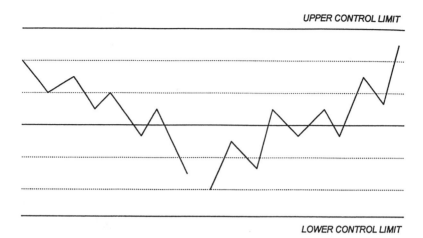

FIGURE 9.15   Trend Pattern

$\overline{X}$ chart (R chart must be in-control)

1. Tool wear
2. Seasonal effects, including temperature and humidity
3. Operator fatigue
4. Increases or decreases in production schedules
5. Gradual changes in standards
6. Gradual change in the proportion of defective in each lot
7. Poor maintenance or housekeeping procedures

R chart

Increasing trend

1. Dulling of a tool
2. Various types of mixture
3. Something loosening or wearing gradually

Decreasing trend

1. Gradual improvement in operator technique
2. Effect of better maintenance program
3. Effect of process controls in other areas
4. Product more homogeneous (less affected by mixture)

It should be noted that care must be taken in the interpretation of trends. This is due to the fact that it is easy to imagine trends where none actually exist. To the untrained eye, the irregular up-and-down fluctuations that occur in a natural pattern are often mistaken for trends.

Cycles

Cycles are "short trends in the data which occur in repeated patterns" (AT&T, 1985, p. 161). An assignable cause is indicated when the pattern exhibits any tendency to repeat. This tendency is illustrated by a series of high portions or peaks interspersed with low portions or troughs. This is an indication of an assignable cause since the major characteristic of a random pattern is that it does not repeat. A pattern with a cycle present is illustrated in Figure 9.16.

The phenomenon of cycles is caused by processing variables which come and go on a relatively regular basis, such as shift changes or seasonal conditions. Some of the more common causes of cycles are:

$\overline{X}$ chart (R chart must be in-control)

1. Seasonal effects such as temperature and humidity
2. Worn positions or threads on locking devices
3. Operator fatigue
4. Rotation of people on the job
5. Difference between gages used by inspectors
6. Difference between day and night shift

R chart

1. Maintenance schedules
2. Operator fatigue
3. Wear of tool or die causing excessive play
4. Tool in need of sharpening
5. Difference between day and night shift (AT&T, 1985, p. 162)

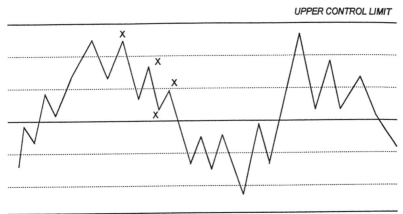

FIGURE 9.16   Cycle Pattern

Basically, cycles are identified by determining the time intervals of the cycle peaks (or troughs) and relating them back to the process. Unless good documentation is done during the data collection phase (e.g., noting shift changes, tool changes, etc.), then identification of the cycle causes could become difficult.

Mixtures

A mixture pattern is identified by the points tending to fall near the upper and lower control limits with an absence of normal fluctuation near the middle (see Figure 9.17). A mixture pattern is actually a combination of two different patterns on the same chart. This may result in a bimodal distribution which can be difficult to detect. A mixture pattern can display two different tendencies. The first tendency is to be stable in nature. This occurs when the component distributions in the mixture maintain the same relative positions and proportions over a period of time (see Figure 9.18). In stable mixtures, the causes producing the distributions tend to be permanent in nature. Typical causes that may produce stable mixtures are:

$\overline{X}$ chart (R chart must be in-control)

1. Different lots of material in storeroom
2. Large quantities of piece parts mixed on the line
3. Differences in test sets or gages
4. Consistent differences in material, operators, etc.

R chart

1–3. Same as above

4. Frequent drift or jumps in automatic controls (AT&T, 1985, p. 171)

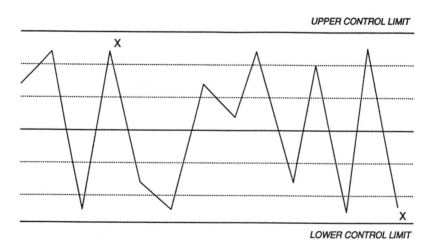

FIGURE 9.17   Mixture Pattern

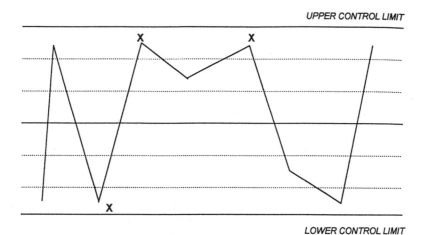

FIGURE 9.18   Stable Mixture Pattern

Stable mixtures usually occur when the product is inspected at the end of the line instead of during manufacture.

The second tendency is to be unstable in nature. This occurs when the relative positions of the component distributions do not remain constant (see Figure 9.19). Some of the more common causes of unstable mixtures are:

$\overline{X}$ chart (R chart must be in-control)

1. Breakdown in facilities or automatic controls

2. Overadjustment of the process

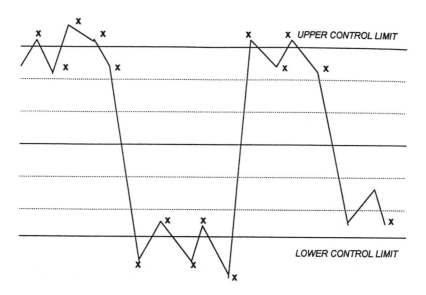

FIGURE 9.19   Unstable Mixture Pattern

3. Carelessness in setting controls

4. Differences in materials, operators, etc.

R chart

1. Two or more materials, machines, operators, etc.

2. Mixture of material

3. Too much play in a fixture

4. Operator fatigue

5. Machine or tools in need of repair (AT&T, 1985, p. 180)

Unstable mixtures are one of the most common and important types of patterns. This is because once the causes of unstable mixtures have been identified and eliminated, other patterns (which may exist) are much easier to interpret. Overall, unstable mixtures are more common than stable mixtures.

Shifts

A sudden shift in level is shown by a positive change in one direction which causes a number of x's to appear on one side of the chart only (see Figure 9.20). Some of the typical causes of shifts are:

$\overline{X}$ chart (R chart must be in-control)

1. Change due to a different kind of material

2. New operator, inspector, machine, etc.

3. Change in set-up or method

4. Chipped or broken cutting tool

5. Damage to fixture

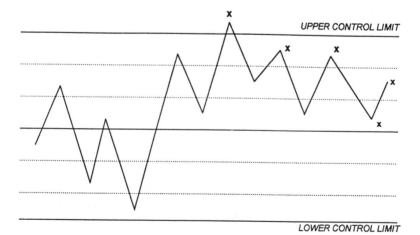

FIGURE 9.20   Shift Pattern

R chart

1. Change in motivation of operator

2. New operator or equipment

3. Change due to different material or supplier (AT&T, 1985, p. 174)

A sudden shift in level is one of the easiest patterns to interpret on any chart.

Stratification

Stratification is a form of stable mixture which has an unnatural consistency. A stratification pattern tends to hug the center line with very few deviations. In other words, it does not fluctuate as one would naturally expect (with random sampling), with occasional points approaching the upper and lower control limits (see Figure 9.21). Stratification usually shows up more readily on the R chart than on the $\overline{X}$ chart. However, the most common causes for stratification on the $\overline{X}$ chart are things that are capable of causing mixtures. Most frequently, however, stratification on the $\overline{X}$ chart may be due to an incorrect calculation of the control limits. Causes associated with the R chart are the same causes that are listed under stable mixtures.

Systematic Variables

A systematic pattern is one in which the pattern becomes predictable (for example, a low point is always followed by a high point or vice versa). The most common appearance of a systematic pattern is shown in Figure 9.22. A systematic pattern indicates the presence of a systematic variable. Some of the more common causes of systematic variables are:

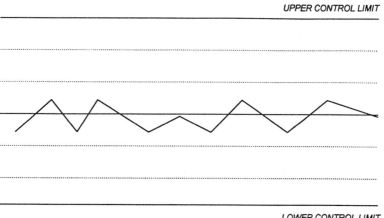

UPPER CONTROL LIMIT

LOWER CONTROL LIMIT

FIGURE 9.21   Stratification Pattern

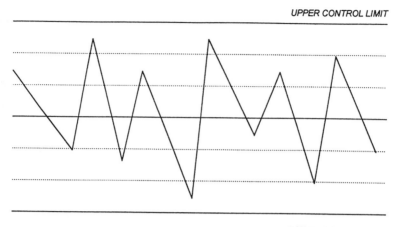

UPPER CONTROL LIMIT

LOWER CONTROL LIMIT

FIGURE 9.22   Systematic Pattern

$\overline{X}$ chart (R chart must be in-control)

1. Differences between shifts
2. Differences between test sets
3. Differences between assembly lines where product is sampled in rotation
4. Systematic manner of dividing the data

R chart

1. This effect is generally due to a systematic manner of dividing the data (AT&T, 1985, p. 175)

These are just six of the more common unnatural control patterns.

Analysis of Variables Control Charts

It is clear from the previous discussion that control charts indicate when a process needs adjustment. But can they indicate whether the product made will meet the customer's requirements? The answer is definitely yes. In fact, this is the true power of control charts.

Meeting Specifications

Manufacturing specifications are given in terms of a nominal dimension and a tolerance dimension. The nominal dimension is what the customer really wants. The tolerance dimension is the amount of variation from the nominal the customer is willing to accept. For example, a customer's specification for the diameter of a rod is

$$0.500 \pm 0.005 \text{ inches}$$

The 0.500 is the nominal dimension and the ±0.005 is the tolerance dimension. What this specifications means is that the customer will accept any rod with a diameter between 0.495 and 0.505 inches.

It is important to note that specifications are set externally from the process. They are set by an external customer, by the design department, etc. Specifications are seldom a reflection of what the process can actually produce.

Recall that the control limits on the variables charts are a function of the process ($\mu \pm 3\sigma_{\bar{x}}$ where $\sigma_{\bar{x}}$ is found from $\frac{\sigma}{\sqrt{n}}$). The relationship between the specification limits, the control limits, and the natural tolerance limits is illustrated in Figure 9.23. As can be seen from this figure, there is no relationship between the specification limits and the control limits. This is

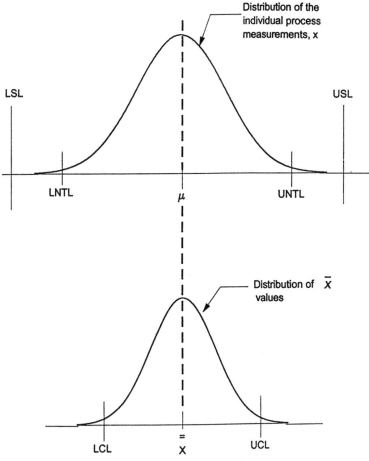

Spec Limits (LSL, USL) => set externally from the process
natural tolerance limits (LNTL, UNTL) = $\mu \pm 3\sigma$ or $\hat{\mu} \pm 3\hat{\sigma}$
control limits (LCL, UCL) = $\bar{\bar{x}} \pm 3\sigma_{\bar{x}}$ or $\hat{\mu} \pm 3\frac{\hat{\sigma}}{\sqrt{n}}$

FIGURE 9.23 Relationship between Specification Limits, Control Limits, and Natural Tolerance Limits

because specification limits are set as a measure for individual items and control limits are set as a measure for a subgroup of items. Thus, a process that is producing within specifications does not imply that the process is in-control. Similarly, a process that is in-control does not imply that the process is producing within specifications. A process that is both in-control and producing within specifications is optimum. How to determine if a process is in-control was discussed in the previous section. How to determine if a process is producing within specifications is the focus of this section.

Because theoretically there is no relationship between the specification limits and the control limits, specification limits should not be drawn on a control chart because they can be misleading. Therefore, another method is needed to determine if the process is capable of meeting specifications. Recall that the process mean and standard deviation can be estimated from $\overline{\overline{X}}$ and $\frac{\overline{R}}{d_2}$, respectively. The process capabilities can now be determined by calculating the **natural tolerance limits** (NTLs) of the process:

$$\text{NTLs} = \hat{\mu} \pm 3\hat{\sigma} = \overline{\overline{X}} \pm \frac{3\overline{R}}{d_2} \qquad 9.45$$

Because the natural tolerance limits represents the nature of the individual items, the specifications can be compared directly with them.

When comparing the specifications with the natural tolerance limits, there are three possible scenarios.* These different scenarios are illustrated in Figure 9.24. The first scenario indicates that the process spread (UNTL–LNTL = 6σ) falls within the specification limits. This would be the optimum scenario—process in control and producing within specifications. The second scenario indicates that the natural tolerance limits are approximately equal to the specification limits. In this case, because the natural tolerance limits are set at $\pm 3\sigma$, from the normal distribution table we know that the process is producing approximately 0.27% non-conforming or defective product. In the third scenario, the process spread is wider than the specification limits. In this case, the process is not capable of meeting specifications and is producing an unacceptable amount of non-conforming product.

At this point, the question as to whether the process can meet the customer's specifications can be answered. If the answer is no (the process cannot meet specifications), an additional question might be "What proportion of non-conforming product is being produced?" This question can be answered using our knowledge of the normal distribution. The following example illustrates this point.

Example 7

An automatic screw machine produces bolts with a specific shank diameter of 8.50 ± 0.25 mm. The process has been operating in-control at an

---

* These scenarios assume that the underlying process is in-control.

Scenario 1

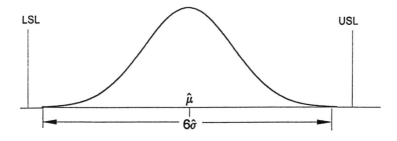

Scenario 2

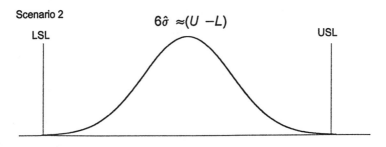

Scenario 3

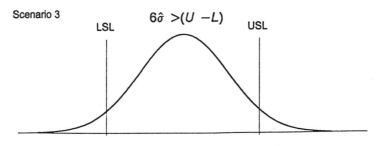

FIGURE 9.24 Specification Limits Compared to Natural Tolerance Limits

estimated mean of 8.50 mm and an $\overline{R}$ of 0.31 mm. The sample size is five.

a. Calculate the $\overline{X}$ and R chart control limits.

R chart

$$\text{center line} = 0.31$$

$$\text{UCL} = D_4 \overline{R} = (2.114)(0.31) = 0.66$$

$$\text{LCL} = D_3 \overline{R} = (0)(0.31) = 0$$

$\overline{X}$ chart

$$\text{center line} = 8.50$$

$$\text{UCL} = \overline{\overline{X}} + A_2 \overline{R} = 8.50 + (0.577)(0.31) = 8.68$$

$$\text{LCL} = \overline{\overline{X}} - A_2 \overline{R} = 8.50 - (0.577)(0.31) = 8.32$$

b. Is the process capable of meeting specifications?

natural tolerance limits $= \mu \pm 3\sigma$

$$\hat{\mu} = \overline{\overline{X}} = 8.50 \text{ mm}$$

$$\hat{\sigma} = \frac{\overline{R}}{d_2} = (0.31)/(2.326) = 0.13 \text{ mm}$$

$$\text{UNTL} = 8.50 + 3(0.13) = 8.89 \text{ mm}$$

$$\text{LNTL} = 8.50 - 3(0.13) = 8.11 \text{ mm}$$

The specification limits are (8.25 mm, 8.75 mm). The natural tolerance limits are wider than the specification limits. Therefore, the process is not capable of meeting specifications.

c. What percentage of non-conforming product is being produced by the process? To answer this question, we must determine how much of the process is falling outside of the specification limits. The situation is illustrated in Figure 9.25. The shaded area represents the amount of product being produced that is non-conforming. From normal distribution theory, the shaded area can be found from:

$$\% \text{ non–conforming} = P(x \leq \text{LSL}) + P(x \geq \text{USL})$$

$$= P(x \leq 8.25) + P(x \geq 8.75)$$

$$= \Phi\left[\frac{(8.25 - 8.50)}{0.13}\right] + 1 - \Phi\left[\frac{(8.75 - 8.50)}{0.13}\right]$$

$$= \Phi(-1.92) + 1 - \Phi(1.92)$$

$$= 0.0274 + 1 - 0.9726$$

$$= 0.0548$$

or 5.48% non-conforming is being produced by this process

Detecting Shifts in Mean

In addition to determining the percent non-conforming a process is producing, the probability of detecting a shift in the mean of the process can also be determined. In many instances, a process is operating in-control and for some reason (a tool breaks, incoming material changes, etc.) the process suddenly shifts. Typically, the first place this shift appears is on the control chart. The shift will appear as a point either above the upper control limit or below the lower control limit. (Recall from rule 1 of the AT&T run rules that any point that falls either above the upper control limit or below the lower control limit signals that the process is out-of-control.) Therefore, knowledge of normal distribution theory will allow you to determine the probability of detecting a sudden shift in process

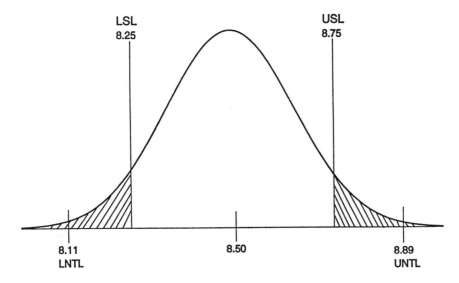

FIGURE 9.25   Percent Non-Conforming Product for Example 7c

mean. Because detection of the shift occurs on the control chart, there are several points that need to be noted. First, the standard deviation used is the standard deviation associated with the $\overline{X}$ chart, $\sigma_{\overline{x}}$ or the standard deviation of the $\overline{X}$'s. Second, the mean used is the new shifted mean because that is the current mean of the process. Third, the control limits are used.

Example 8

Using the previous example, suppose that the process mean shifts to 8.70 mm due to a change in incoming material.

Determine the probability of detecting a shift in the process mean from 8.50 mm to 8.70 mm. This situation is illustrated in Figure 9.26. The shaded area represents the probability of detecting the shift.

$$\sigma_{\overline{x}} = \frac{\hat{\sigma}}{\sqrt{n}} = \frac{0.13}{\sqrt{5}} = 0.06$$

$$
\begin{aligned}
P(\text{detecting shift}) &= P(X \leq \text{LCL}) + P(X \geq \text{UCL}) \\
&= P(X \leq 8.32) + P(X \geq 8.68) \\
&= \Phi\left[\frac{(8.32 - 8.70)}{0.06}\right] + 1 - \Phi\left[\frac{(8.68 - 8.70)}{0.06}\right] \\
&= \Phi(-6.33) + 1 = \Phi(-0.33) \\
&= 0 + 1 = -0.3707 \\
&= 0.6293
\end{aligned}
$$

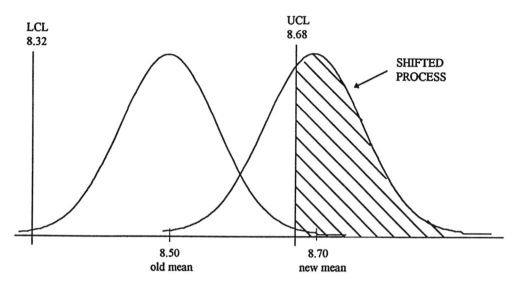

LCL
8.32

UCL
8.68

SHIFTED
PROCESS

8.50
old mean

8.70
new mean

FIGURE 9.26   Percent Non-Conforming Product after Shift for Example 7c

or 62.93% probability of detecting the shift in mean on the first subsequent sample.

Process Capability Indices

Process capability means that if all the points in the sample fall within the natural tolerance limits, then the process should be capable of meeting the customer's specifications. A process capability index is "an attempt to provide in a single number a meaningful measure of uniformity around a target for a given product or process characteristic" (Case et al., 1987, p. 107). In other words, a process capability index is found by comparing the natural tolerance limits of a process with the specification limits. There are two commonly used process capability indices: C_p and C_{pk}.

C_p is determined by

$$C_p = \frac{(\text{USL} - \text{LSL})}{6\sigma} \qquad 9.46$$

C_{pk} is determined by

$$C_{pk} = \min\left[\frac{(\text{USL} - \overline{\overline{X}})}{3\sigma} ; \frac{(\overline{\overline{X}} - \text{LSL})}{3\sigma}\right] \qquad 9.47$$

C_p is a valid index only if the process is centered at the center of the specifications because C_p does not take into account the centering of the process. On the other hand, C_{pk} does account for the centering of the process. Therefore, C_{pk} is valid all the time, thus making it the more popular index. The differences in C_p and C_{pk} are illustrated in Figure 9.27. In scenario 1, the process is centered at the center of the specifications and

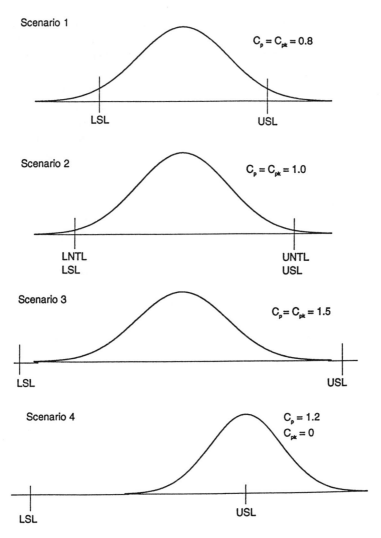

FIGURE 9.27   Difference between C_p and C_{pk}

the spread of the process (UNTL–LNTL) is greater than the spread of the specifications (USL–LSL). Because the process is centered at the center of the specifications, then $C_p = C_{pk}$. Because the spread of the process is greater than the spread of the specifications, then C_p and C_{pk} have a value less than one. An index value less than one indicates that the process is not capable of meeting specifications. In scenario 2, the process is centered at the center of the specifications and the spread of the process is exactly equal to the spread of the specifications (natural tolerance limits = specification limits). Whenever the natural tolerance limits equal the specification limits and the process is centered at the center of the specifications, $C_p = C_{pk} = 1.0$. An index value of 1.0 indicates that the process is just able to meet specifications. (From normal distribution theory, we know that the process is producing 0.27% non-conforming components.) In scenario 3, the process is centered at the center of the specifications and the spread of the natural tolerance limits is smaller than the spread of the specification limits. This gives values of C_p and C_{pk} greater than 1.0. An index value greater than 1.0 indicates that the process is indeed capable of meeting specifications (provided the process is centered at the center of the specifications). In scenario 4, the process is centered about the upper specification limit. Because the spread of the process is less than the spread of the specifications, C_p has a value greater than 1.0. If this were the only index used, a false interpretation of the capability of the process would be made, namely, that because the index is greater than 1.0, the process is capable of meeting specifications. However, by looking at the process in relationship to the specifications, we see that the process is producing 50% non-conforming components. The C_{pk} value for this situation was less than 1.0, which indicates that the process is not capable of meeting specifications. Because C_{pk} accurately reflects the situation regardless of where the process is centered, it is the more commonly used index.

A few general points can help when using C_p and C_{pk}:

1. $C_{pk} > 1.0$ indicates that the process is capable of meeting specifications.

2. $C_{pk} < 1.0$ indicates that the process is not capable of meeting specifications.

3. C_{pk} is always less than or equal to C_p.

4. $C_p = C_{pk}$ only when the process is centered at the center of the specifications.

5. $C_{pk} = 0$ whenever the process is centered at either the upper specification limit or the lower specification limit.

6. C_p and C_{pk} can only be used on processes that are in-control.

7. $C_{pk} < 0$ indicates that the process is centered either below the lower specification limit or above the upper specification limit.

EXERCISES

Questions

9.1 What does the $\overline{X}$ chart measure? Why is this important?

9.2 What does the R chart measure? Why is this important?

9.3 What is the underlying distribution of the $\overline{X}$ chart?

9.4 What is the relationship between specification limits and control limits?

9.5 What is the relationship between natural tolerance limits and control limits?

9.6 On which control chart (if any) can specification limits be put?

9.7 What is the difference between σ and $\sigma_{\bar{x}}$?

9.8 When is C_p a valid index?

9.9 When is C_{pk} a valid index?

9.10 What do capability indices represent?

9.11 Who first suggested the use of control charts?

9.12 What are the three basic uses of control charts?

9.13 What is the special notation used to denote the normal distribution?

9.14 What factors need to be decided when preparing to use variables control charts?

9.15 What is a rational subgroup?

9.16 What is one of the most widely used methods for determining whether or not instability exists in a control chart?

9.17 What are some of the more common patterns observed in control charts?

9.18 What do the nominal dimension and the tolerance dimension represent in a customer's specifications?

9.19 What are natural tolerance limits?

Problems

9.1 We have a random variable x that is normally distributed with a mean of 145 and a standard deviation of 7.

   a. What is the probability that x is less than 135?

   b. What is the probability that x is greater than 150?

   c. What is the value of x that would give a probability of 25%?

   d. What is the probability that x will fall between 150 and 130?

9.2 Apply the AT&T run rules to the following charts:

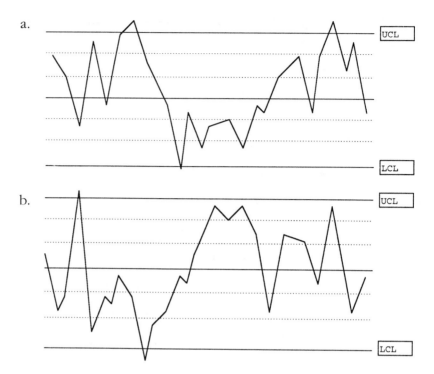

9.3 Consider the following 20 samples:

Sample	Observations				
1	42	59	38	28	24
2	32	22	22	25	41
3	38	40	31	52	40
4	22	52	33	27	37
5	46	32	20	50	43
6	27	29	24	15	24
7	31	4	34	60	37
8	32	46	30	32	40
9	35	20	34	46	39
10	55	25	33	54	41
11	22	44	51	42	36
12	14	24	12	33	22
13	36	52	19	47	50
14	29	21	17	9	21
15	33	31	26	18	7
16	40	34	17	27	23
17	23	41	21	29	20
18	28	22	35	21	45
19	32	27	16	30	16
20	23	29	31	42	13

a. Determine the control limits for the $\overline{X}$ and R charts.

b. Plot the $\overline{X}$ and R charts. Apply the AT&T run rules.

What can you conclude about the process?

9.4 A process is currently operating in-control. The control limits for the $\overline{X}$ bar and R charts are:

$\overline{X}$ **chart**	**R chart**
UCL = 47.69	UCL = 54.99
LCL = 15.23	LCL = 0
$\overline{\overline{X}}$ = 31.46	$\overline{R}$ = 22.26

The sample size is 4.

a. What are the natural tolerance limits of the process?

b. Suppose an S chart were to be substituted for the R chart. What would be the appropriate parameters of the S chart?

9.5 A process has been found to be in-control as evidenced by the $\overline{X}$ and R charts. The upper control limit of the R chart is 24.54. The sample size is 5.

a. Estimate the process standard deviation.

b. If specifications are at 88 and 112, at what value should the process be centered to minimize the fraction non-conforming?

c. Specifications are at 88 and 112. Anything above the upper specification limit results in scrap. Anything below the lower specification limit results in rework. Scrap is very costly and rework is relatively cheap. At what value should the process be centered in order to minimize rework and ensure only 0.135% scrap?

9.6 Samples of size 8 are used with $\overline{X}$ and R charts. The process has been determined to be in-control with $\overline{X}$ = 150 and $\overline{R}$ = 14.75.

a. What is the probability of detecting a shift in the next sample taken?

b. What are the natural tolerance limits of the process?

c. If specifications are 155 ± 10, what percentage non-conforming product is being produced?

9.7 A process has a known mean of 100.0 and a known standard deviation of 2.5. The process is in-control. $\overline{X}$ and R charts with samples of size 6 are being used to monitor the process.

a. What are the values of the $\overline{X}$ and R chart control limits?

b. What is the alpha error on the $\overline{X}$ chart?

c. Suddenly the process shifts downward to 97.0. What is the probability of a point falling outside the $\overline{X}$ control limits on the first sample taken after the shift occurs?

9.8 A particular part has specifications of 110.50 ± 0.25. Parts produced outside of specifications are scrapped. Two different machines produce this particular part at a rate of 150 parts per hour each. Items from both machines are discharged into the same collection box. Every half hour, the inspector selects a sample of size 6 from the collection box. A single $\overline{X}$ and R control chart is kept using the inspector's samples.

a. After 40 samples have been taken, $\Sigma \overline{X} = 4162.33$ and $\Sigma R = 8.66$. Determine the control limits for the $\overline{X}$ and R charts.

b. Calculate the natural tolerance limits of the process.

c. Calculate C_p and C_{pk}. Interpret these values.

d. Assuming no points outside the control limits on either chart and no significant runs are apparent, based on a normal distribution of this characteristic what would you estimate the fraction non-conforming to be?

e. What serious mistake is being made in the situation described in the statement of this problem?

9.9 $\overline{X}$ and S control charts are maintained for a certain quality characteristic. The sample size is 9. After 50 samples, we have $\Sigma \overline{X} = 9810$ and $\Sigma S = 1350$.

a. Calculate the control limits for the two charts.

b. Assuming that both charts exhibit control, what are the natural tolerance limits?

c. If the quality characteristic is normally distributed and the specifications are 200 ± 26, calculate C_p and C_{pk} and interpret these values.

d. Estimate the fraction non-conforming being produced.

e. Assuming the variance remains constant, where should the process mean be located in order to minimize the fraction non-conforming?

f. Suppose an R chart were to be substituted for the S chart. What would the control limits for the R chart be?

9.10 If the mean shifts to 210, what is the probability that the shift will be detected on the first subsequent sample?

9.11 Tensile strength is an important quality characteristic for bridge bolts. The bolts are made of a mild steel (ASTM A36). Because a tensile strength test destroys the bolt and each bolt is expensive, a sample of size 1 was selected, and 20 bolts were tested. The results are as follows:

Bolt	Tensile strength (psi)	Bolt	Tensile strength (psi)
1	57,500	11	74,000
2	77,750	12	60,000
3	85,000	13	77,000
4	57,560	14	59,900
5	62,000	15	64,500
6	69,900	16	71,000
7	79,800	17	80,500
8	75,300	18	69,700
9	64,500	19	78,000
10	70,500	20	68,900

a. Set up the X chart and the MR chart. Is the process in-control?

b. If the specification limits are 58,000 and 80,000 psi, what can you say about the process?

9.12 A process has been operating in-control at a mean of 6.5 inches. The upper control limit on the $\overline{X}$ chart is 6.77 inches. The lower control limit is 6.23 inches. The sample size is 5. The process standard deviation is 0.20 inches. Specifications on the dimension are 6.5 ± 0.65 inches.

a. Calculate C_p and C_{pk} and interpret these values.

b. What percent (if any) non-conforming is the process currently producing?

c. If the mean shifts to 6.6 inches, what is the probability that the shift will be detected on the first sample taken after the shift occurs?

d. Calculate C_p and C_{pk} at this new mean and interpret these values.

e. What percent non-conforming is being produced at this new mean?

BIBLIOGRAPHY

AT&T Statistical Quality Control Handbook. Delmar, Charlotte, N.C., 1985.

Case, Kenneth E., David H. Brooks, and James S. Bigelow, "Proper Use of Process Capability Indices in SPC," in *1987 IIE Integrated Systems Conference Proceedings.* Institute of Industrial Engineers, Norcross, Ga., 1987, p. 107(5).

Grant, Eugene L. and Richard S. Leavenworth, *Statistical Quality Control.* 6th ed., McGraw-Hill, New York, 1988.

McMillen, Nevin, *Statistical Process Control and Company-Wide Quality Improvement.* IFS Publications, Bedford, England, 1991.

Montgomery, Douglas C., *Introduction to Statistical Quality Control.* 2nd ed., John Wiley & Sons, New York, 1991.

$$\text{LCL} = \bar{p} - 3\sqrt{\frac{\bar{p}(1 - \bar{p})}{n}}$$ 10.14c

Equation 10.14c may give a value less than zero for the lower control limit. Whenever this occurs, a lower control limit of zero is used.

Example 1

A manager wants to keep track of the number of non-conforming circuit testers being produced. There are six types of defects which can cause a circuit tester to be considered defective or non-conforming:

1. Mechanical defect

2. Short

3. Open

4. Peak inverse voltage (PIV)

5. Voltage forward (VF)

6. Reverse polarity (RP)

The manager sets up a data collection sheet and begins to collect the information on the defective circuit testers being produced. The manager sets the sample size at 2000. The data collected for a period of 23 days are given in Table 10.1. The average fraction non-conforming can be determined using Equation 10.13:

$$\bar{p} = \frac{\sum\limits_{i=1}^{m} D_i}{\sum\limits_{i=1}^{m} n_i} = \frac{5851}{46000} = 0.1272$$

The control limits for the p chart can be found from Equations 10.14b and 10.14c:

$$\text{UCL} = \bar{p} + 3\sqrt{\frac{\bar{p}(1 - \bar{p})}{n}} = 0.1272 + 3\sqrt{\frac{0.1272(1 - 0.1272)}{2000}} = 0.1496$$

$$\text{LCL} = \bar{p} - 3\sqrt{\frac{\bar{p}(1 - \bar{p})}{n}} = 0.1272 - 3\sqrt{\frac{0.1272(1 - 0.1272)}{2000}} = 0.1048$$

The p chart for the fraction non-conforming is displayed in Figure 10.1. The process appears to be in-control. However, the average fraction non-conforming is 12.72%, which the manager feels is too high. The manager

TABLE 10.1 Data Collected on Non-Conforming Circuit Testers

Day	Mechanical defect	Short	Open	Peak inverse voltage	Voltage forward	Reverse polarity	Total defective	Total inspected	Fraction non-conforming
1	38	50	67	78	7	1	241	2000	12.05
2	47	61	78	90	3	2	281	2000	14.05
3	42	51	89	99	5	0	286	2000	14.30
4	50	50	76	103	4	0	283	2000	14.15
5	12	47	72	98	2	1	232	2000	11.60
6	11	64	88	87	8	0	258	2000	12.90
7	5	49	71	93	12	1	231	2000	11.55
8	15	52	69	92	14	2	244	2000	12.20
9	13	63	70	98	7	3	254	2000	12.70
10	9	72	76	87	9	5	258	2000	12.90
11	8	67	77	86	13	0	251	2000	12.55
12	12	59	71	80	11	0	233	2000	11.65
13	22	62	74	82	9	1	250	2000	12.50
14	9	61	63	90	6	2	231	2000	11.55
15	17	83	64	97	8	1	270	2000	13.50
16	19	65	68	98	7	1	258	2000	12.90
17	18	50	79	104	4	0	255	2000	12.75
18	14	51	64	118	3	1	251	2000	12.55
19	20	57	77	96	7	0	257	2000	12.85
20	17	60	63	98	5	0	243	2000	12.15
21	16	68	79	114	3	1	281	2000	14.05
22	14	61	71	92	11	0	249	2000	12.45
23	10	68	78	89	8	1	254	2000	12.70

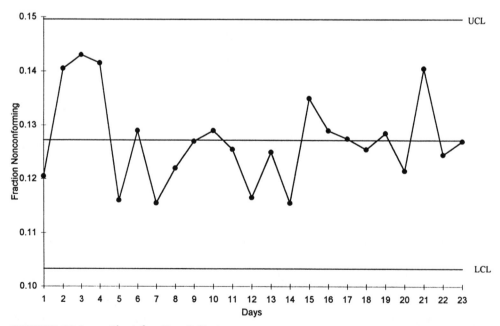

FIGURE 10.1 p Chart for Circuit Testers

studies the data collected for this chart, which are given in Table 10.1. From Table 10.1 it appears that the biggest problem is PIV or peak inverse voltage. After further study, an adjustment is made at the soldering station. The manager then collects more data to find out whether the adjustment reduced the fraction non-conforming. The new set of data is shown in Table 10.2 and the accompanying p chart is displayed in Figure 10.2. It appears that the adjustment reduced the number of non-conforming due to peak inverse voltage, which reduced the total fraction non-conforming. The total fraction non-conforming is 8.97%, which is still higher than the manager would like. Therefore, the manager has decided to continue working on the problem.

In Example 1, the sample size was constant. Many times, however, the sample size is not constant, especially if 100% inspection is being performed. With 100% inspection, inspection is typically performed on units produced during some defined sampling period, such as a shift, a day, or a production run. Many factors influence the number of units produced during a sampling period. Therefore, it is very difficult to produce exactly the same number of items every time.

Since the control limits for the p chart are a function of the sample size, some modifications need to be made to ensure that the chart is properly interpreted. The three most common modifications are:

TABLE 10.2   Data Collected after Adjustment

Day	Mechanical defect	Short	Open	Peak inverse voltage	Voltage forward	Reverse polarity	Total defective	Total inspected	Fraction non-conforming
1	33	47	62	19	5	2	168	2000	8.40
2	42	63	67	26	4	1	203	2000	10.15
3	41	61	72	22	3	1	200	2000	10.00
4	40	68	76	22	6	1	213	2000	10.65
5	30	50	72	16	3	0	171	2000	8.55
6	25	61	83	14	7	1	191	2000	9.55
7	15	65	69	21	4	0	174	2000	8.70
8	7	60	78	18	10	0	173	2000	8.65
9	6	57	67	23	6	1	160	2000	8.00
10	18	50	71	25	10	2	176	2000	8.80
11	17	59	78	20	5	3	182	2000	9.10
12	21	65	71	24	6	1	188	2000	9.40
13	11	62	63	17	4	4	161	2000	8.05
14	15	59	64	22	3	0	163	2000	8.15
15	27	58	71	35	5	0	196	2000	9.80
16	9	64	79	21	3	1	177	2000	8.85
17	16	53	77	24	4	0	174	2000	8.70
18	11	57	82	28	3	1	182	2000	9.10
19	12	51	81	23	6	2	175	2000	8.75
20	7	63	66	20	4	0	160	2000	8.00

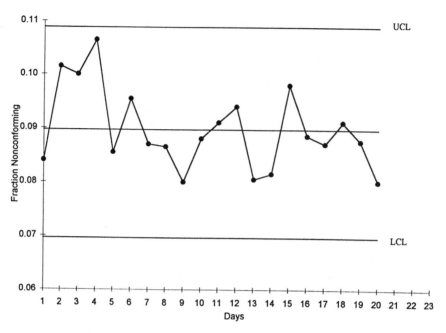

FIGURE 10.2   p Chart after Adjustment

1. Compute separate control limits for each sample based on its specific sample size. This is the more accepted approach. Interpretation of the chart is straightforward. However, it does require continued calculation of the control limits. Also, the plotting of different control limits for each sample looks a little messy. This is not a problem if done on a computer. If it is done by hand, this modification can be tedious.

2. Compute the control limits based on an average sample size. This method is easier, but it is only appropriate if the sample sizes do not vary greatly. An accepted rule of thumb is if the sample sizes vary less than 20%, then an average sample size can be used. The major concern when using this modification is ensuring that the chart is interpreted properly. For example, if the actual sample size is greater than the average sample size used, then a point may indicate in-control when in fact it is actually out-of-control. Conversely, if the actual sample size is smaller that the average sample size used, then a point could plot above the upper control limit when in fact it would not be above its own true upper control limit.

3. Compute the control limits based on a standardized fraction non-conforming. This method stabilizes the plotted value, but it is difficult to set up and interpret.

Because computers are so readily available these days and because it is the easiest to interpret, the first modification is recommended.

of opportunity varies, thus making it difficult for the area of opportunity and the inspection unit to be the same.

Statistical Base

The development of the c chart is based on the **Poisson distribution**. In statistics, "a Poisson random variable is used to 'count' the number of occurrences of low probability events in situations that involve large number of trials" (Farnum, 1994, p. 134). As applied to attributes control charts, a Poisson random variable is used to "count" the number of non-conformities per inspection unit (or given area of opportunity).

The Poisson distribution, as applied to control charts, assumes that:

1. The opportunity for the occurrence of a non-conformity is large.

2. The probability of getting a non-conformity at a specific point is small.

3. The opportunity space for non-conformities to occur is constant from sample to sample.

4. Non-conformities occur randomly and are independent of one another.

The Poisson random variable, X, is described by the parameter, λ (lambda). The Poisson distribution is unique in that λ represents both the mean and the variance.

$$\mu = \sigma^2 = \lambda \qquad\qquad 10.16$$

Once λ is known, any probability concerning the Poisson random variable can be evaluated by

$$P(X = k) = \frac{e^{-\lambda}\lambda^k}{k!} \qquad k = 0, 1, 2, \ldots \qquad 10.17$$

where e represents the base of the natural logarithm, 2.71828....

c Chart

The c chart plots the number of non-conformities that occur in a **constant** area of opportunity or inspection unit. The constant means that the area of opportunity and the inspection unit are equal. Examples of a constant inspection unit are fixed length, area, and quantity. Fixed length could be a section of road, a roll of paper, etc. Fixed area could be the hood of a car, a defined portion of a circuit board, etc. Fixed quantity could be a work week, three computers, etc.

In most applications, the center line, or mean, of the c chart is based on the average number of non-conformities per inspection unit. This can be determined by:

$$\mu = \bar{c} = \frac{\sum\limits_{i=1}^{k} c_i}{k} = \frac{\text{total number of non–conformities found}}{\text{number of inspection units}} \qquad 10.18$$

where c_i is the observed number of non-conformities found in inspection unit i. The control limits are determined by

$$\text{control limits} = \mu \pm 3\sigma$$

Therefore, the control limits for the c chart are determined from

$$\text{center line} = \bar{c} \qquad\qquad 10.19a$$

$$\text{UCL} = \bar{c} + 3\sqrt{\bar{c}} \qquad\qquad 10.19b$$

$$\text{LCL} = \bar{c} - 3\sqrt{\bar{c}} \qquad\qquad 10.19c$$

Recall that the mean and the variance of a Poisson random variable are equal. As with the p and np charts, if the calculation of the lower control limit is less than zero, then the lower control limit is set to zero.

Example 4

A production line supervisor decides to count the number of non-conformities that exist on the 3.5-inch floppy disks being produced by process line 2. The production rate is approximately 500 per hour. For reasons of convenience, the supervisor takes a sample of 75 per hour. In other words, the inspection unit is 75 floppy disks. The supervisor collects data for three days. The number of non-conformities observed over the three days is displayed in Table 10.5.

Table 10.5 shows that there were a total of 472 non-conformities in the 24 samples. From Equation 10.18, the mean can be determined by

$$\bar{c} = \frac{\sum\limits_{i=1}^{k} c_i}{k} = \frac{472}{24} = 19.67$$

The control limits can be determined using Equations 10.19b and 10.19c:

$$\text{UCL} = \bar{c} + 3\sqrt{\bar{c}} = 19.67 + 3\sqrt{19.67} = 32.97$$

$$\text{LCL} = \bar{c} - 3\sqrt{\bar{c}} = 19.67 - 3\sqrt{19.67} = 6.36$$

The c chart is shown in Figure 10.5. As can be seen, all points fall within the control limits and the pattern appears to be random. Therefore, no lack of control is indicated.

TABLE 10.5 Number of Non-Conformities for 3.5-Inch Floppy Disks

Sample number	Number non-conformities	Sample number	Number non-conformities
1	14	13	24
2	18	14	22
3	21	15	23
4	32	16	32
5	30	17	20
6	18	18	28
7	21	19	8
8	11	20	15
9	18	21	12
10	12	22	16
11	17	23	24
12	15	24	21
TOTAL			472

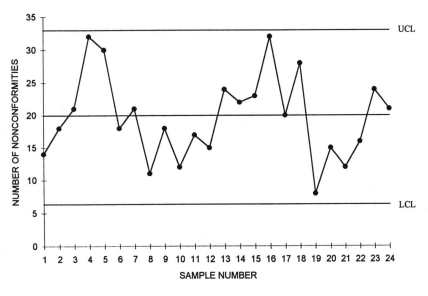

FIGURE 10.5 c Chart for 3.5-Inch Floppy Disks

u Chart

In many applications, the area of opportunity varies. This violates the constant opportunity space assumption upon which the c chart is based. Therefore, it becomes necessary to create a standardized statistic. This standardized statistic is defined as u and is the average number of non-conformities per inspection unit. It is determined by

$$u = \frac{c}{n} \qquad 10.20$$

where c is the number of non-conformities per area of opportunity and n is the number of inspection units in the area of opportunity inspected. In this case, the inspection unit is not equal to the area of opportunity. This means that there will typically be multiple inspection units for a given area of opportunity. It also means that n will not always be an integer. For example, let's say that the inspection unit is 10 feet of paper. The process that makes the paper produces the paper in rolls that vary in size from 100 to 125 feet. Because the paper is produced in rolls, it is inspected for non-conformities by rolls. Thus, the area of opportunity is one roll. The number of inspection units in a given area of opportunity (a roll of paper) would vary from 10 to 12.5 units.

The characteristic that is plotted for this type of inspection is u determined from Equation 10.20. This gives the u chart. As with all control charts, a center line and control limits must be established. The mean or center line is found by

$$\bar{u} = \text{mean} = \text{center line} = \frac{\sum\limits_{i=1}^{k} c_i}{\sum\limits_{i=1}^{k} n_i} \qquad 10.21$$

$$= \frac{\text{total number of non–conformities}}{\text{total number of inspection units}}$$

where c_i is the observed number of non-conformities in opportunity area i, n_i is the number of inspection units in opportunity area i, and k is the number of opportunity areas inspected.

The control limits are obtained from $\bar{u}$. Note that each $c_i = u_i n_i$ follows a Poisson distribution whose parameter λ_i can be estimated from $\bar{u} n_i$. Therefore, the control limits for the u chart are

$$\text{UCL} = \bar{u} + 3\sqrt{\frac{\bar{u}}{n}} \qquad 10.22a$$

$$LCL^* = \bar{u} - 3\sqrt{\frac{\bar{u}}{n}} \qquad\qquad 10.22b$$

where n is the number of inspection units in the given area of opportunity.

If the number of inspection units varies from opportunity area to opportunity area, the control limits will also vary because the control limits are a function of the number of inspection units.

Example 5

A copy shop manager notices that the number of complaints on completed jobs has increased. The manager realizes that the total number of completed jobs per day has also increased. The manager wants to determine if the increase in complaints should be expected due to the increase in total number of jobs or if the quality of work has really decreased. The manager decides to inspect all completed jobs for defects on a daily basis and does so for three weeks. The results of the manager's inspections are shown in Table 10.6.

Since the size of each completed job varies only slightly, the manager lets one completed job be the inspection unit. Since the area of opportunity (or completed jobs) varies, the manager develops a u chart. This means that the control limits vary from day to day. Table 10.6 also shows the development of the u chart. Equation 10.21 was used to calculate average number of defects per unit. Equations 10.22a and 10.22b were used to calculate the individual control limits. The plotted u chart is illustrated in Figure 10.6.

The average number of defects per completed job is 16.88. All points fall within control limits and the pattern appears random. Therefore, the manager concludes that the process is operating in-control. However, the manager feels that an average of 16.88 defects per completed job is too high. Therefore, the manager decides to form a task team to lower the average number of defects per completed job.

SUMMARY

Control charts for attributes are widely used in non-manufacturing applications. They are very easy to use. Also, the concept of number non-conforming or number of defects is readily understood by most people, thus making these charts easy to understand.

---

* If the lower control limit is less than zero, then it is set equal to zero.

TABLE 10.6 Development of u Chart for Complaints Received

Date	Number of completed jobs, n_i	Number of complaints, c_i	Non-conformities per unit, $u_i = c_i/n_i$	LCL $\bar{u} - 3\sqrt{\dfrac{\bar{u}}{n_i}}$	UCL $\bar{u} + 3\sqrt{\dfrac{\bar{u}}{n_i}}$
1	21	375	17.86	19.57	14.19
2	17	244	14.35	19.87	13.89
3	28	421	15.04	19.21	14.55
4	25	478	19.12	19.34	14.41
5	20	388	19.40	19.63	14.12
6	29	511	17.62	19.17	14.59
7	22	345	15.68	19.50	14.25
8	25	477	19.08	19.34	14.41
9	31	566	18.26	19.09	14.66
10	28	414	14.79	19.21	14.55
11	23	364	15.83	19.45	14.31
12	27	444	16.44	19.25	14.50
13	26	435	16.73	19.29	14.46
14	29	533	18.38	19.17	14.59
15	23	433	18.83	19.45	14.31
16	30	497	16.57	19.13	14.63
17	23	356	15.48	19.45	14.31
18	26	388	14.92	19.29	14.46
19	22	403	18.32	19.50	14.25
20	28	467	16.68	19.21	14.55
21	24	355	14.79	19.39	14.36

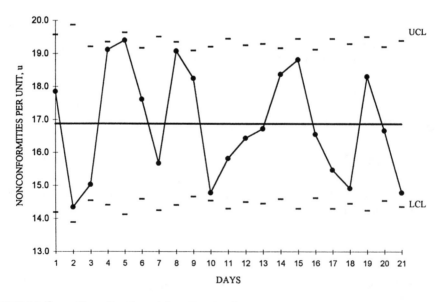

FIGURE 10.6   u Chart for Complaints Received

EXERCISES

Questions

10.1 List the four types of attributes control charts and what each chart plots.

10.2 What is attribute data?

10.3 What is the difference between non-conforming and non-conformity?

10.4 What is/are the advantage(s) of using attributes charts?

10.5 Identify the probability distribution on which each type of attribute chart is based.

10.6 Which control chart(s) is/are used when the sample size is not constant?

10.7 What happens to the control limits when the sample size is not constant? How does this affect interpreting the chart?

10.8 When the sample size varies, the np chart and the c chart are not appropriate for use. Explain why.

Problems

10.1 A process produces silicon wafers. The wafer is 0.01 inches thick and 10 cm in diameter. There are 250 integrated circuits or chips on each wafer. At the end of the process, the wafer is inspected. The data below give the number of non-conforming chips per wafer. Construct a fraction non-conforming control chart for these data. What can you conclude about the process?

Wafer number	# non-conforming	Wafer number	# non-conforming
1	17	19	18
2	14	20	13
3	11	21	15
4	13	22	19
5	16	23	11
6	18	24	17
7	20	25	21
8	15	26	13
9	12	27	16
10	17	28	12
11	16	29	15
12	22	30	19
13	11	31	17
14	19	32	11
15	15	33	13
16	11	34	20
17	14	35	14
18	15	36	16

10.2 Construct a np chart for the data in Problem 10.1. Which type of chart do you prefer? Why?

10.3 The data below represent the number of dishes that are broken at a restaurant while loading and unloading the dishwasher. The total number of dishes washed varies daily. Construct a p chart for these data. What can you conclude about the situation? Do you have any recommendations?

Day	Total number of dishes washed	Number of broken dishes	Day	Total number of dishes washed	Number of broken dishes
1	465	51	13	465	39
2	425	42	14	425	41
3	500	55	15	500	51
4	500	53	16	500	47
5	425	44	17	425	38
6	425	41	18	425	44
7	425	39	19	425	41
8	465	47	20	465	48
9	500	56	21	465	42
10	500	43	22	500	47
11	425	46	23	500	51
12	465	49	24	465	36

10.4 A process produces overhead projectors. Each projector is inspected for defects or non-conformities. Typical defects found are scratches, dents, paint blemishes, improper labeling, etc. The supervisor wants to keep track of the defects being produced and decides to set up a u chart. The inspection unit the supervisor uses is 10% of all projectors produced per day. Since the number of projectors produced per day varies, so does the inspection unit (or sample size). The data given below were collected over the first four weeks. Develop a table similar to Table 10.6 given in the chapter. Plot the u chart. Does this process appear to be in-control? What are your recommendations?

Day	Sample size	Number of defects	Day	Sample size	Number of defects
1	100	654	11	110	667
2	120	688	12	125	777
3	95	544	13	120	644
4	115	592	14	95	466
5	120	721	15	110	632
6	110	652	16	100	584
7	90	502	17	120	669
8	125	756	18	115	623
9	115	570	19	100	567
10	100	633	20	100	678

10.5 For the situation in Problem 10.4, assume the supervisor used a constant sample size of 110 projectors. Use the data given below to set up and plot a c chart. Does the process appear to be in-control?

Day	Sample size	Number of defects	Day	Sample size	Number of defects
1	110	632	11	110	627
2	110	644	12	110	717
3	110	548	13	110	648
4	110	579	14	110	586
5	110	701	15	110	632
6	110	652	16	110	554
7	110	582	17	110	659
8	110	655	18	110	613
9	110	578	19	110	667
10	110	639	20	110	618

10.6 Set up and plot a u chart for the data in Problem 10.5.

10.7 A process is being monitored with a p chart. The average fraction non-conforming of the process is 0.05.

a. Assuming the sample size is 350, calculate the 3 sigma control limits for the p chart.

b. What is the smallest sample size that will give a positive lower limit?

10.8 For the process in Problem 10.7, calculate the 3 sigma control limits for a np chart with a sample size of 350.

BIBLIOGRAPHY

Farnum, Nicholas R., *Modern Statistical Quality Control and Improvement*. Duxbury Press, Belmont, Calif., 1994.

Gitlow, Howard, Shelly Gitlow, Alan Oppenheim, and Rosa Oppenheim, *Tools and Methods for the Improvement of Quality*. Richard D. Irwin, Boston, 1989.

Hines, William W. and Douglas C. Montgovery, *Probability and Statistics in Engineering and Management Science*. John Wiley & Sons, New York, 1980.

Montgomery, Douglas C., *Introduction to Statistical Quality Control*. John Wiley & Sons, New York, 1991.

11

WHEN TO USE THE DIFFERENT CONTROL CHARTS

INTRODUCTION

How to develop and interpret the different control charts was discussed in detail in the previous two chapters. In this chapter, a simplified aid is provided for deciding which control chart is appropriate for a given circumstance. In the past, this decision had to be made by someone experienced in the use of control charts. However, the increased awareness of quality in the workplace has meant that more and more people are being introduced to the various tools of quality, including control charts. Thus, the need exists for a basic aid in choosing the correct control chart.

The flowchart in Figure 11.1 is a very simple and easy-to-use aid when determining which control chart is needed for a given situation. There are several flowcharts of this nature. However, the distinguishing features of this flowchart are:

1. It is simple and easy to use.

2. Only a basic understanding of statistics is required.

3. It can be used (and, more importantly, understood) by personnel at all levels.

EXAMPLES

Numerous examples to illustrate how the flowchart works are provided in this section.

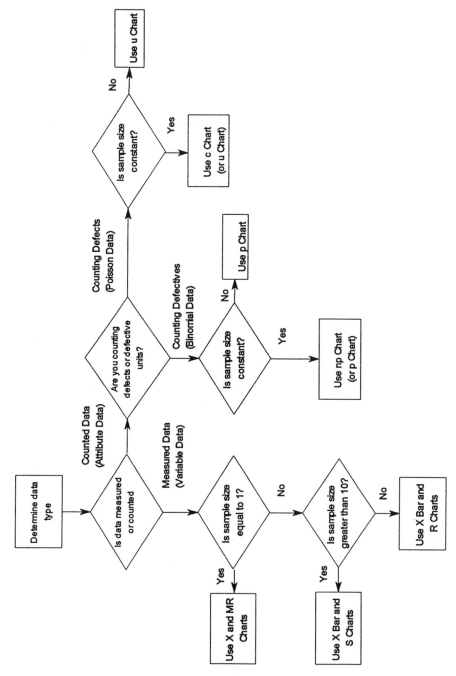

FIGURE 11.1   Decision Flowchart (©1994 J.A. Swift)

Example 1

A ceramic tile manufacturing company has just secured a contract with NASA to supply the tiles for the new space shuttle. The manufacturing process is long and detailed, and only 20 to 25 tiles can be manufactured per day. NASA requires that the tiles be subjected to specific measured tests to prove that they are capable of withstanding repeated exposure to extreme high temperatures. The tests required are destructive tests. Because the tests are destructive tests and the production output per day is low, the manufacturing company has decided to use a sample size of one. Which chart should be used?

Solution (refer to Figure 11.1)

data are measured $\rightarrow$ sample size = 1 $\rightarrow$ use X and MR charts

Example 2

Mr. Fence runs a small alterations shop. Recently, there has been an increase in the number of complaints about the work done in his shop. He has decided that at the end of each day, he will inspect all the work completed that day for defects. Which chart should Mr. Fence use?

Solution

data are counted $\rightarrow$ counting defects $\rightarrow$

sample size varies (a different number of alterations

are completed each day) $\rightarrow$ use a u chart

Example 3

A boot manufacturer wants to check a certain style of boot for possible defects in the sole stitching. The defects include missed stitches, loose threads, and any other observed defects. This particular style of boot is produced at a rate of 100 pairs per hour. The manager suggests checking ten pairs per hour. Which chart should be used?

Solution

data are counted $\rightarrow$ counting defects $\rightarrow$

sample size is constant (10 parts/hour) $\rightarrow$ use a c chart

Example 4

A carpenter at a local door manufacturing company is responsible for making sure that the lengths of the doors being produced meet specifications. Twenty doors are produced per hour. The carpenter collects and measures five doors hourly. Which chart should the carpenter use?

Solution

data are measured (length of doors) $\rightarrow$ sample size > 1 $\rightarrow$

sample size < 10 $\rightarrow$ use $\overline{X}$ and R charts

Example 5

A computer manufacturer inspects all chips that are produced. The number of chips produced in one day varies. Chips are inspected on a good/bad basis. The good chips are sold. The bad chips are unusable and are thrown away. If the manufacturer wants to keep track of the unusable chips produced per day, which chart should he use?

Solution

data are counted $\rightarrow$ counting defectives (unusable chips) $\rightarrow$

sample size varies $\rightarrow$ use a p chart

Example 6

The cruise ship King Titan wants to keep track of the number of non-gambling customers it carries each cruise. The cruise ship defines a non-gambling customer as anyone under the age of 21. King Titan has a passenger capacity of 750, and it is always booked to capacity. Upon boarding, each passenger must present proof of age. Those over 21 are issued a bracelet which allows them to gamble. Those under 21 are not issued a bracelet. A tally is kept on the number of passengers under the age of 21. Which chart should the cruise ship use to track the number of non-gambling customers?

Solution

data are counted $\rightarrow$ counting defectives (non–gambling customers) $\rightarrow$

sample size is constant (750 passengers per cruise) $\rightarrow$ use a np chart

Example 7

A medical supplier specializes in intravenous (IV) needles. The outer diameter of the IV needles is a critical parameter, and it has very tight specification limits. The medical supplier wants to set up a control chart to determine if the process producing the needles is in-control. The process to be studied produces 200 IV needles per hour. The process supervisor suggests inspecting 20 IV needles per hour. Which chart should be used?

Solution

$$\text{data are measured (outside diameter)} \rightarrow \text{ sample size } > 1 \rightarrow$$

$$\text{sample size } > 10 \rightarrow \text{ use } \overline{X} \text{ and S charts}$$

SUMMARY

As seen from the previous examples, using Figure 11.1 makes the decision as to which chart to use in a given situation relatively easy. Once an appropriate chart has been identified for use, the previous two chapters can be used to aid in setting up the chart and interpreting it.

EXERCISES

For the following situations, use Figure 11.1 and the solution formats given in the examples in the chapter to determine the appropriate control chart.

11.1 A process that packages a ready-to-make cake mix automatically weighs each bag of mix before placing it into its respective box. The specification for each bag of mix is 8 ± 0.01 ounces. If a bag weighs outside of specs, it is automatically separated from the rest. Which chart should be used?

11.2 A hardware store has recently changed its supplier of wood products. In order for the store to sign a permanent contract with this new supplier, the products must pass some quality standards. At the present time, the products are ordered weekly and order quantity varies from week to week. All items ordered are received at the beginning of the week following placement of the order. The company tracks quality by inspecting 20% of all items ordered and tracking the number of defects (scratches, dents, blemishes, etc.). Which chart should be used?

11.3 A T-shirt outlet in Miami Beach wants to keep track of the number of unsellable T-shirts it receives from its supplier. A T-shirt is considered unsellable if the design is faded, peeling, crooked, etc. The number of T-shirts delivered per week varies. The T-shirt outlet does a 100% inspection of every delivery. Which chart should be used?

11.4   Mrs. Green is a gymnastics coach. She wants to keep track of the number of technical errors made by one of her students during a certain floor routine. Due to time constraints, the student can only perform the floor routine twice a day. Which chart should Mrs. Green use?

11.5   FWS Water Company produces bottled water. Because the company is located in the Middle East, it must use saltwater as its source. The company has recently developed a new and significantly cheaper process to remove the salt. The new process produces 200 one-liter bottles per hour. The process manager inspects 15 bottles every hour. For each bottle inspected, he determines the percent of salt remaining in the water. Which chart should the process manager use?

11.6   A clinic is trying to determine the number of patients it treats for the flu each day. The number of patients that come into the clinic varies from day to day. Which chart should be used?

11.7   An airline manager in Memphis wants to track the number of late plane arrivals from Tampa. The manager wants to track the late arrivals on a weekly basis. Due to the air route licensing agreement this airline has, the number of planes leaving Tampa for Memphis per week is constant. Which chart should be used?

11.8   A furniture company produces kitchen tables. The length of the table legs has very tight tolerances in order to keep the finished table from wobbling. The process produces 80 table legs per hour and 8 per hour are inspected. Which chart should be used?

11.9   Mr. Henderson has the tedious job of proofreading all drafts that are being sent to the local print shop. To make his work more meaningful and satisfying, he has decided to record how often the name of the company is misspelled in the documents. If he wanted to plot his findings on a chart to show his boss, which chart should he use?

11.10   A job placement office wants to know the average number of errors that walk-in applicants make on the typing exam. The number of errors made per applicant will be recorded. Which chart should be used?

11.11   A diamond-cutting firm wants to keep track of the final size (carat) of each diamond it cuts. Which chart should be used?

11.12   A motorcycle exhaust manufacturer wants to determine if the process that makes the Z2 exhaust pipes is in-control. The critical parameter of the exhaust pipe is the level of sound (measured in decibels) emitted from the pipe. Five exhaust pipes are randomly selected each hour, and the level of sound emitted is measured. Which chart should be used?

12

QUALITY IMPROVEMENT STORIES

WHAT IS A QUALITY IMPROVEMENT STORY?

A quality improvement (QI) story is a step-by-step guide for problem solving (or process improvement). It is called a story because it organizes the work a team does in such a way that their story is told. It tells who they are, when and why they got together, where and what they worked on, and how they solved their problem. By having every team use the same storytelling technique, communication is standardized. This standardization allows for easier transfer of ideas between teams, departments, and even companies. It also provides a framework for training all employees in the application of the basic quality control tools.

A QI storyboard is a visual display of the QI story. The storyboard is typically mounted (or hung) in the area where the problem is occurring. This allows everyone to see what problem is being worked on and how far along in the problem-solving process the team has advanced.

There are four main reasons for using a QI story. First, it helps the team organize, gather, and analyze the data in a logical fashion. In this sense, all team members are speaking the same language and working on the same problem. Second, it monitors the team's progress. When a QI storyboard is visible, team members (as well as non-team members) can see exactly where the team is in the problem-solving process. Third, it facilitates understanding by non-team members. This is helpful in that non-team members may be able to provide useful feedback that the team may have missed or not thought of. Because everyone in the company is interested in problem/process improvement, feedback is desirable. Fourth, it standardizes presentations to management. Because management is (or should be) already familiar with the use of QI stories, management can concentrate on the problem being presented, which saves valuable time. It also lets the team speak with facts (something that strongly influences management).

A QI story follows several basic steps for solving a problem:

1. Identify the problem area

2. Observe and identify causes of the problem

3. Analyze, identify, and verify root cause(s) of the problem

4. Plan and implement preventive action

5. Check effectiveness of action taken

6. Standardize process improvement

7. Determine future actions

The relationship between the QI process and the PDCA cycle is depicted in Figure 12.1.

Within each step, certain tasks are performed to ensure that the team does not miss an important point. In the remainder of this chapter, each step is discussed and a case study is presented.

STEP 1: IDENTIFY THE PROBLEM AREA

Purpose

The purpose of this step is to identify the general problem to be worked on and to recognize the importance of the problem. There are many problems, both large and small, that could be worked on. However, because resources and time are limited, only the most important problems can be addressed. The best way to identify the most important problems is through the use of "good data." With good data, it is easy to quantify the significance of the problem and consequently solve it.

The reasons for working on a problem can stem from many sources. The problem could have arisen from a process that was being tracked. The problem could come from customer complaints. It could also come from upper management. Whatever the source or reason, once a problem area has been defined, data must be gathered to substantiate the importance of the problem. One of the best ways to demonstrate the importance of a problem is to show the loss in performance (time, money, etc.) that is occurring at the present time and how much it should improve by correcting the problem. Identifying who the customers of the process are and how the problem affects them also demonstrates the significance of the

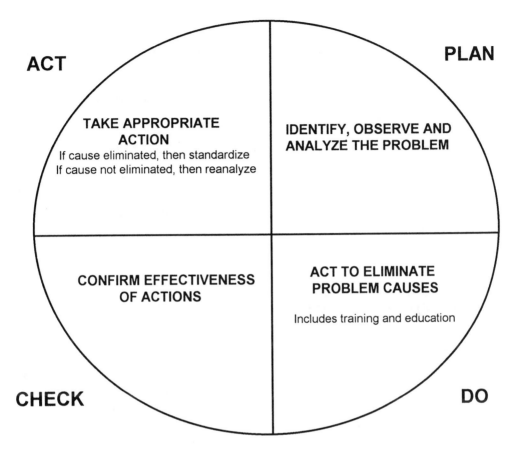

FIGURE 12.1 Relationship between the Quality Improvement Process and the PDCA Cycle

problem. With the problem identified and its importance substantiated, the team can proceed to the next step.

Tools*

The tools that are the most helpful in this step are brainstorming, multivoting, flowcharts, graphs, and control charts. Brainstorming helps the team identify problem areas (if one has not already been mandated). If the list is too long, multivoting can be used to reduce the list. Flowcharts help identify a trackable indicator that will show the variability and improvement of the process over time. Graphs and control charts indicate the magnitude (or importance) of the problem.

---

* The tools listed here are not intended to be all-inclusive. They are the tools that are most often used to implement the specific step.

Results

There are several results that should be achieved in this step before continuing:

1. The problem area has been clearly defined and understood.

2. The importance of the problem has been substantiated.

3. The customers and how the problem affects them have been identified.

4. A trackable indicator that shows the impact of any changes made to the process has been identified.

5. An estimated budget and schedule for completion of the project have been developed.

STEP 2: OBSERVE AND IDENTIFY CAUSES OF THE PROBLEM

Purpose

The purpose of the observation step is to evaluate the present status of the problem and identify the factors that could be causes of the problem. This is done by investigating the specific features of the problem. This step takes the initial tracking indicator and stratifies it to the point where the team can take action. This stratification is done by investigating the four points that define the features of the problem: time, place, type, and symptom. (Additional data typically must be collected at this point.) Once the initial tracking indicator has been broken down and causes of the problem have been identified, a specific problem statement can be formulated and the team can proceed to the next step.

Step 2 initially appears very similar to Step 1. However, the purpose of Step 1 was to identify the general problem area and recognize its significance. The purpose of Step 2 is to identify the factors that are causes of the problem.

Tools

The tools that will be most useful in this step are check sheets, Pareto charts, histograms, flowcharts, graphs, and control charts. The initial tracking indicator is illustrated using graphs and control charts. Flowcharts are used to identify where in the process data can be easily collected. Check sheets are used to collect the additional data when investigating the features (time, place, type, and symptom) of the problem. Pareto charts and histograms help stratify the data to the point where the causing factors can be identified and prioritized.

Results

The expected results of this step are as follows:

1. The factors that cause the problem have been identified and prioritized.

2. A specific problem statement has been formulated which distinguishes the causing factor that will be corrected.

STEP 3: ANALYZE, IDENTIFY, AND VERIFY ROOT CAUSE(S) OF THE PROBLEM

Purpose

The purpose of the analysis step is to determine the main or root cause(s) of the specific problem identified in the previous step. It is very important that causes, and not symptoms, of the problem are identified because treating or fixing a symptom does not eliminate the problem. The problem can only be eliminated if the cause is eliminated. Much like taking aspirin for a toothache, it may relieve the ache temporarily, but if the cause of the ache is not treated, the ache usually returns. The best way to identify the root cause(s) is to construct a cause-and-effect diagram. The cause-and-effect diagram takes the problem identified in the previous step and makes it the "effect" portion of the diagram. Now the root cause analysis begins. All elements that seem to relate to the effect are identified and put on the cause-and-effect diagram. The potential root cause(s) are compared with the actual causes using the information obtained in the observation step. (The cause-and-effect diagram will typically undergo several iterations at this point.) The root cause(s) that appear to have the greatest impact are highlighted on the cause-and-effect diagram. At this point, the analysis step is only half done. Verification of the main root cause(s) must be done. The biggest mistake teams make is to proceed to the next step without verifying the root cause(s). In order to verify that the correct root cause(s) have been identified, additional new data must be collected. Once the root cause(s) have been verified, the team then proceeds to the next step.

Tools

The tools that can be used in this step are cause-and-effect diagrams, brainstorming, cheek sheets, Pareto charts, graphs, control charts, and scatter diagrams. Brainstorming is used in developing the cause-and-effect diagram. Check sheets are used in collecting the additional data needed when verifying the root cause(s). Scatter diagrams are used to verify the causes by establishing or rejecting relationships between probable causes and the effect. Graphs and control charts are used to continue tracking the process.

Results

The major result of this step is that the root cause(s) of the problem have been identified and verified with new data.

STEP 4: PLAN AND IMPLEMENT PREVENTIVE ACTION

Purpose

The purpose of this step is to plan and implement actions that will eliminate the root cause(s). There are two types of action. The first type is corrective action. **Corrective action** is action taken to correct or to temporarily fix the problem, like taking aspirin to relieve a toothache (treating the symptom instead of the cause). This temporarily fixes the problem, but does nothing to prevent it from recurring. The second type of action is preventive action. **Preventive action** is action taken to prevent the problem from happening again, in this case treating the cause of the toothache.

Preventive action eliminates the cause of the problem and prevents it from recurring. Therefore, preventive action is the best way to solve a problem. It is also the reason the team came together in the first place. Determining an appropriate preventive action takes time. Therefore, it may be necessary to implement temporary corrective actions in order to minimize the impact of the problem while an appropriate preventive action is being determined.

Care must be taken when developing actions to eliminate the root cause. This is because many actions may cause other problems not foreseen, like side effects from drugs. To prevent the unwanted side effect, the proposed preventive action must be thoroughly evaluated before implementing it. Because people are always part of the process and typically resistant to change, unwanted people side effects need to be anticipated and avoided. Active cooperation of all involved is essential for success.

Because action means change and change mean additional money or resources, a cost/benefit analysis needs to be performed. The cost/benefit analysis should take into account both tangible and intangible benefits. A cost/benefit analysis ensures that the preventive action to be implemented does not cost more than just leaving the problem alone.

Once all factors concerning the proposed preventive actions have been investigated, an action plan is developed and the preventive action is implemented. Tracking of the previously selected key indicators is also initiated.

Tools

The major tool used in this step is a cost/benefit analysis. A cost/benefit analysis illustrates to management the cost and impact of any action taken.

Results

The major results are as follows:

1. Preventive action to "eliminate" the problem has been identified.

2. A cost/benefit analysis has been done for the proposed preventive action.

3. An action plan has been developed, with specific assignments and expected completion time defined.

4. The selected preventive action is implemented, and tracking of the chosen key indicators is initiated.

STEP 5: CHECK EFFECTIVENESS OF ACTION TAKEN

Purpose

The purpose of the check step is to ensure that the main cause(s) of the problem have been eliminated. This is done by comparing the data obtained after the preventive action has been implemented with the data obtained before implementation. The same format (tables, graphs, charts), the same time frame (weeks, months), and the same indicator that was used to show the status prior to implementing the preventive action are used in the comparison.

If the preventive action did not eliminate the problem, then something is happening in the process that was not properly identified, and the problem needs to be reanalyzed. If the results of the preventive action are not as good as expected, then the reasons why need to be investigated and fully documented. In short, the problem-solving process has failed and the team must return to the observation step.

If the preventive action appears to have eliminated the problem, then the team can proceed to the standardization step.

Tools

The tools used in this step are graphs, control charts, and Pareto charts. The graphs and control charts use the same indicator as used in the beginning of the study to illustrate the overall impact of the preventive action. The Pareto charts use the same causes of the problem that were used in the beginning of the study so that the before and after Pareto charts accurately illustrate any improvement.

Results

The major result of this step is the decision to standardize the preventive actions taken or to reanalyze the problem.

STEP 6: STANDARDIZE PROCESS IMPROVEMENT

Purpose

The purpose of this step is to eliminate the cause of the problem permanently. This is done by replicating and documenting the preventive action taken in Step 4. Within the new standard, who, what, when, where, why, and how must be clearly identified. This is essential in communicating the reasons for the new standard and ensuring active cooperation from all workers involved. In addition, education and training are needed for all the workers involved so that the new standard becomes part of their thoughts and habits. If proper education and training are not provided, the new standard will not be carried out properly and problems will begin to recur.

Tools

The tools that can be used are graphs, control charts, and flowcharts. Flowcharts are used to illustrate the new process. Graphs and control charts are used to continue tracking the process.

Results

1. New work procedures are developed and documented.

2. A new process flowchart is developed.

STEP 7: DETERMINE FUTURE ACTION

Purpose

The purpose of this step is to provide a summary of the story. This is done by reviewing the problem-solving process just completed and determining any future action that needs to be taken. By reviewing the problem-solving process just completed, the team can determine such things as what was done well, what could have been done better, and what could have been done differently. This reflection allows for team as well as individual growth. (After all, every problem attacked, whether solved or unsolved, is a learning experience which better prepares each individual to solve the next problem.)

In determining future action, the team establishes by whom and how often the process indicator needs to be checked to ensure that the preventive action is still working. The team also identifies any remaining problems and lays out a plan to solve them. If the remaining problems are outside of the team's direct control, then the team makes suggestions for their improvement. If there are no direct problems the team can begin working on, then the team is disbanded. Typically, the individual team members will quickly become involved in other teams since the overall company goal is continuous improvement.

Tools

The primary tool used in this step is the PDCA cycle. Applying the PDCA cycle to the problem aides the team in the quest for continuous improvement.

Results

The result of this step is the development of a timetable. This timetable establishes by whom and how often the process indicator is to be checked. The process indicator is checked primarily to ensure that the new standard is being implemented properly. Another result could be development of an action plan detailing how any remaining problems will be addressed.

OTHER CONSIDERATIONS

Time Frame

The QI story provides an organized framework to solve any problem. By having a structure to follow, a team can expect to reduce the amount of wasted time typically spent in the problem-solving process. It is important to note that the QI story framework is not a shortcut. The seven steps in the process help ensure that no aspect of the problem is ignored. Depending on the complexity of the problem, it will still take anywhere from several months to over a year to completely solve it.

Quality Improvement Story Requirements

The proper use of a QI story requires many things. First, it requires knowledge of the quality control tools. These tools could be the seven basic tools, they could include the seven management tools, or they could even more be advanced statistical tools like design of experiments. Whatever tools are required, it is important that the team members are properly trained in their use. Typically, everyone in the company is trained in the use of the seven basic tools. As the need arises, more advanced training is provided. For example, most managers need training in the seven management tools because they deal more with ideas than data. If a team feels that a certain tool could be effectively used and no team member is trained in its use, then support and guidance must be available to the team. Otherwise, the team will feel lost and may give up.

Second, the QI story requires that team members be able to effectively communicate their ideas. They must be able to communicate verbally in order to present their ideas. They must also be able to communicate their ideas in writing. This also requires training and support in the form of in-house short courses and guidance personnel.

Third, knowledge about the actual construction of a QI story is needed. This too requires training and support. The best training for this comes from experience. The more stories a team works on, the easier the process becomes. The best support comes from an experienced person acting as team leader. Every team should include one or more experienced people. This ensures that the team does not become discouraged and quit.

Finally, the QI story requires teamwork. Working as a team member does not come naturally to most people. Therefore, all employees need to be trained in how to work as a team. They need to know how to interact as a team, how to delegate work to other team members, and how to trust and respect everyone on the team. This may seem to be a trivial matter, but more teams have failed not because the problem was too difficult, but because the team members themselves could not work together.

In summary, the QI story is a very effective means of addressing a problem. It requires the use of a variety of tools, the ability to communicate and persuade, and the ability to work as a team. With proper training and support, the goal of continuous improvement can be achieved through the use of QI stories.

EXERCISES

12.1 What is a QI story?

12.2 Discuss several reasons for using a QI story.

12.3 List the basic steps of a QI story. What are the expected results of each step?

12.4 What is one of the best ways to demonstrate the importance of a problem to management?

12.5 What are the two types of action that can be taken? Give an example of each type.

12.6 What are the basic requirements of a QI story?

12.7 Within your own work environment, identify a problem that you (or your team) can work on. Use the QI story to address and document the problem-solving effort.

BIBLIOGRAPHY

FPL Quality Improvement Program, *QI Story and Techniques*. Florida Power and Light Company, Miami, 1987.

Gitlow, Howard S., Shelly J. Gitlow, Alan Oppenhelm, and Rosa Oppenhelm, "Telling the Quality Story," *Quality Progress*. September 1990, pp. 41–46.

Kume, Hitoshi, *Statistical Methods for Quality Improvement*. The Association for Overseas Technical Scholarship, Japan, 1985.

CASE STUDY*
Improvement in the Process of Administering Prophylactic Antibiotics in Cardiac Surgery through the Use of the Continuous Improvement Story

by Elizabeth Rall Mazzei, RN, BSN, CIC

PROLOGUE

This case study was prepared from a medical environment. The medical world has terminology unique to its environment which is used throughout this case study. The quality improvement story technique that was used was adapted from the methodology presented in Chapter 12. The successful results of this case study further demonstrate the versatility of the quality improvement story technique for analyzing problems and implementing corrective action in the service sector.

BACKGROUND

Continuous quality improvement methods have been used in the field of hospital infection control/epidemiology since the early 1970s. Data collection, including measurements, analysis of the data, and feedback, is a basic concept in infection control programs. Improvement efforts are usually

---

* This study was conducted through the Florida Consortium for Infection Control (FCIC). The hospital is anonymous. Permission to publish the study here is granted by N. Joel Ehrenkranz, M.D., FCIC Director.

targeted toward procedures of high volume or high risk to patients and/ or health care workers.

Surveillance of patients having undergone cardiac surgery is a common component of infection control programs. Cardiac surgery is considered to be a potentially high-risk procedure.

A recent medical record audit of cardiac procedures identified flaws in the timing and the documentation of administration of antibiotics. The appropriate administration of antibiotics is a generally accepted method to reduce the occurrence of wound infections. In this audit, the following factors were evaluated: appropriate choice of antibiotic, including efficacy and cost; timeliness of administration; and avoidance of unnecessary post-op doses. Required components of documentation are name of the drug, the dose, the route, the time given, and signature or initials of the person administering it.

IDENTIFYING THE PROBLEM AREA AND THE CAUSES OF THE PROBLEM (STEP 1)

If complete documentation of administration of a drug (as described in the previous section) is lacking, a surgeon or hospital could be in a position of possible liability. This means that if even one of the required components is not properly recorded, it could be concluded (in a court of law) that the drug was not given at all. The medical record audit revealed that a potential liability problem existed due to improper documentation. The medical audit reviewed three types of cardiac operations: coronary revascularization (CRV), valve replacements, and coronary revascularization with valve replacement (CRV/valve). As can be seen in Figure 1, the results of this audit indicated that a large percentage of the charts audited lacked complete documentation of the prophylactic antibiotic administration.

A continuous improvement team was formed to examine the extent and distribution of the documentation deficits. The team's goals were to investigate and improve the process to ensure (1) the appropriate timing of drug administration and (2) the complete documentation of all required components related to the drug's administration.

OPERATION DATES	PERCENTAGE OF CASES WHICH LACKED FULL DOCUMENTATION			
	CRV	VALVE	CRV/VALVE	TOTAL
6/92 - 2/93	84.4%	94.1%	100%	89.0%

FIGURE 1 Summary of Initial Chart Audit for Cardiac Surgery

OPERATION DATES	PERCENTAGE OF CASES WHICH LACKED FULL DOCUMENTATION			
	CRV	VALVE	CRV/VALVE	TOTAL
3/93 - 5/93	83.3%	33.3%	100%	78.0%

FIGURE 2   Summary of Second Chart Audit for Cardiac Surgery

One issue that immediately arose was the use of the term "on call to the operating room (OR)" by surgeons for timing the pre-operative administration of antibiotics. Interpretations of "on call to the OR" could mean giving the drug on leaving the patient's room, on entering the pre-op suite, or upon entering the OR. The situation was complicated by the fact that many individuals were involved in the care of patients immediately prior to the operation, including the floor nurse, pre-op nurse, internist, cardiothoracic surgeon, anesthesiologist, and surgical team (scrub nurse, circulating nurse, surgeon assistants, and perfusionist [operator of heart/lung machine]).

An antibiotic administered for surgical prophylaxis should be given within 30 minutes prior to the incision. Since time spent in the pre-op suite could take more than an hour, the team felt that administering it in the patient's room or in the pre-op suite would be administering the antibiotic too early. Therefore, a decision was made to define "on call to the OR" to mean that the drug would be given in the OR. This policy change was implemented immediately.

After three months, a medical record audit was performed to determine if the timing of the drug administration had improved. The results of the audit showed that the change in the interpretation of "on call to the OR" decreased the variations in the timing of administration. However, no significant decrease in the lack of full documentation was evident after this intervention (see Figure 2). At this point, the team felt that further analysis was needed.

ANALYSIS, IDENTIFICATION, AND VERIFICATION OF ROOT CAUSES OF THE PROBLEM (STEP 2)

Individuals from Infection Control, Pharmacy, Nursing, Anesthesia, Pre-op Suite, and Surgery concerned with the problem met, and through discussion and interaction (brainstorming), potential causes of the problem were identified. A non-traditional fishbone diagram was developed* (see Figure

---

* A traditional fishbone diagram usually has a problem statement at the head and all the spines answer the question "why" in terms of how they contribute to the problem.

3). In this diagram, the major categories (spines) are delineated as those areas in which personnel participate in the process of getting the antibiotic to the location where the patient is and administering it.

Prior to this step, it was difficult to have a clear understanding of how everyone's responsibility fit into the process. From the fishbone diagram, the team determined that the anesthesiologist would be the most likely candidate to administer and document that the antibiotics had been given properly. It was recognized that having anesthesiology represented on the team would facilitate the improvement of the problem.

Once anesthesiology joined the team, a flowchart was drawn to further analyze the problem (see Figure 4). The flowchart illustrated the process tasks from the time the order for an antibiotic was written to the time of administration and documentation. It also clearly identified gaps that existed in communication and current unassigned responsibilities. From the flowchart, the decision to assign the responsibility for the administration and documentation of the antibiotic to the anesthesiologist was confirmed and agreed to by all departments represented on the team. It also indicated why assigning this task to any other individual in the process would result in less than 100% compliance in proper timing of the drug administration.

PLANNING AND IMPLEMENTING PREVENTIVE ACTION (STEP 3)

The anesthesiologist agreed to administer the prophylactic antibiotics for a six-month pilot period. A rubber stamp with the required information (see Figure 5) was developed to use on the Anesthesia Record while the project was being piloted. This stamp provided a consistent means of recording the required information. It also allowed the use of existing anesthesia record forms, which permitted the team to immediately implement the suggested improvement plan. The team agreed on a six-month pilot program.

CHECKING EFFECTIVENESS OF ACTION (STEP 4)

At the end of the six-month pilot program, another medical record audit was done to see if any improvement had been made. The audit revealed (see Figure 6) that the administration of antibiotics in the appropriate time frame now occurred 100% of the time. Also, the number of documentation errors (or possible liability cases) was dramatically reduced. In the CRV cases, documentation errors were reduced by 79%. In the valve cases, documentation errors were reduced by 26%. In the CRV/valves, documentation errors were reduced by 93%.

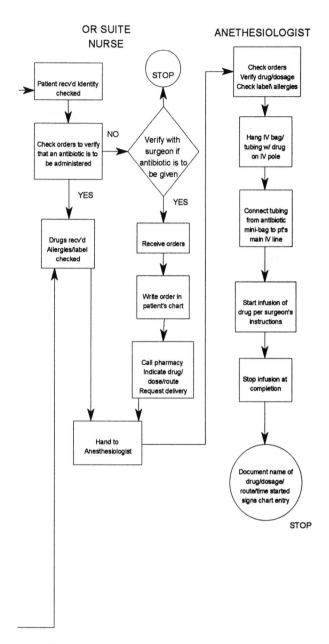

FIGURE 4 (continued)

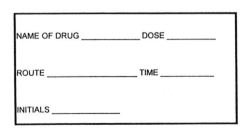

FIGURE 5   Rubber Stamp Used to Facilitate Documentation

OPERATION DATES	PERCENTAGE OF CASES WHICH LACKED FULL DOCUMENTATION			
	CRV	VALVE	CRV/VALVE	TOTAL
6/93 - 11/93	3.6%	7.1%	6.9%	5.1%

FIGURE 6 Summary of Chart Audit after Implementation of Changes

STANDARDIZATION (STEP 5)

Due to the extremely successful outcome of the pilot project, the team felt that the improvement to the process could now be standardized. In this case, standardization started with the redesigning of the anesthesia record to include the information from the rubber stamp. Also, education and training began for the OR staff. This included the pre-op nurses, the surgical team, and the anesthesiologists. Finally, the results of the quality improvement story were shared with others in the hospital as a means of demonstrating the effectiveness of the quality improvement story process.

FUTURE ACTION (STEP 6)

In order to assess the continued measure of compliance, periodic reviews are being conducted. Retraining is scheduled to be given when needed.

SUMMARY

This study evolved over a nine-month period of time. Personnel from six different departments participated. The primary result was that the legal liability due to lack of full documentation of antibiotic administration had been significantly reduced. Also, the results of this continuous improvement story are being studied and considered for replication in all FCIC hospitals.

ENDNOTE

I wish to thank Dr. Ehrenkranz for asking me to participate in this project, his advice, statistical support, and editorial contributions to this case study.

13

THE SEVEN QUALITY MANAGEMENT TOOLS

INTRODUCTION

This chapter is intended to acquaint the reader with the seven quality management tools. Due to the nature of these tools, only an introduction to the tools is provided.

HISTORY

On April 26, 1972, the newly formed Japanese Society of Quality Control Technique Development* held its first meeting. "The Society's activities consisted of identifying and evaluating various management control techniques used in areas such as operations research (OR) and value engineering (VE), diverse creativity techniques, and other company-wide QC techniques, looking for those which had proven most effective" (Mizuno, 1988, p. xi). The society identified seven new management control techniques:

1. Relations diagram
2. KJ method®
3. Systematic diagram
4. Matrix diagram
5. Matrix data-analysis
6. Process decision program chart (PDPC)
7. Arrow diagram

---

* This society was sponsored by the Japanese Federation of Science and Technology.

TABLE 13.1 Original and Modified Names of the Seven Quality Management Tools

Original title	Modified title
1. KJ method*	1. Affinity diagram
2. Relations diagram	2. Interrelationship digraph
3. Systematic diagram	3. Tree diagram
4. Matrix diagram	4. Matrix diagram
5. Matrix data-analysis	5. Prioritization matrix
6. Process decision program chart	6. Process decision program chart
7. Arrow diagrams	7. Activity network diagram

* The KJ method® is a registered trademark held by the Kawayoshida Research Center. The KJ method was developed by Mr. Jiro Kawakita. Mr. Kawakita is a Japanese anthropologist and founder of Kawayoshida Research Center.

The society called these tools the "Seven New QC Tools." In 1979, JUSE Press published *Kanrishi to Sutaffu no Shin-QC-nanatsu-dogu,* edited by Shigeru Mizuno, which described these seven new tools. (In 1988, an English version of the Mizuno book, entitled *Management for Quality Improvement: The 7 New QC Tools,* was published by Productivity Press.)

In the early 1980s, the seven quality management tools were introduced in the United States. Some of the original titles were modified. The original names of the seven tools, along with their respective modified names, are listed in Table 13.1.

The seven management tools are used primarily for problems that are qualitative in nature. They help identify problems and determine and establish plans for corrective action. They are most often used by middle and upper management.

The remainder of this chapter provides an introduction to each of the seven quality management tools.

AFFINITY DIAGRAM (KJ METHOD®)

Description

The affinity diagram is a very effective means of collecting a large amount of verbal data and organizing it into natural clusters in a relatively short amount of time. The clusters represent the intrinsic structure of the problem being investigated.

The development of an affinity diagram is a very creative process. Typically, a group of people (or a team) identify a problem to work on.

Each individual in the group thinks about the problem and verbalizes his or her thoughts (the thoughts can be facts, opinions, or even experiences). Each individual thought is captured (typically on 3 × 5 note cards) either by the individual or the team leader. After all thoughts have been recorded, all of the individual thoughts (represented by note cards) are placed on a surface. Then every individual in the group participates is arranging the thoughts into similar or related groups. Each group is then given a heading. The entire process should take less than an hour.

An affinity diagram that identifies the components of a particular company's self-assessment is illustrated in Figure 13.1. Notice that the strengths of the company are identified in the diagram by shading. The unshaded boxes are those areas in the company that need attention. For example, "Long Development Cycles" within the Process area needs attention. This particular area will be investigated further using the next tool. Notice also that the thoughts are narrative in nature rather than quantitative.

Application

The affinity diagram is especially useful when collecting thoughts on unknown or unexplored areas. It is also useful when the problem:

1. Is complex in nature

2. Is in a disorganized or chaotic state

3. Has not improved through the use of more traditional methods

4. Has a large number of ideas to be organized

5. Requires a team effort

6. Requires a creative approach

Affinity diagrams are not particularly useful when the problem is simple and easy to understand.

RELATIONS DIAGRAM (INTERRELATIONSHIP DIGRAPH)

Description

The relations diagram clarifies complex cause-and-effect relationships (or complex objectives to means relationships) by displaying the logical relationships that exist between factors. In many instances, the affinity diagram provides the input for the relations diagram.

The process for developing a relations diagram requires that the main problem be identified and written down. The next step is for every individual in the group to identify what he or she thinks are possible causes. These possible causes are written down (typically on 3 × 5 note cards). These cards are then laid out under the main problem. Next, one

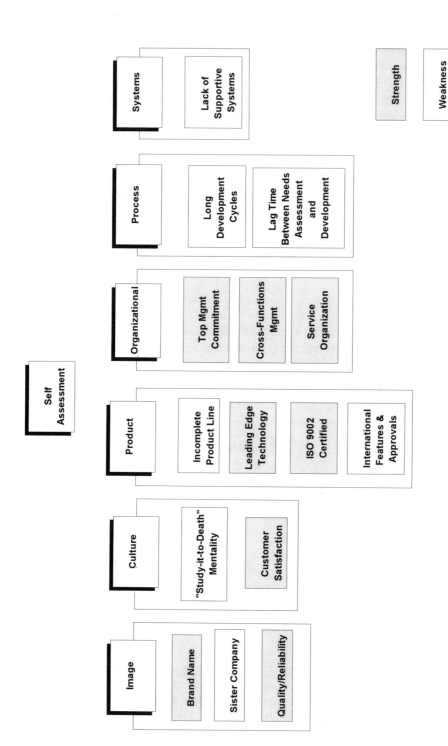

FIGURE 13.1   Affinity Diagram (KJ Method®)

by one, the note cards are reviewed by asking "Does the topic on this card cause or influence any of the topics on the other cards?" If the answer is yes, a one-way arrow is drawn to illustrate the cause or influence. The key cause factor is identified as the box with the most arrows extending from it. The key effect factor is identified as the box with the most arrows pointing toward it. Both the key cause factor box and the key effect factor box are highlighted.

A relations diagram for the problem of long development cycles identified in the affinity diagram in Figure 13.1 is displayed in Figure 13.2. In this example, the key cause factor is poor management because it has the most arrows extending from it. The key effect factor is low development productivity because it has the most arrows pointing toward it. Notice that both the key cause factor and the key effect factor have been highlighted (in this case, they are shaded). This makes it easier to recognize the key factors in presentations to various groups.

Application

The relations diagram is very useful when the root cause(s) needs to be identified and quantitative data are unavailable to determine it. It is also useful when there are a large number of interrelated issues that need to be better defined and understood. Because the relations diagram is not restricted to a specific framework, the development of ideas is enhanced and preconceptions are eliminated.

SYSTEMATIC DIAGRAM (TREE DIAGRAM)

Description

The systematic diagram is also called a dendrogram. Its more common usage is in family tree charts and organizational charts. As a quality management tool, it is used to illustrate the means needed to achieve specific goals and objectives. It provides an overview of the whole situation at a single glance.

The basic structure of a systematic diagram is illustrated in Figure 13.3. Reading the figure from left to right, the first objective is the primary objective. The next level is the means of achieving the primary objective. If these means are not fundamental means (or achievable actions), then they become secondary objectives. This cascading of means and objectives continues until a set of fundamental means is obtained.

An example of a systematic diagram is presented in Figure 13.4. The primary objective is "personnel having the proper skill set for the job" they are performing. Figure 13.4 shows that there are four means of reaching the primary objective, one of which is to "train existing personnel." This is not a fundamental means and, therefore, becomes a secondary objective. There are two means of obtaining the secondary objective as shown in Figure 13.4, one of which is to "identify outside training courses." This

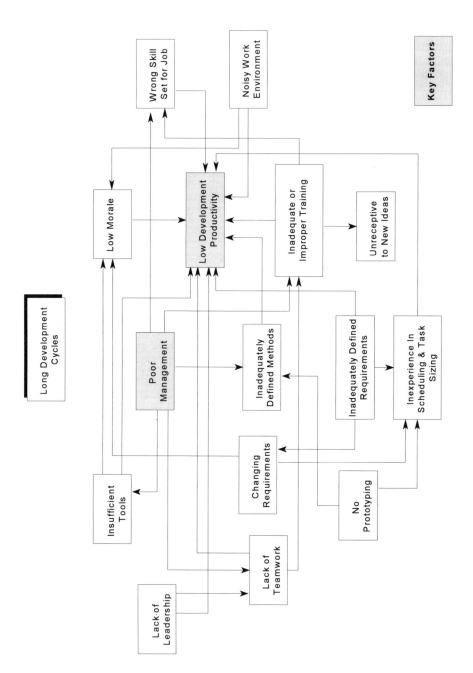

FIGURE 13.2 Relations Diagram (Interrelationship Digraph)

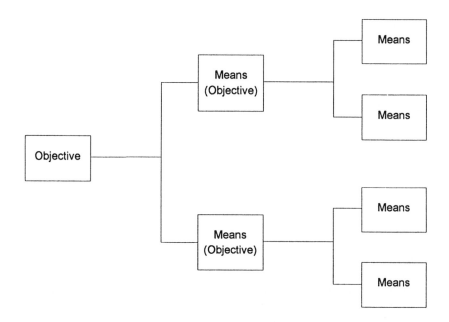

FIGURE 13.3   Basic Structure of a Systematic Diagram

becomes a tertiary objective with two means: "schedule out-of-town courses" and "schedule local off-site courses." These two means are the fundamental means for this branch.

Application

The systematic diagram is most useful in breaking down broad problems into specific executable details. At the lowest level, the fundamental means represent a set of assignable tasks and prioritizable options.

MATRIX DIAGRAM

Description

The matrix diagram is used to expedite the problem-solving process through multidimensional thinking by indicating the existence and strength of a relationship between two or more sets of factors. The five types of matrix diagrams are:

1. L-shaped matrix

2. T-shaped matrix

3. Y-shaped matrix

4. X-shaped matrix

5. C-shaped matrix

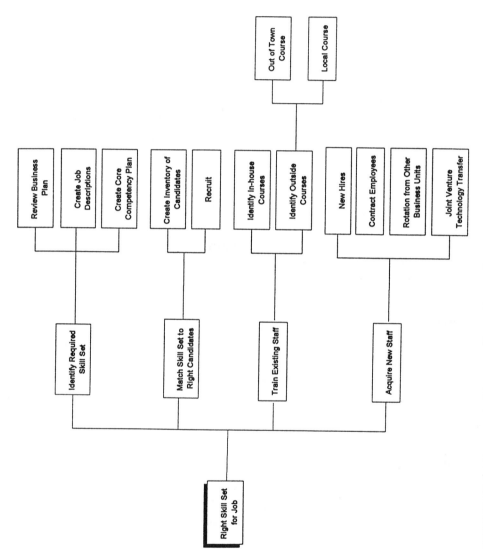

FIGURE 13.4 Systematic Diagram (Tree Diagram)

Organizational Task Assignments

	Fred	Samantha	Andrew	Sharon
Administration	✧	O		
Product Management	✧			
Product Requirements	O		σ	✧
Development Plan	σ		✧	O
Training Plan	σ	✧		
Quality Plan	σ	σ	✧	
Staffing Plan		✧	σ	
Project Scheduling and Tracking	σ	σ	✧	O

✧　Primary Responsibility

O　Secondary Responsibility

σ　Communication Needed

FIGURE 13.5　L-Shaped Matrix Diagram

The L-shaped matrix is the most commonly used matrix diagram. The L-shaped matrix is a two-dimensional chart (rows and columns) that explains the interrelationship between two variables. The most common use of the L-shaped matrix is to define the relationship between goals and the means of achieving them. An L-shaped matrix that defines the organizational tasks of a company and who is responsible for each task is illustrated in Figure 13.5. As seen from Figure 13.5, a matrix diagram is very useful in identifying and assigning responsibility for the various tasks associated with an implementation plan.

Application

Matrix diagrams are used to clarify the relationship between two or more factors. They aid in identifying, assigning, and monitoring the actions taken to correct a problem.

MATRIX DATA-ANALYSIS (PRIORITIZATION MATRICES)

Description

The matrix data-analysis method extends the use of the matrix diagram by providing a more detailed analysis of the interrelationships defined in the matrix diagram. The matrix data-analysis method arranges the matrix diagram previously developed and quantifies the relationships. This is done by obtaining numerical data for intersecting cells. Once quantified, the tasks or actions can be prioritized in order to identify the most desirable or effective options. This is the only one of the seven management tools that is a numerical analysis tool. One of the variations of this technique utilizes principal-component analysis, which is a multivariate analysis technique. In fact, the reason this method was identified as one of the seven management tools by the Japanese was "so managers and staff could become more familiar with multivariate analysis techniques" (Mizuno, 1988, p. 38). Further discussion of this tool is not provided here because it requires considerable knowledge of statistical theory.

Application

The matrix data-analysis method is very useful in analyzing factors that are elaborately intertwined. It provides a means of organizing and categorizing raw data that are difficult to interpret. It also provides more information than can be obtained by studying the basic data.

PROCESS DECISION PROGRAM CHART

Description

The process decision program chart (PDPC) helps prepare for any unexpected problems that may arise when executing a plan. It identifies likely contingencies and appropriate countermeasures to include in a given implementation plan. A simple PDPC for a three-day cross-state bicycle trip is displayed in Figure 13.6. The items within the rectangles represent the "what ifs" or possible unexpected problems. The circles represent the appropriate reactions to the unexpected problems. The preferred or selected countermeasures are identified by an O underneath them. The impossible or difficult countermeasures are identified by an X underneath them.

Application

The PDPC is useful in developing contingency plans. It is most helpful when the process or product is unfamiliar, if the environmental conditions are unknown, or if the time requirements to complete given tasks are unknown. It is also quite useful in evaluating alternative implementation plans.

ARROW DIAGRAMS (ACTIVITY NETWORK DIAGRAM)

Description

Arrow diagrams are used to schedule the most suitable completion plan for a project and its subordinate tasks. They provide a time-sequenced action

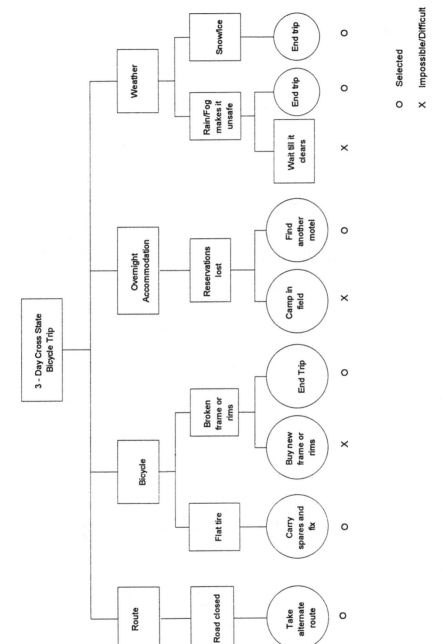

FIGURE 13.6 Process Decision Program Chart

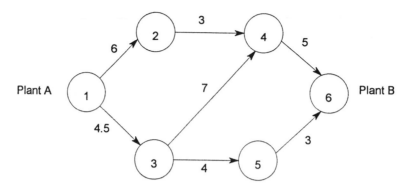

FIGURE 13.7   Simple Arrow Diagram (Activity Network Diagram)

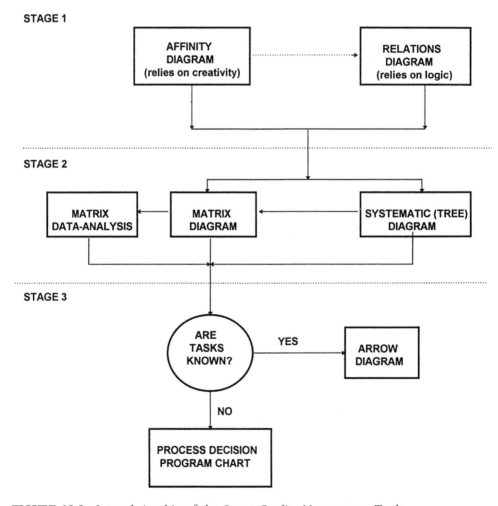

FIGURE 13.8   Interrelationship of the Seven Quality Management Tools

plan for all aspects of the project. They display every task necessary for completing a project through the use of an arrow network. They also determine the total implementation time and identify any key subordinate tasks which may need special monitoring.

A very simple arrow diagram is shown in Figure 13.7. It represents electricity being sent from plant A (node 1) to town A (node 6). The electricity must pass through relay substations (nodes 2 to 5). The distance between nodes (in miles) is shown above the arrow that connects the two nodes. For example, the distance between plant A and substation 2 is six miles. The utility company wants the electricity being sent from plant A to town A to travel the minimum possible distance. The shortest path is nodes $1 \rightarrow 2 \rightarrow 4 \rightarrow 6$, for a total of 14 miles. However, if node 2 is out of service for some reason, there are still two alternate routes for the electricity to travel. This simple illustration indicates the power of arrow diagrams. They allow you to obtain accurate information promptly if one part of the process is delayed or becomes inoperable. They allow you to judge the priorities of the process. They allow for an accurate overview of the entire project or process if the project or process becomes larger (or smaller). They also enable you to better cope with changes in the plan.

Two of the more commonly used arrow diagrams are program evaluation and review technique (PERT) and critical path method (CPM). Both are very powerful and have been used for years in project planning.

Application

Arrow diagrams are best used when the project or process:

1. Is well defined

2. Has clearly sequenced activities or tasks

3. Has a definite beginning and ending point

4. Is complex

5. Has simultaneous implementation paths

6. Has a critical completion schedule

   Arrow diagrams are most helpful in determining:

1. Which tasks can be easily eliminated

2. Which tasks can be done simultaneously

3. Which tasks must be completed on schedule

4. Which tasks can tolerate a delay

5. The completion time for each task

SUMMARY

The seven quality management tools discussed in this chapter are primarily used in the *plan* step of the PDCA cycle. The *plan* step can be divided into three stages:

Stage 1   Clarify and identify the nature of the problem

Stage 2   Identify means and clarify their relationship to the objectives

Stage 3   Develop contingency plans and time sequencing for implementing the means identified in Stage 2

The use of the seven management tools, their relationship to one another, and in which stage of the *plan* step they are most effective are illustrated in Figure 13.8.

EXERCISES

13.1   Who originally put the seven quality management tools together?

13.2   When are the seven quality management tools used?

13.3   What is the overall purpose of the tools?

13.4   Have you ever used any of the tools? If so, when?

13.5   When would the affinity diagram be preferred over the relations diagram?

13.6   What is the other name for the affinity diagram? How did it get this name?

13.7   What are the three stages in the *plan* step of the PDCA cycle?

13.8   In your job, identify an area where one or more of the seven quality management tools can be used? Try it.

BIBLIOGRAPHY

Brassard, Michael, *The Memory Jogger+: Featuring the Seven Management and Planning Tools*. GOAL/QPC, Methuen, Mass., 1989.

Gitlow, Howard S., *Planning for Quality, Productivity, and Competitive Position*. Dow Jones-Irwin, Homewood, Ill., 1989.

Mizuno, Shigeru (Ed.), *Management for Quality Improvement: The 7 New QC Tools*. Productivity Press, Cambridge, Mass., 1988.

PART IV

OTHER
QUALITY ISSUES

14 QUALITY FUNCTION DEPLOYMENT

HISTORY

The first formal use of quality function deployment (QFD) can be traced to the Kobe Shipyard, Mitsubishi Heavy Industries, Ltd., Japan in 1972. In 1977, Toyota began using QFD extensively. It wasn't until 1983 that QFD was introduced to American companies. In 1983, Ford and several supplier companies went to Japan and had several meetings with Dr. Ishikawa and other member of the Union of Japanese Scientists and Engineers. It was at these meetings that the power of QFD was recognized. In 1984, Dr. D. Clausing, then of Xerox, introduced the operating mechanism of QFD to Ford and the supplier companies. Also in 1984, the American Supplier Institute organized three Japanese Study Missions for several U.S. supplier companies. The purpose of the study missions was to review Toyota supplier QFD case studies, which in turn would aid in the transfer of the technique to U.S. industries. The study missions took place in December 1984, June 1985, and April 1986. It was during the last study mission that two of the supplier companies, Budd Company and Kelsey Hayes, presented the first U.S. QFD case studies. In 1987, Ford and General Motors began QFD training in their plants. Since that time, QFD has been studied and implemented by companies all across the United States (Sullivan, 1987, p. 1; Morrell, 1987, p. 1).

WHAT IS QUALITY FUNCTION DEPLOYMENT?

The overall objective of QFD is "to improve (reduce) the product development cycle while improving quality and delivering the product at lower

249

costs" (Sullivan, 1987, p. 3). QFD itself is a systematic and structured approach used to translate the voice of the customer into the appropriate technical requirements and actions for each stage of product or service development and production. In other words, it connects customer requirements to production or service requirements. QFD is driven by the voice of the customer, which is the customer's requirements expressed in the customer's own words.

METHODOLOGY

Two major components make up the heart of QFD: product quality deployment and deployment of the quality function. Product quality deployment encompasses the activities associated with translating the voice of the customer into technical quality characteristics and features. These technical quality characteristics and features are known as the final product or service control characteristics. Deployment of the quality function encompasses the activities associated with ensuring that customer-required quality is actually achieved. Included in these activities is the assignment of specific quality responsibilities to specific groups or departments.

The QFD process (see Figure 14.1) is driven by the "voice of the customer." Therefore, the process begins by capturing the "voice of the customer" or the customer requirements. Because these requirements are usually stated in qualitative terms, they must be translated or converted into technical or company terminology. This translation results in the formulation of the product/service design characteristics. These characteristics need to be measurable because it will be the monitoring of these characteristics that determines whether the customer's requirements are being satisfied. However, these product/service design characteristics need to be broken down further for proper implementation. Therefore, the design characteristics are translated into specific parts, with the critical characteristics of these parts identified. When the critical part characteristics have been identified, the required manufacturing/service operations are then determined. The critical process parameters are also identified so that checks can be made to ensure that the critical part characteristics are being met. Also at this stage, any constraints, such as new equipment needed or limited capital, are identified and dealt with. When the manufacturing/service operations have been specified, the operating instructions are developed. These instructions constitute the entire set of procedures and practices that will be used to consistently make products that satisfy customer requirements.

This process appears to be simple. However, the fundamental problem is that the initial customer requirements do not get properly translated into the final product. Another problem is that some customer requirements often conflict with one another. The concept of QFD is based on four key documents which aid in avoiding these problems:

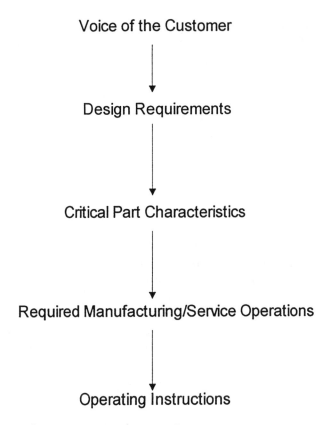

Voice of the Customer

Design Requirements

Critical Part Characteristics

Required Manufacturing/Service Operations

Operating Instructions

FIGURE 14.1 Quality Function Deployment Process

1. Overall customer requirement planning matrix

2. Final product characteristic deployment matrix

3. Process plan and quality control charts

4. Operating instructions (Sullivan, 1986, pp. 40–41)

The planning matrix translates the "voice of the customer" into specific final product/service control characteristics. The deployment matrix takes the final product/service control characteristics and translates them into critical part characteristics, thus moving the customer requirements deeper into the design process. The process plan and quality control charts identify the critical product, service, and process parameters that are vital to meeting the critical part characteristics. They also identify check points for each of the critical parameters. The operating instructions constitute the entire set of procedures and practices that will be performed by all personnel to ensure that the critical parameters are achieved. The main purpose of these documents is to translate and deploy the customer's requirements throughout the product/service design, development, and production process of an organization. The customer's requirements are ultimately addressed by the operational personnel who produce the product and deliver the services. The flow and relationship of these documents is illustrated in Figure 14.2.

RELATIONSHIP MATRIX CONSTRUCTION

The basic design tool of QFD is the relationship matrix, which is shown in Figure 14.3. The following steps outline the construction of the first relationship matrix, called the planning matrix.

Step 1.   Determine the customer's requirements. These requirements are typically first stated in qualitative terms such as "easy to use," "looks nice," "comfortable," etc. They come from a variety of sources: marketing research, sales department, customer service department, surveys, etc. They also come from non-end-user customers such as retailers, vendors, regulators, etc. These types of requirements are very important to the customer but are typically difficult to quantify or act on.

Proper execution of this step is critical to the overall success of the QFD process. If the "true" customer requirements (not what the team thinks or feels the customer requires) are not properly captured and expressed, then the final outcome might not satisfy many customers. Because these customer requirements come from a variety of sources, this step is probably the most difficult one.

1.a.   Take the initial customer requirements and list them as the WHATs that are to be accomplished. It is important to note that some customer requirements may take the form of "does not," such as "does not make a mess" or "does not cost much."

1.b.   Expand these WHATs into secondary requirements in order to obtain a more definitive list. Repeat this step until the characteristics are thoroughly defined and any vagueness has been clarified (see Figure 14.4 as an example).

1.c.   Take the final list of customer requirements and place them in the WHAT section of the planning matrix (Figure 14.3).

Step 2.   Translate the customer's requirements into final product/service control characteristics (or design requirements). These characteristics must be quantifiable and actionable.

2.a.   For each WHAT item, list one or more HOWs. These HOWs are the design characteristics that should exist in order to satisfy customer requirements. Because these design characteristics are deployed throughout the process, they must be measurable and actionable. If each HOW item is not actionable, then each non-actionable HOW item is further defined by treating it as a WHAT item and listing more detailed HOWs for it (see Figure 14.5 for an example). The final list of HOWs becomes the final product/service control characteristics.

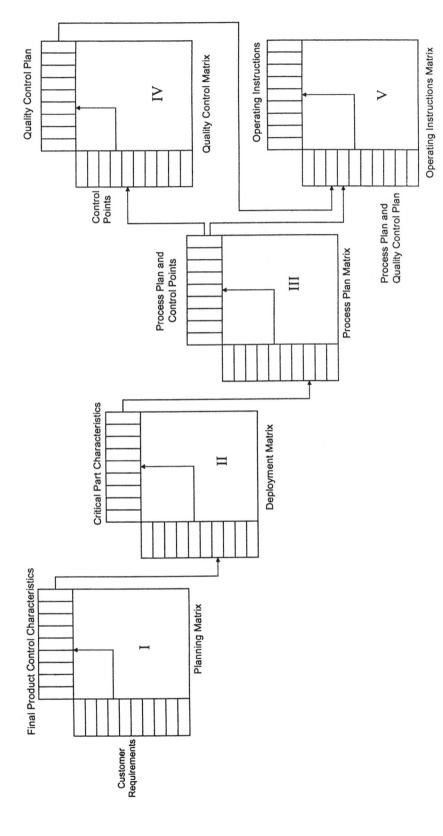

FIGURE 14.2 Flow and Relationship of the Quality Function Deployment Documents

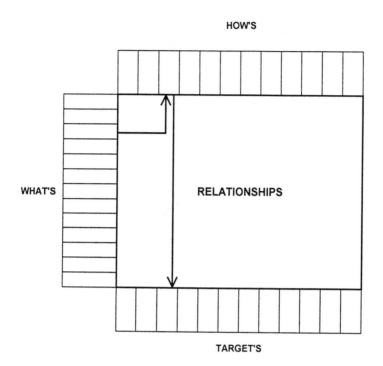

FIGURE 14.3   The Relationship Matrix

2.b.   Take the list of final product/service control characteristics and place them in the HOW section of the planning matrix (Figure 14.3).

Step 3.   Develop the relationship matrix between the customer requirements (WHATs) and the final product/service control characteristics (HOWs). This is done by placing one of the following symbols at the intersection of each WHAT and HOW that are related. The following symbols are used to depict the strength of the relationship:

no symbol		**no** relationship
triangle	Δ	**weak** relationship
circle	O	**medium** relationship
solid circle	●	**strong** relationship

This step allows the team to cross-check its thinking. If there is an absence of symbols or a majority of weak relationship symbols, then the translation of WHATs into HOWs as not been completed properly. If this happens, the team needs to return to Step 2 and further modify or supplement the HOWs. This step also helps identify any conflicting design requirements.

Step 4.   Establish the target values. The target values provide specific objectives for the subsequent design and also provide a means of assessing

Extensions

Several extensions to the basic QFD matrix enhance its usefulness. The first extension is the correlation matrix. The correlation matrix is a triangular table put on top of the HOWs (see Figure 14.7). By using the symbols defined below, the interrelationships between the HOWs can be established.

solid circle	●	**strong positive** relationship
circle	○	**positive** relationship
cross	+	**negative** relationship
double cross	++	**strong negative** relationship

When one HOW supports another HOW, then there is a positive relationship. When one HOW adversely affects another HOW, then there is a negative relationship. A negative relationship identifies when a trade-off should be considered. If there are no negative relationships, then examine the matrix to ensure that errors were not made and the analysis is complete.

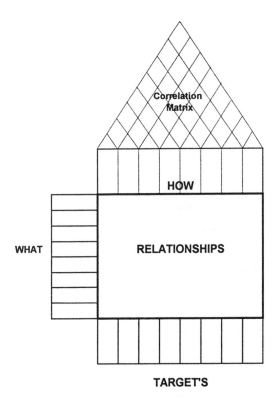

FIGURE 14.7   The House of Quality

The correlation matrix appears to give the basic matrix a roof, which makes the entire matrix look like a house. Therefore, the basic QFD matrix is also known as the House of Quality.

Another extension is the technical difficulty assessment for each HOW. This assessment is usually done on a scale of 1 to 5 (low to high). It is a measure of the relative difficulty of accomplishing each HOW. This row is typically placed between the relationship matrix and the TARGETs (see Figure 14.8).

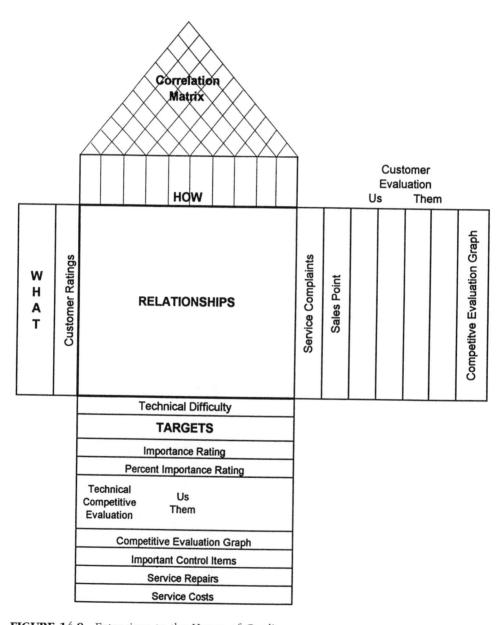

FIGURE 14.8   Extensions to the House of Quality

Another extension is the customer importance rating. This extension has two components. The first component is the customer's rating of each WHAT item. This rating represents the level of importance each WHAT item has to the customer. Typically, a scale of 1 to 5 is used to represent this level of importance. This information usually comes from surveys, customer complaints, etc. This customer rating is usually placed in a vertical column between the WHATs and the relationship matrix (Figure 14.8). The second component is the importance rating of each HOW item. This is found by taking the symbol in each HOW column, weighting it, multiplying this weight value times the customer rating value of each WHAT item, and adding them all together. This is done for each HOW column. Therefore, the importance rating is usually a row placed beneath the TARGETs (Figure 14.8). Because these values by themselves have no direct meaning, an additional row called the percent importance rating is usually added. This is found by taking an individual HOW importance rating and dividing it by the sum of all the importance ratings (Figure 14.9). The percent importance ratings is a useful aid in prioritizing efforts and making any trade-off decisions that might be necessary.

Another useful extension is the competitive evaluation. The competitive evaluation is a pair of graphs that illustrate, item for item, how the present company's product compares to the competition's product. It shows how the product being evaluated is viewed by the customers and how well a company and the competitors are meeting the customer's expectations. The competitive evaluation of the WHATs comes from customer-oriented information such as surveys, media, marketing feedback, sales feedback, etc. and is typically evaluated on a scale of 1 to 5. The rating for each WHAT item is placed in the customer evaluation table according to company. Each rating point is plotted on the competitive evaluation graph, and the company's rating points are connected (Figure 14.9). Competitive evaluation of the HOWs is done in a similar manner, except the evaluation comes from technical-oriented sources, such as engineers or technical benchmarking of the competition's product. The competitive evaluations are useful in determining the values of the TARGETs.

Another extension that may be required is the important control items. These are associated with the HOWs and represent additional requirements that must be met, such as design constraints and government regulations.

Several extension used on occasion are the service complaint column, the service repairs/cost row, and the sales point column. The service complaint column represents the number of complaints received per WHAT item. This is useful in determining where significant customer problems may exist. The service repairs row represents the number of repairs per item made for a given HOW item. The service costs row represents the cost per item incurred for a given HOW item. This helps identify which HOWs are more reliable and less costly. The sales point column represents the significance (or importance), if any, of a given WHAT item. This helps prioritize the WHATs. The general layout of a QFD matrix with the extensions is depicted in Figure 14.8, and a working

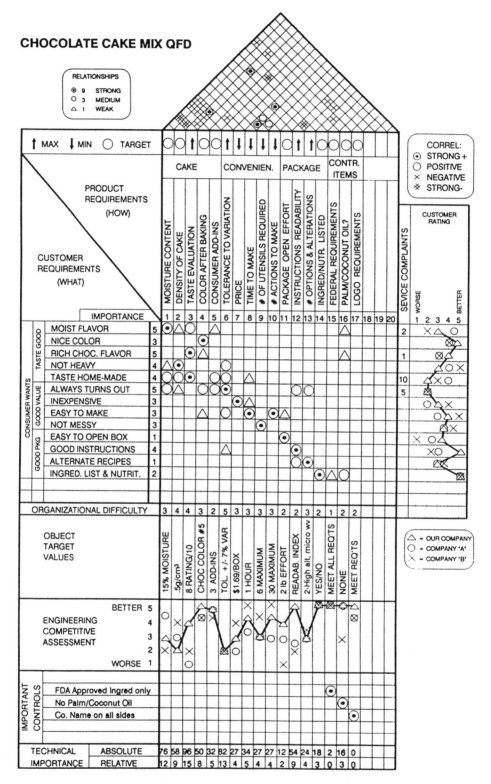

FIGURE 14.9 Example of House of Quality with Extensions (Copyright ©American Supplier Institute, Inc., Allen Park, Michigan. Reproduced by permission under License No. 941201.)

example of a QFD matrix with most of the extensions mentioned is illustrated in Figure 14.9.

Other popular extensions are currently being used, but this discussion is not intended to be all-inclusive. Any extensions desired can become part of the basic QFD matrix. The only limitation is the team's creativity.

House of Quality

As previously mentioned, each of the four key documents can be represented by a relationship matrix. However it is the planning matrix that provides the focus for the entire QFD effort, which makes it the key document. The planning matrix illustrates the customer's requirements, design parameters, and the perceived and real differences between a business and its competitors. For this reason, a majority of the extensions discussed are commonly part of the planning matrix (see Figure 14.9). Therefore, it is the most complex relationship matrix. It is also the reason why many refer to the planning matrix as the House of Quality.

RESULTS

The results of QFD can be measured using a variety of parameters. These parameters include the number of engineering changes required during product development, total cycle time to market, start-up costs, production cost, and overall market share. The quality of the final product can also be determined by tracking the number of customer complaints and warranty claims. All of these parameters can be measured and quantified, which makes it easy to justify using QFD.

BENEFITS

By using QFD, many benefits are realized:

1. QFD makes product quality a function of product design. Quality is built in, and product quality is no longer the result of quality control efforts.

2. Total product development time is reduced. (The actual time to define the product typically increases, but the total design cycle is reduced.)

3. Products are produced at lower cost with higher quality (product design is better).

4. The number of start-up problems is reduced.

5. Documentation and communication between groups and departments are improved, which results in an improved working environment.

6. Any conflicting design requirements are usually identified early. Also, any omissions that are typically the result of oversight are avoided.

7. The critical quality characteristics that need to be controlled are identified.

8. Customer requirements are identified and translated directly into product characteristics, which leads to increased customer satisfaction. It also reduces misinterpretation of customer requirements during subsequent stages.

9. The technology and job functions required to carry out the design are identified and assigned to specific individuals or groups.

10. Specific tools and techniques that will provide the greatest payoff are identified.

11. The organization's means of satisfying customer requirements is documented.

12. A historical database is established. This is a very valuable resource for future design and process improvements.

QFD has a major downside in that it requires extensive training and can be very laborious. However, there is a hidden benefit to the extensive training. Once training is completed, all of the functional areas are using the same approach and criteria. Hence, they are speaking the same language.

CONCLUSION

Several points need to be kept in mind when using QFD. First, it is applicable to more than new product design. It can be used effectively for existing design or process improvements. Second, QFD can be applied to any process within the organization, especially service processes. Third, it is not a tool restricted to the quality department. It is a valuable tool for everyone.

EXERCISES

14.1 Where and when was QFD first used?

14.2 What is the objective of QFD?

14.3 Discuss the two major components of QFD.

14.4   What are the four key documents of QFD? What is the purpose of each document?

14.5   What is the basic design tool of QFD?

14.6   Identify a simple item (like chicken soup, a wooden chair, etc.) and develop a basic planning matrix for it.

14.7   Which extensions to the basic QFD matrix would be useful to you? Can you think of any additional extensions?

14.8   Which matrix provides the focus for the entire QFD effort? What is another name for this matrix?

14.9   What parameters can be used to measure the results of a QFD effort?

14.10   What are the benefits of using QFD?

14.11   What is the major downside to QFD? Is there a hidden benefit to this downside? If so, what is it?

BIBLIOGRAPHY

Conti, Tito, "Process Management and Quality Function Deployment," *Quality Progress.* December 1989, p. 45(4).

Denton, Keith D., "Enhance Competition and Customer Satisfaction—Here's One Approach," *Industrial Engineering.* May 1990, p. 24(7).

DeVera, Dennis, Tom Glennon, Andrew A. Kenny, Mohammad A.H. Khan, and Mike Mayer, "An Automotive Case Study," *Quality Progress.* June 1988, p. 35(4).

Fortuna, Ronald M., "Beyond Quality: Taking SPC Upstream," *Quality Progress.* June 1988, p. 23(6).

Gopalakrishnan, K.N.; Barry E. McIntyre, and James C. Sprague, "Implementing Internal Quality Improvement with the House of Quality," *Quality Progress.* September 1992, p. 57(4).

Hauser, John R. and Don Clausing, "The House of Quality," *Harvard Business Review.* May–June 1988, p. 63(11).

Kogure, Maseo and Yoji Akao, "Quality Function Deployment and CWQC in Japan," *Quality Progress.* October 1983, p. 25(5).

McElroy, John, "QFD: Building the House of Quality," *Automotive Industries.* January 1989, p. 30(3).

Morrell, Norman E., "Quality Function Deployment," In *Quality Function Deployment: A Collection of Presentations and QFD Case Studies.* American Supplier Institute, Dearborn, Mich., 1987.

Quality Function Deployment: Executive Briefing. American Supplier Institute, Dearborn, Mich., 1987.

Sullivan, Lawrence P., "Quality Function Deployment," *Quality Progress*. June 1986, p. 39(12).

Sullivan, Lawrence P., "Quality Function Deployment (QFD): The Beginning, the End and the Problem In-Between," In *Quality Function Deployment: A Collection of Presentations and QFD Case Studies*. American Supplier Institute, Dearborn, Mich., 1987.

Sullivan, Lawrence P., "Policy Management through Quality Function Deployment," *Quality Progress*. June 1988, p. 18(3).

CASE STUDY
TQM and Quality Function Deployment: Application to Electronic Component Design

by Marilyn Liner, Elvira N. Loredo,
Howard S. Gitlow, and Norman G. Einspruch*

ABSTRACT

This paper describes the use of total quality management (TQM) and quality function deployment (QFD) by Raychem Corporation to attain the corporate goal to "delight the customer." The circumstances that led Raychem Corporation to implement a TQM program and the steps taken to coordinate and integrate TQM practices are outlined. The role of QFD in Raychem's TQM program is highlighted through the description of the first QFD study conducted at Menlo Park, California site of Telecom Division of Raychem. The approach used in developing a cable television (CATV) connector and the results attained by the Telecom Division cross-functional team are detailed in a series of charts and the team's evaluation of its experience using QFD.

TOTAL QUALITY MANAGEMENT AT RAYCHEM

Raychem Corporation, a Fortune 300 company headquartered in Menlo Park, California, develops and manufactures high-performance industrial products based on its expertise in product design, materials science, and manufacturing process technologies. Rising competition and a market shift toward commercial rather than military applications have increasingly

---

* This article is reprinted with permission of the authors.

influenced Raychem's "invent–make–sell" business units. These changes in the business environment placed increasing pressure on profitability and led Raychem's senior management to commit to becoming a total quality management (TQM) company. As an integral part of TQM, quality function deployment (QFD) has provided an important framework for supporting that commitment by promoting the design of customer needs and wants into company products and services in a cost-effective manner.

Raychem views TQM as a means to "delight our customer," i.e., to meet and exceed both external and internal customer needs and expectations for products and services. To accomplish this goal, Raychem's independent business units have implemented various TQM processes based on the quality improvement philosophies and methodologies of Deming, Juran, and Crosby.

Senior management has coordinated the implementation of TQM in the independent business units by:

- Appointing a quality executive to the Management Council, the senior leadership body of the company

- Promoting learning and use of TQM methods and tools

- Endorsing the standardization of procedures for company-wide processes including New Product Introduction, Design Review Requirements, and the Quarterly Executive Summary

- Defining and reviewing key metrics to measure progress in achieving quality objectives

- Promoting the use of quality tools (such as QFD) and customer focus in all processes

A result of the direction provided by senior management has been the integration of QFD elements into the Raychem New Product Introduction Guidelines illustrated in Figures 1a and 1b.

QFD APPLICATION: TELECOM DIVISION

Introduction

The first QFD study conducted by the Raychem Telecom Division in Menlo Park, Calif. started in August 1989. The product development team's purpose was to develop a new cable television (CATV) connector for indoor use. Customers for the product were approximately 100 CATV system operating companies in the U.S., which controlled approximately 8000 cable systems nationwide. Cable system operating company technicians install the indoor CATV connector (Figure 2a) onto coaxial cable (Figure 2b) to connect cable television services to home video, television, and cable connector equipment. The push-on connector designed by Raychem allows cable subscribers to easily disconnect and correctly reconnect their own equipment,

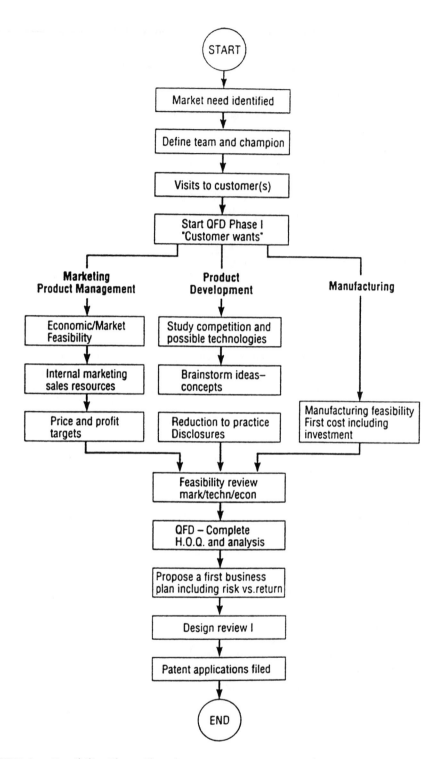

FIGURE 1a   Feasibility Phase Flowchart Incorporating QFD Elements

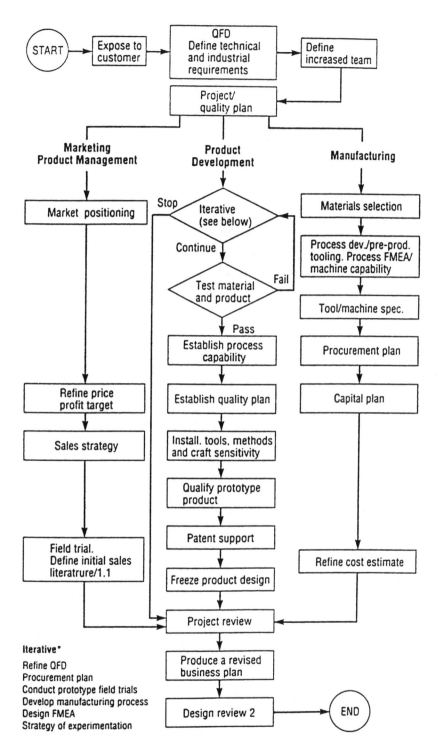

FIGURE 1b   Development Phase Flowchart Incorporating QFD Elements

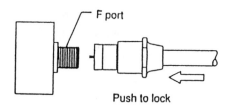

FIGURE 2a   Sketch of Indoor CATV Connector

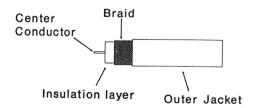

FIGURE 2b   Coaxial Cable

resulting in fewer trouble and service calls to the CATV system operators. The connector is also designed to reduce the initial installation time needed by cable operators.

Development work on the CATV connector had begun some months before the QFD study was started. The Raychem Corporate Technology Group, which had been responsible for the initial concept development, was ready to transfer a design to the Telecom Division for detailing, manufacturing, and marketing. However, the existing design did not satisfy Telecom development and manufacturing engineers, who wanted to systematically re-evaluate it using QFD.

The Project Team

A nine-member project team was formed consisting of one engineer each from Marketing, Sales, Manufacturing, and Quality; three engineers from Development; and two from Corporate Technology. The mission statement developed by the team was to "Develop a CATV connection system for indoor use in the U.S. market, to fit all U.S. cable and port sizes, for installation by cable operators."

Defining Customer Requirements

As a first step in the QFD study, the project team set out to gather data on the "Voice of the Customer"—customer needs as expressed in customer language. Sales and marketing team members conducted telephone interviews with two dozen familiar customers representing different-sized CATV operators and different geographical areas. As preparation for the inter-

Strong	●	9		
Moderate	O	3		
Weak	△	1		

		MANDREL						RING		ETC		
TARGET		xxx in +/- xxx	xxx in +/- xxx	xxx in +/- xxx	xxx in +/- xxx	ddd	ttt	xxx in +/- xxx	compound xx-xx	kkk	hhh	
PART FEATURES		Leaf wall thickness	Port end I.D.	Plating Hardness	Radius at thread tip	etc.	etc.	Wall thickness	Material	etc.	etc.	Technical Reqt. Importance Wt.
TECHNICAL REQ'TS	**TARGET VALUES**											
etc.	aaa		●						O			4
etc.	bbb			O				●				5
Force to install	x lbs.	O	O			O			△			3
Force to remove	x lbs.	●	O	●		●		●	O			4
RF Shielding	xxx		O	O	●				●		△	5
etc.	yyy		O	O				●	●			3
etc.	zzz							O		●		2
Forces on Equipment Panel	xx lbs,s in-lbs.	PROPRIETARY RELATIONSHIPS										
No. of installation modes	1 mode											
No. of installation steps	x steps											
etc.	mmm		●						O			4
etc.	nnn	△		●								4
Weighted Importance of Part Features		171	63	132	90	198	200	153	39	25	150	

FIGURE 5 QFD Matrix of Technical Requirements vs. Part Characteristics for Connector-to-Part Interface

Testing and Design Optimization

Using designed experiments to determine specification limits for key part characteristics—such as part dimension and material properties—increases the team's understanding of the range of values required for optimal performance. The target values determined for the part features were entered into the "Technical Requirements vs. Part Characteristics" matrix columns as shown in Figure 5.

Using designed experiments, the team explored various design alternative with respect to key TRs. For example, the target value range for the TR Pull-out Force drove the analysis of the performance of various designs. By testing different connector designs for pull-out force performance, Raychem engineers determined the distribution of the pull-out force performance on cables with varying braid counts. Testing of many design variations and analysis of tradeoffs led to a design selection.

Benchmarking the Competition

The team analyzed competing products from the external customer perspective and from the internal technical perspective. Prior to the introduction of QFD, Raychem had not systematically conducted point-by-point analyses of competing products from the customer's perspective. However, the company did maintain close informal communication with customers about competitive products. In addition, prototypes of the new CATV connector had been given to a small number of selected customers to provide data on customer response to the new design. This background, supplemented by conversations with customers regarding various connectors on the market, enabled the sales and marketing team members to rate each connector on its ability to satisfy the requirements on the list of customer needs. Figure 6 illustrates their format, which used a 1–5 ascending scale of customer satisfaction to compare three competitive products, an existing Raychem connector, and the new concept.

The team completed a second competitive analysis from an internal viewpoint (see Figure 7). The development and marketing team members collaborated to develop a Pugh concept selection table comparing several competitors' designs with an existing Raychem exterior CATV connector and a number of design variations of the new indoor connector. The comparison criteria were a combination of important technical and customer requirements, including sale price. The team members compared each connector to a reference design on its ability to meet the comparison criteria. For each criterion, a design received a "+" for "better than," a "–" for "worse than" and an "s" for "same as" the reference design. Laboratory performance testing provided data for rating the competing connectors on their relative ability to meet key technical requirements.

This internal comparison indicated that the current Raychem design was superior to competing connectors in many areas, but was more expensive while offering similar but not superior RF shielding performance. RF

	Existing Connectors				New CATV Connector
	A	B	C	D	
Function/Reliability					
etc.	4	4	2	1	5
etc.	3	3	3	4	4
etc.					
Convenient Installation					
etc.	3	3	4	4	4
etc.	3	4	4	4	5
etc.	3	2	4	4	3

FIGURE 6 Analysis of the Competition: Customer Perspective

Concept / Comparison Criteria	Reference concept (Design)	Design 1	Design 2	Design 3	Design 4	Design 5	Design 6	Design 7
xxx		-	-	-	s	s	★	★
yyy	D	-	s	+	s	s	★	★
zzz		-	s			-	★	★
	A	+	+	+	s	-	★	★
		+	+			-	★	★
	T	+	+	-	-	+	★	★
		★	★	★	★	★	★	★
	U	★	★	★	★	★	★	★
		★	★	★	★	★	★	★
	M	★	★	★	★	★	★	★
Totals +'s		★	★	★	★	★	★	★
Totals -'s		★	★	★	★	★	★	★

```
+ = Better than reference design
- = Worse than reference design
s = Same as reference design
★ = Propreitary information
```

FIGURE 7   Analysis of the Competition: Team Perspective Using a Pugh Concept Selection Table

shielding performance was one of the most important customer needs. Accordingly, the designers concentrated on developing methods to reduce manufacturing costs and increase RF shielding; these efforts resulted in design improvements.

Developing the Manufacturing Process

Outside suppliers manufacture the CATV connector parts, which the Telecom production group subsequently assembles. The CATV connector team developed and documented the production process according to usual company practices. A process flowchart was created, along with detailed part drawings and purchase specifications. During process development for the connector shell, engineers worked with polymer suppliers and vendor manufacturing plants to select materials and to determine appropriate process parameters. Purchasing representatives, who joined the team temporarily during process development work, arranged visits with die casting vendors to discuss production and design alternatives for the metal mandrel part.

While in-process controls are an important element of quality plans for Telecom products manufactured in-house, developing detailed process control plans in partnership with vendors remains a future goal. A Quality Plan was drawn up in the form of tables outlining requirements, functional tests, measured characteristics, sampling methods, measurement tools, and relevant document numbers.

The team did not formally use QFD in developing the manufacturing process. However, the earlier QFD work on TRs and part features did facilitate process development by providing a better understanding of part tolerance requirements.

Product Introduction

The product was formally introduced approximately two years after initial inception and ten months after the start of the QFD study. In the opinion of the team, the QFD process had improved the product without delaying the schedule. Several team members had been concerned that using QFD would lead to major schedule delays.

Based on the number and the importance of the improvements made as a result of QFD, the management of the Telecom Division regards the connector project a successful first application of QFD. The connector, while less than perfect at product introduction, was significantly better than it would have been otherwise. The QFD study led to fewer late design changes, higher manufacturing yields, and increased customer satisfaction. The availability of a push-on connector delivering the performance of a traditional connector clearly delighted some important customers.

Evaluating the QFD Process

The team analyzed what went right and what went wrong during the first application of QFD and listed their suggestions for future work. High on the list of benefits was improved communication and a greater ease in making decisions based on fact rather than opinion. The team's evaluation of their experience using QFD follows.

Advantages/Insights Gained Using QFD

The Team Process:

- Forced the prioritizing of requirements
- Kept group members involved and connected
- Made observations rational rather than emotional
- Helped identify differences of opinion and reach consensus

The Product:

- Matrices outlined objectives more clearly than lists
- Forced direct technical group contact with customers early in the project

- Identified areas where more customer information was needed
- Forced looking at the competition, point by point
- The product was improved

Key Problems Using QFD

The Environment:

- Development events and timing squashed the process
- The design concept had been chosen; relatively few changes could be made
- Lack of buy-in to the process by all team members
- Lack of meeting attendance
- Normal manning practices did not allow enough resources

The Tool:

- First matrix was too large
- Mixed in tests with the TRs
- Too much numerology on customer data
- Took a long time
- Late in distinguishing "world-class" performance from required target values

Suggestions for Future Work with QFD

Customer Interaction:

- Apply QFD early, not after choosing the design concept
- Involve all group members in visiting/gathering customer data
- Gather customer data scientifically to get consistency (e.g., how questions were phrased)
- Do not announce the product introduction date too early
- Don't show the product prematurely and thereby encourage competition

The Tool:

- Take a quick cut at the House of Quality early and then refine it
- Use fewer, broader Customer Needs and TRs

Project Management:

- Spend more time on feasibility and alternative designs
- Clearly identify the target values required to go to market

- Spend more time understanding interactions among TRs
- Don't expect a shorter time to product introduction, but expect a better product

CONCLUSION

TQM at Raychem has been defined as exceeding external and internal customer requirements and expectations for products and services. The use of TQM tools such as QFD is an integral part of Raychem's commitment to becoming a total quality management company. In alignment with the company's commitment to "delight the customer," a product development team in Raychem's Telecom Divisions used QFD in conjunction with other TQM tools to develop an indoor cable television connector. The team used QFD methods to listen to and analyze the "Voice of the Customer" and to detail and prioritize technical requirements and part design characteristics. Benefits of using QFD included product improvements, fewer design changes, easier process scale-up, improved communication and teamwork, and increased customer satisfaction. This successful use of QFD by the Telecom Division has led to the integration of QFD into the Raychem New Product Introduction Guidelines and has generated enthusiastic support for QFD's ability to help Raychem become a recognized practitioner of total quality management.

15

BENCHMARKING*

INTRODUCTION

Benchmarking has recently become one of the most popular management tools in today's modern business. One reason for its popularity is that it can be a simple and inexpensive process; on the other hand, it can also be complex and extensive. In light of the value and importance of competitive benchmarking, it is easy to understand the virtual explosion of its use.

According to a Chinese proverb attributed to a Chinese general over 2000 years ago, "if you know your enemy and know yourself, you need not fear the results of a hundred battles" (Sun Tzu, 1983). This proverb (whether true or mythical) can be paraphrased here and used as sound advice for managers: "If you know your own product and your own company well enough, you need not fear competition from other companies." It has become a truism that one must study and know more about all aspects of one's own company, because in this modern age, at the dawn of the 21st century, knowledge is power.

Benchmarking is becoming increasingly useful, especially in the all-important aspect of quality. It is important to be competitive with the "best of the best," and it must be understood that this is a dynamic and continuous business process.

HISTORY

Since 1979, the concept of benchmarking has taken on a radical new meaning. Before that time, benchmarking simply meant comparing various components of the company to the previous year's performance. In the

---

* This chapter was written by Dr. Fred W. Swift, Florida International University.

earliest use of benchmarking, *Webster's* definition was sufficient: "...a surveyor's mark...of previously determined position...and used as a reference point." A company would simply decide which measures of performance to follow and measure itself from year to year. The most common measures were related to cost and included profits, sales volume, expenses, some type of performance ratio, or some other economic parameter. Strategic planners would opt for some percentage increase or decrease. If this goal was met or exceeded, then the unit was declared a success for the period in question.

Most researchers and writers suggest that 1979 was the turning point for benchmarking as a vital management tool. Xerox is given credit for first discovering that it was vital to use benchmarks to compare itself to other competitors as well as to reference points within its own organization. At that time, Xerox's manufacturing unit decided to compare unit manufacturing costs and features of its copying machines to those of competitor machines. What Xerox discovered was that the competition was selling copiers for what it was costing Xerox to manufacture them. Xerox took these findings and made them its improvement targets. This drove Xerox to make drastic changes which have brought Xerox back to the forefront. Thus began the concept.

DEFINITION

Improvement goals based on the company's own past performance are no longer sufficient. In fact, the definition itself has undergone a revolution. In 1979, Xerox realized that the old *Webster's* definition was no longer sufficient and adopted a new one:

> The continuous process of measuring our products, services, and business practices against the toughest competitors or those companies recognized as industry leaders.
>
> D.T. Kearns, Xerox CEO (Camp, 1989, p. 10)

Another definition proposed by Robert Camp as a working definition is:

> Benchmarking is the search for industry best practices that lead to superior performance. (Camp, 1989, p. 12)

Both definitions emphasize that benchmarking is a continuous process of searching out, understanding, and implementing the best industry practices to improve one's own business. Both definitions also emphasize that benchmarking is not restricted to the end product, but can (and should) be applied to all areas of the business.

THE BENCHMARKING PROCESS

Benchmarking can be conducted by following the ten-step process outlined in *Industry Week*:

1. Identify the function to benchmark.

2. Identify the best-in-class company in that function. Often, a trip is made to the selected company.

3. Identify the key performance variables to measure, and collect the data. Agree with the cooperating company on the type of data being collected to insure that accurate comparisons can be made.

4. Analyze and compare the data. In addition to collecting quantitative data, describe key management approaches that differ between the companies, and identify the critical success factors.

5. Project future performance levels of the benchmarked company. Since it will take some time to adopt many of the techniques used by the benchmarked company, project what that company's performance level will be in five years, then plan to match or exceed that level in your own company.

6. Establish functional goals. The team of benchmarking specialists presents its final recommendations to top management on ways in which the organization must change to reach the new goals.

7. Communicate benchmark findings. Senior management shares portions of the benchmarking study's findings with employees to build enthusiasm and support for the new strategies.

8. Develop action plans. The benchmarking team develops specific action plans for each objective.

9. Implement specific actions and monitor progress. Collect data after a period of time to determine new performance levels. Adjustments to the action plans should be made if goals are not being met, and problem-solving teams may be formed to work out snags.

10. Recalibrate benchmarks. Over time, the benchmarks should be reevaluated and updated to insure that they are based on the latest data and best targets. (Altany, 1990, p. 18)

This is by no means the only way to implement benchmarking. Other methodologies, such as Camp's (Camp, 1989, p. 17), Alcoa's, and AT&T's (Bemowski, 1991, pp. 20–23), should be studied before choosing one. Ideally, the benchmarking process a company uses should be one that takes the best practices of others and incorporates them into a process that will work specifically for the company.

The key to implementing any benchmarking process is to make sure that (1) the environment within the company is conducive to benchmarking, (2) all homework (team selection, benchmarking topic selected, own process analyzed, etc.) is done prior to benchmarking another company, and (3) the information gained from the benchmarking process is used (Bemowski, 1991, p. 22).

SPECIAL CONSIDERATIONS

Performance Indicators

Attention must be given to the measures used to determine the current health of the company. Historically, there has been a search for those internal, quantifiable parameters which indicate a company's short-term financial condition. While these studies were sufficient in static markets, intense worldwide competition has mandated that better indicators be found to ensure that a company stay competitive within its environment.

Prior to the 1970s, the process was simple and straightforward. Top management decided which department or function to benchmark and compared its performance from year to year or for some other comparable time period. The measure was generally an economic indicator or an indicator that measured productivity. In the late 1970s and early 1980s, when Xerox and others decided to make a more comprehensive analysis and compare themselves to competitors, benchmarking took on more significance, but it also became more comprehensive, more complex, and vital.

Through the 1980s, the tendency was to determine what should be benchmarked and then compare oneself to direct competitors. This process became more difficult because a leading company was reluctant to share vital information with a competitor who was not too far behind. Thus, the vital information had to come from a third party or intensive research, such as searching public records or hiring a marketing analyst.

Now, performance indicators have taken on a whole new meaning and have changed and evolved rapidly. While everyone agrees that it is of prime importance to decide what will be benchmarked, hardly anyone agrees on which performance indicators should be used. On further study, this is understandable, because functions are unique within a corporate culture or a corporation. Some indicators are standard across the business world and some are common. If possible, these should be researched and used as a model. Internal benchmarking should be a must, so that management always knows its own company. The standards of economic indicators, performance indicators, productivity indicators, etc. are the easiest to deal with, the easiest to obtain data on, and are of vital importance to any business. Any company that is just starting this technique should begin at this point and benchmark a few important parameters set by management. Then it should move quickly into competitive benchmarking but should again begin modestly. What to benchmark can be the most difficult and important step in the process. To stay compatible with the total quality management (TQM) criteria, it is suggested that the functions of the enterprise be examined and categorized as input to the service or process, the process itself and all its steps, and finally the outputs. If this can be modeled for a company, or a class of companies, then the rest of the task becomes straightforward.

BIBLIOGRAPHY

Altany, David, "Copycats," *Industry Week.* November 5, 1990, p. 11(4).

Bemowski, Karen, "The Benchmarking Bandwagon," *Quality Progress.* January 1991, p. 19(6).

Camp, Robert C., *Benchmarking: The Search for Industry Best Practices that Lead to Superior Performance.* ASQC Quality Press, Milwaukee, 1989.

Camp, Robert C., "A Bible for Benchmarking, by Xerox," *Financial Executive.* July–August 1993, p. 23(5).

Colman, Lester E. and Donald G. Reynolds, "Benchmarking Customer Satisfaction," *Chief Executive (U.S.).* April 1994, p. 24(4).

DeToro, Irving J., "Strategic Planning for Quality at Xerox," *Quality Progress.* April 1987, p.16(5).

Furey, Timothy R., "Benchmarking: The Key to Developing Competitive Advantage in Mature Markets," *Planning Review.* September/October 1987, p. 30(3).

McGonagle John J. Jr. and Denise Fleming, "New Options in Benchmarking," *The Journal for Quality and Participation.* July–August 1993, p. 60(8).

Main, Jeremy, "How to Steal the Best Ideas Around," *Fortune.* October 19, 1992, p. 102(3).

Pryor, Lawrence S., "Benchmarking: A Self-Improvement Strategy," *The Journal of Business Strategy.* November/December 1989, p. 28(5).

Spendolini, Michael J., "The Benchmarking Process," *Compensation and Benefits Review.* September–October 1992, p. 21(8).

Sun Tzu, *The Art of War.* Delacorte Press, New York, 1983, p. 84.

Swanson, Roger, "Quality Benchmark Deployment," *Quality Progress.* December 1993, p. 81(4).

Swift, Fred, Tim Gallwey, and Jill A. Swift, "Benchmarking—The Neglected Element in Total Quality Management," Presented at the Workshop on Benchmarking—Theory and Practices. Trondheim, Norway, June 1994 (10 pp).

Tucker, Francis G., Seymour M. Zivan, and Robert C. Camp, "How to Measure Yourself Against the Best," *Harvard Business Review.* January–February 1987, p. 8(4).

Vaziri, H. Kevin, "Using Competitive Benchmarking to Set Goals," *Quality Progress.* October 1992, pp. 81(5).

CASE STUDY 1
Benchmarking:
The Key to Developing
Competitive Advantage in Mature Markets

by Timothy R. Furey*

Many U.S. businesses face slower economic growth, increased foreign competition, and customers who are increasingly sensitive to price. As a result, a brilliant strategy is no longer enough to guarantee marketing success. Rather, U.S. corporations are increasingly focusing on developing an operational competitive advantage in R&D, manufacturing, sales, and marketing. In response to this challenge, strategic planners at such corporations as Xerox, Ford, and GTE have begun to introduce a new planning tool called "benchmarking."

HOW IT WORKS

Benchmarking is an analytical process for rigorously measuring a company's operations against the best-in-class companies inside and outside its markets. The goals of the benchmarking process are to:

- Identify key performance measures for each function of a business' operations

- Measure one's own company's internal performance levels as well as the leading competitors'

- Compare performance levels and identify areas of competitive advantage and disadvantage

- Implement programs to close the gap between internal operations and the companies

While the concept of benchmarking is not revolutionary, recent experience has shown that the companies using this process are more likely to achieve significant operating competitive advantages than those that count on the benchmarking process happening by itself.

* This article is reprinted from *Planning Review*, Vol. 15, No. 5 (September/October 1987), with permission from The Planning Forum, The International Society for Strategic Management and Planning.

The potential power of benchmarking is shown in the two case studies that follow. The company identities have been disguised. Both companies have successfully implemented the process.

CASE NUMBER ONE: MANUFACTURING

Company X, a national leader in the production of widely used plastic components, was increasingly being underpriced by a small regional manufacturer. To discover the source of its competitor's price advantage, Company X began benchmarking each cost component of the manufacturing function. As a result, it managed to track down four key cost performance measures:

- The price paid for the major raw material used

- The material yield

- The number of man-hours needed to produce 100 units

- The average wage rate

Company X benchmarked these costs against both the small regional competitor and its largest national competitor. The results are shown in Table 1.

TABLE 1   Manufacturing Benchmarking

	Company X*	Regional competitor	National competitor
Raw material			
Price paid per pound (index = 100)	100	85	109
Yield (pounds/1000 units)	× 100	× 94	× 95
Relative cost index	100	80	104
Cost as % of Company X sales price	45%	38%	47%
Company X margin advantage/(disadvantage)	—	(9%)	2%
Labor			
Man-hours/1000 units	100	118	91
Cost/man-hour	× 100	× 94	× 100
Relative cost index	100	111	91
Cost as % of company sales price	32%	36%	29%
Company X margin advantage/(disadvantage)	—	4%	(3%)
Total margin			
Advantage/(disadvantage)	—	(5%)	(1%)

* Company X used an index of 100 for its cost and developed a relative index for its competitors.

From the benchmarking process, Company X determined that the regional competitor was using fewer pounds of a lower quality, less expensive raw material to produce the same number of units, which gave the regional competitor an overall 10 percent cost advantage. However, once product quality performance was measured, it was found that the regional competitor's product did not meet customers' specifications in several critical areas. As a result, Company X's sales force was able to make a strong case with their customers for buying their product—at a premium price.

When Company X took a look at its leading national competitor, it noticed that while its own purchasing department had successfully negotiated lower raw material prices, the national competitor's raw material yields and labor productivity were significantly better. This initiated a manufacturing process review that identified several potential productivity improvements.

Ultimately, Company X was able to identify several areas of competitive advantage and disadvantage. This information proved so valuable that R&D, sales and distribution, and marketing all used the technique to determine cost and quality performance and to work on areas of competitive advantage and disadvantage.

CASE NUMBER TWO: SALES

Company Y, a major vendor of telecommunications equipment, was concerned about the cost and productivity of its sales force. By benchmarking itself against its largest direct competitor and the best-in-class vendor of data-processing equipment, the company was able to develop the comparisons shown in Table 2.

TABLE 2   Sales Force Benchmarking

	Company Y	Direct competitor	"Best-in-class" competitor
Cost benchmarks			
Average total sales rep. compensation	$38,000	$44,000	$55,000
Percent of compensation earned from commission	10%	15%	30%
Revenues/sales rep.	$835,000	$900,000	$1,200,000
Compensation as % of revenues	4.6%	4.9%	4.6%
Performance benchmarks			
Average number of calls/week/rep.	16–18	13–16	20+
Revenue quotas	Yes	Yes	No
New account quotas	Informal	No	Yes

hospitals. The focus on measuring core processes and identifying best practices can be widely applied to operations throughout all of a hospital's services. Two of the most valuable benefits of benchmarking are that it encourages organizations to look outward for improved practices instead of inward and that it provides measurement of processes that had previously been evaluated subjectively.

Health care institutions, and particularly doctors, are often viewed as highly resistant to innovative management practices. Yet the doctors who were involved in this project proved to be enthusiastic advocates of benchmarking. One of the main reasons for the successes achieved here was the thoroughness of the planning and data gathering before any offsite visits and information exchanges were made. Managers are often in such a hurry to visit other plants, offices, and facilities that they give little time to advance preparation. In addition, time spent in planning and collecting data on one's own processes helps build the commitment and knowledge for a successful exchange with other organizations.

Benchmarking is in the early stages of adoption in some leading hospitals and health care institutions. It is likely to secure a firmer hold in those hospitals where senior management considers it part of strategic planning and where measures of process improvement are found to be just as important as financial measures of performance.

The crucial concerns are determining which processes have the most direct influence on competitive advantage and which benchmarks are the best overall measures of these processes. Senior managers in many of the hospitals in this study singled out patient flow through the emergency room as the core process with the most strategic significance and identified cycle time or speed as the critical measure of this process. The introduction of best practices should enhance these business processes and create competitive advantage. They should either improve customer satisfaction and increase revenues or they should improve some aspect of operations that will lower costs or increase productivity.

A possible concern with this pilot project is how many of the best practices improved patient care and satisfaction, as well as how many increased admissions or improved productivity and lowered costs. Some of the enhancements that reduced cycle times through the emergency room could have improved both patient satisfaction and staff productivity. But some of the changes could have improved neither one.

Critical to any long-term commitment to benchmarking is establishing clearer relationships between organizational changes and measurable results in areas of strategic importance. Minimally, senior management needs to assure itself that the increased revenue and lowered costs obtained by introducing new practices exceed the staff time and capital invested.

16

QUALITY TEAMS

BACKGROUND

The concept of quality teams originated in Japan in the early 1960s. At the time, company-wide quality control efforts were being implemented throughout Japan. The Union of Japanese Scientists and Engineers (JUSE) was offering short courses in the use of statistical techniques, holding seminars, and publishing articles, books, and magazines. However, the bulk of the effort was directed toward engineers and managers. Material for shop foremen and line workers was scarce. In July 1961, many Japanese foremen attended a quality seminar. It was at this seminar that they indicated an interest in seeing a publication that their line workers could easily understand and use. JUSE heard of this request and immediately began working on the idea. The effort was headed by Dr. Kaoru Ishikawa.

In April 1962, the first issue of *Gemba-To-QC* (*Quality Control for the Foreman*) was published. This periodical was specifically designed for the people in the workshop. In order to maintain the worker focus of the magazine, the editorial staff established three main policies for the magazine:

1. To facilitate education, training and propagation of QC techniques, and to help first-line supervisors and foremen improve their QC ability.

2. To encourage foremen and workers to subscribe to the magazine on their own account.

3. To organize at the workshop level a group called "QC Circle" headed by a foreman and participated in by his subordinate workers; to encourage them to study QC using the magazine as a

textbook, and to make such a group function as a core of QC in each workshop. (Ishikawa, 1980, pp. 6–7)

The magazine set forth three main objectives of organizing quality control circles:

1. To foster study groups in which foremen and workers study the magazine together.

2. To apply the results of their study to their workshops in order to more effectively manage and to improve the work environment.

3. To expand the personality of foremen and workers. (Ishikawa, 1980, p. iii)

In May 1962, the first quality control circle was registered with the QC Circle Headquarters (a subgroup of JUSE). In November 1962, the first QC Circle conference was held. Since that time, the number of registered quality control circles has continued to grow. By 1980, there were over 100,000 registered circles.

In the 1980s, the concept of quality circles was brought to the United States. At that time, many top managers felt that quality circles were one of the secrets to the success of the Japanese. Therefore, top managers mandated that the work force participate in quality circles. Since top managers showed no commitment to quality circles and since they were not voluntary (both fundamental principles of the success of Japanese quality circles), a majority of the initial quality circle efforts failed.

In the late 1980s and early 1990s, quality circles reemerged in the United States as quality teams. This time they were being implemented with top management support and were succeeding.

The purpose and fundamental principles of quality teams are discussed in the remainder of this chapter. Different types of teams, responsibilities of team members, and guidelines for successful team meetings are also discussed.

WHAT ARE QUALITY TEAMS?

A quality team is a small group of individuals who voluntarily meet to work toward a common beneficial objective. Typically, the individuals come from the same work environment and strive to solve a common problem. All quality teams work as an integral part of the company's quality improvement effort. In this way, quality teams:

1. Contribute to the improvement and development of the company

2. Contribute to the establishment of a happy, friendly work environment which is meaningful to work in

3. Provide a means of displaying and recognizing worker capabilities, which allows for individual growth

The purpose of quality team activities is threefold:

1. To promote leadership, management abilities, and quality improvement capabilities among the work force and to encourage improvement through self-development

2. To increase the level of worker morale and create an environment in which everyone is increasingly aware of quality issues and problems and the need for improvement

3. To act as the nucleus of a company's quality improvement effort by acting as the focal point for quality improvement directions set by top management

Several fundamental criteria must be met in order to successfully run and manage quality teams. Participation on quality teams must be voluntary. Top management must take an active role in recognizing and promoting team activities, and opportunities for self-development must exist.

Voluntary participation ensures that everyone on the team is interested in solving the problem at hand. It means that the team is for the most part self-directed and motivated to solve an existing problem or improve a given situation. It requires that management trust the workers enough to be self-directed in deciding what problems to work on and how best to solve them. People naturally work well if they feel they are trusted. Those workers who do not initially choose to work on a team should not be forced to do so. In time, those workers will recognize the benefits derived from working as a part of a team and decide to join in. Basically, respect for workers' voluntary efforts is equivalent to the fundamental tenet of total quality management: respect for people. Those companies that do not respect their people will eventually lose their best ones.

Top management involvement is critical to the success of quality teams. If quality teams fail, the company's quality effort typically fails. Therefore, it is in the best interest of top management to promote and encourage team participation. The best way to promote participation is by example. If top management utilizes the team concept to solve its own problems, it is indicating that it truly believes in the effectiveness and usefulness of quality teams. It is also important that top management appropriately recognize the efforts of the work force teams. An excellent means of recognition is to properly evaluate the recommendations of the different teams and implement them. Implementing the work force teams' recommendations indicates that top management values their efforts and recognizes them as contributing to the company-wide goal of continuous improvement. It also indicates that top management is interested in employees developing their mental skills in addition to their job skills. People naturally develop their work abilities as they are given the opportunity to develop and use their mental abilities. Management that recognizes this recognizes that a continually learning and developing work force enhances a company's ability to improve and grow.

Providing opportunities for self-improvement means that management provides training courses on a continuous basis. The number of courses an employee may take is not limited. Quality teams are characterized by their ability to educate and train people in the use of new techniques. Team participation enhances this education and training in that team members actually use and implement the techniques learned. Providing a forum for individuals to learn and grow enhances individual initiative and creativity, both of which are essential ingredients for a continuously improving environment. Opportunity for self-improvement also means that workers who never thought of themselves as leaders are encouraged and given the opportunity to lead. Quality teams provide a natural forum for developing the people skills, conceptual skills, and decision-making skills needed to be a leader.

TYPES OF TEAMS

There are four major types of teams. Each has a different worker composition and purpose. The four types of teams are:

1. Operational teams

2. Cross-operational teams

3. Assigned teams

4. Directional lead teams

Operational teams are sometimes called functional teams. Operational team members come from the same operating unit. Formation of the teams is, of course, voluntary. The teams are encouraged to select their own problems or improvement opportunities. The problem or improvement opportunity selected normally comes from the team's own work environment.* More importantly, the problem or improvement opportunity is one over which the team has actual control. Upon solving the problem, the team usually is not disbanded. It typically identifies another problem or improvement opportunity to work on. The team may or may not consist of exactly the same members. In many instances, an individual leaves one team to join another that is working on a problem of greater interest to the him or her. Changing teams (as long as it is not in the middle of a problem) should be encouraged. This allows individuals to expand and share their experiences and knowledge. The purpose of operational teams is to address problems that directly affect individuals in their daily lives.

Cross-operational teams are often called cross-functional teams. The

---

* Several topics are not appropriate for operational teams to address, including anything related to personnel such as absenteeism, pay scales, promotions, discipline, etc.

members of cross-operational teams come from more than one operating unit. The purpose of the team is to work on problems or improvement opportunities that cut across operational or functional lines. The cross-functional problem can come from several sources. It could be a problem identified by an operational team, or it could be a problem that just developed. Typically, once the problem is solved, the team is disbanded.

Assigned teams are teams that are formed to solve a specific problem or group of problems. The specific problem has typically been identified by upper management as needing immediate attention. The members of this team usually come from more than one functional area and are assigned by upper management based on individual background and experience. Once the specific problem is solved, the team is disbanded.

Directional lead teams are led by a vice-president, staff manager, plant manager, director, or other appropriate top manager. The purpose of a directional lead team is to function as a steering committee for the teams operating in its area. This team sets policy guidelines, handles overall logistics, coordinates team communication, and develops policy deployment plans and projects for its area. These teams are seldom disbanded.

CORE TEAM PARTICIPANTS

Every type of team has the same core team participants: team members and the team leader.

Team members make up the heart of a team. These individuals gather and analyze data (for operational teams, the data are quantitative; for directional teams, the data are usually qualitative) and recommend, implement, and track the effectiveness of solutions. They also participate in presenting their efforts.

The team leader coordinates the activities of the team. The leader is responsible for leading the team through the problem-solving process, maintaining team momentum, communicating the team's needs, communicating the team's progress, and identifying the need for and training members in various statistical techniques. The team leader does not have to be a manager or supervisor. The team leader does have to be someone who is knowledgeable in the problem-solving process and capable of teaching the team the proper use of the quality tools. Most importantly, the team leader must be someone the team respects.

Another very important person in quality team management is the team facilitator. The team facilitator coaches and supports managers, supervisors, team leaders and team members. The facilitator teaches the quality improvement and problem-solving process and provides training in the various tools and techniques. The facilitator is responsible for promoting the quality improvement program and ensuring the synergism of team efforts. The team leader relies on the team facilitator for special support and direction. It is the team facilitator who settles disputes and maintains the spirit of cooperation toward the common goal of continuous improvement. In many organizations, the job of team facilitator is designated as a full-time job. In many instances, it is a core group of individuals who coordinate training and promotional activities.

SELECTION OF PROBLEM OR IMPROVEMENT OPPORTUNITY

A team should be aware of several criteria when selecting the team project (problem or improvement opportunity). Using these criteria as guidelines will enhance the team's success.

1. The project must be compatible with management policies.

2. A project that is familiar, and of common concern to all team members, should be selected first.

3. The project chosen should be within the team's realm of control.

4. The project should be chosen based on the impact of its solution (reduced rework, reduced costs, etc.).

5. As a general rule, a project that can be solved in three to six months should be chosen.

6. Once a project has been chosen, simple techniques (Pareto chart, check sheets) should be utilized extensively.

TEAM MEETING GUIDELINES

The first time the team meets, it should establish team rules of conduct. Some common rules of conduct are:

1. Criticism of others or their ideas is forbidden.

2. Everyone has complete freedom to express their thoughts and ideas.

Several general guidelines should be followed whenever a team meets:

During the meeting:

1. Team leader reviews progress.

2. Team works together to identify, analyze, and solve work-related problems.

3. Team members are encouraged to make simple, brief presentations before the group. (This builds confidence and team unity.)

4. Team leader should take every opportunity to give praise. (Suggest better ways of doing things after recognizing team members' efforts.)

single team has saved the hospital around 600 bed days or $200,000 per year. The hospital estimates that, due to these savings, its cost for the first year's management reporting system will have been repaid more than 20 times within the first year. The gains in patient and staff satisfaction might be more difficult to measure, but it is easy to see that as the number of teams and hospitals employing these methods increases, the effect of such quality improvement programs will be quite great.

An interesting result of the analysis of the routinely available hospital separation data is that now, through the activities of a quality improvement team, additional specific data are collected; that is, existing data were used to find areas for improvement, but additional data were required to determine the effect of the changes. The research and data collection undertaken by team members have been absorbed into their general duties without any observable disruption to their routine. If this result can be reproduced in other hospitals and teams (which appears likely from other projects), it will not be long before the regular collection of scientific data permeates all facets of the Australian health services. The increasing availability of such data will give managers and clinicians an invaluable base for rational decision making. The quality improvement team approach, as documented in *The Team Handbook*, is an extremely useful method of scientific problem solving in quality of care applications. The team did not adhere to all of the instructions in *The Team Handbook*, but extracted and used those tools that it regarded as most appropriate in the given situation.[7]

ACKNOWLEDGMENTS

The authors would like to thank the following people, who were instrumental in the success of this project. From the HSRG: Lee-Anne Clavarino, Robert Gibberd, and Craig Shaw. From Tamworth Base Hospital: David Briggs, Lyn Bruce, John Davies, John Dearin, Julia Greaves, Marina Griffin, Annette Mitchell, Joy Newcombe, Ruth Turner, Peter Wakeford, Belinda Whitten, Mary Wilcox, and Arthur Wooster.

REFERENCES

1. Report of the Forum on Priorities on National Health, Australian Institute of Health, Canberra, 1991.
2. Brian T. Callopy, "Developing Clinical Indicators: The ACHS Care Evaluation Program," *Australian Clinical Review*, 10:83–85, 1990.
3. NSW Department of Health, Computing and Information Services Branch, "Inventory of Health-Related Data Collections," Department of Health, NSW, 1986.

4. Paul L. Grimaldi and Julie A. Micheletti, *Diagnosis Related Groups: A Practitioner's Guide* (Chicago, IL: Pluribus Press, 1983).
5. Peter R. Scholtes, *The Team Handbook—How to Use Teams to Improve Quality,* Joiner Associates, Inc., Madison, WI, 1988.
6. Ibid.
7. Ibid.

17

ISO 9000

INTERNATIONAL ORGANIZATION FOR STANDARDIZATION

Prior to discussing the ISO 9000 standards, a brief introduction on the International Organization for Standardization is provided.

The International Organization for Standardization (ISO) is a voluntary, non-governmental international organization which was founded in Geneva, Switzerland in 1946. It is funded primarily by industry. The acronym ISO is used to represent the organization. ISO comes from the Greek word *isos,* which means equal.

The organization's objective is "to promote the development of standardization and related work activities with a view to facilitating the international exchange of goods and services and to developing cooperation in the sphere of intellectual, scientific, technological, and economic activity" ("ASQC Standards," undated, p. 3). It is concerned with the standardization of goods and services in technical and non-technical fields (except for electrical and electronic engineering, which is governed by the International Electrotechnical Commission). The organization creates standards, but does not evaluate or enforce them.

Its membership extends to over 90 countries. Each member is the national body "most representative of standardization in its country." In most countries, it is a governmental organization. In a few Western industrial countries, the national standards body is a private organization. For instance, in the United States, the national standards body is ANSI (American National Standards Institute), and in Great Britain, it is the BSI (British Standards Institute).

The work of preparing international standards is usually done through ISO technical committees. There are approximately 180 technical committees. Each technical committee is responsible for discussing, developing,

TABLE 17.1   National Equivalents of ISO 9000 Series

Country	Standard
Australia	AS 3900
Brazil	NB 9000
Denmark	DS/ISO 9000
France	NF-EN 29000
Germany	DIN ISO 9000
Japan	JIS Z 9900
Portugal	FM 29000
Spain	UNE 66 900
U.K.	BS 5750
United States	ANSI/ASQC Q90
European Community	EN 29000

and coordinating global standards for one of many areas of specialization. Each ISO member has the right to be represented on any technical committee in which it has an interest.

Once a technical committee has an international standards draft, that draft is circulated to all member bodies for a vote. Publication as an International Standard requires the approval of at least 75% of its voting members.

ISO 9000

In 1979, ISO established Technical Committee 176 to develop a generic set of quality system management standards. The original committee had 20 participating members and 14 observing members.* This committee relied heavily on the U.K. standard BSI 5750 as a guide to developing the ISO 9000 series of standards. The first ISO 9000 series of standards was published in 1987. A revised version was published in 1994.

The ISO 9000 series of standards has been translated into various languages and is known by different names in different countries. A list of some of the different names by which the ISO 9000 series is known is provided in Table 17.1. Note that most of the national versions bear some code number that includes 9000 or 90. Also note that the European Community[†] has adopted its own version of the standard series, EN 29000.

---

* ISO/TC 176 now has 42 participating members and 21 observing members.
[†] See Appendix A for a history of the emergence of the EC and its governing institutions.

Components of ISO 9000 Standard Series

The standards in the ISO 9000 series are intended to provide a generic core of quality system standards applicable to a broad range of industry and economic sectors. They are not standards for products. Instead, they are standards for governing quality management systems. Therefore, products do not meet ISO 9000 standards; organizations do.

There are five parts to the ISO 9000 series:

Part 1: ISO 9000:1994(E)	**Quality Management Standards**
ISO 9000-1	Part 1: Guidelines For Selection and Use of ISO 9001, ISO 9002, and ISO 9003
ISO 9000-2	Part 2: Generic Guidelines for the Application of ISO 9001, ISO 9002, and ISO 9003
ISO 9000-3	Part 3: Guidelines for the Application of ISO 9001 to the Development, Supply, and Maintenance of Software
ISO 9000-4	Part 4: Guide to Dependability Program Management
Part 2: ISO 9001:1994(E)	**Quality Systems—Model for Quality Assurance in Design, Development, Production, Installation, and Servicing**
Part 3: ISO 9002:1994(E)	**Quality Systems—Model for Quality Assurance in Production, Installation, and Servicing**
Part 4: ISO 9003:1994(E)	**Quality Systems—Model for Quality Assurance in Final Inspection and Test**
Part 5: ISO 9004:1994(E)	**Quality Management and Quality System Elements**
ISO 9004-1	Part 1: Guidelines
ISO 9004-2	Part 2: Guidelines for Services
ISO 9004-3	Part 3: Guidelines for Processed Materials
ISO 9004-4	Part 4: Guidelines for Quality Improvement
ISO 9004-5	Part 5: Guidelines for Quality Plans
ISO 9004-6	Part 6: Guidelines on Quality Assurance for Project Management
ISO 9004-7	Part 7: Guidelines for Configuration Management
ISO 9004-8	Part 8: Guidelines on Quality Principles and Their Application to Management Practices

Briefly, ISO 9000 is a guideline for selecting at which level (9001, 9002, or 9003) to be certified. ISO 9001, ISO 9002, and ISO 9003 are the guidelines for each specific level of certification. ISO 9004 is a management model.

ISO 9000 certification is done on a site basis. In other words, a company cannot get a ISO 9000 certification that covers all sites and facilities of that company. The company must have each individual site and facility independently certified. Certification can be obtained at three different levels: 9001, 9002, or 9003. ISO 9001 certification is the most comprehensive level of certification in the series. Certification at this level requires conformance to all 20 functional areas of the standard. ISO 9002 certification requires conformance to 19 of the 20 functional areas. ISO 9003 requires conformance to 16 elements. The 20 functional areas of standards and which elements are required for each level of certification are listed in Table 17.2.

The Certification and Registration Process

The process of registration requires a review of a site's quality manual against one of the standards (9001, 9002, or 9003). This review must be performed by an accredited certification/registration agency. Since the choice of accrediting agency is up to the site being audited, the experience and reputation of the agency should be carefully assessed. The RAB (Registrar Accreditation Board) accredits organizations based in the United States. In Britain, it is the National Accreditation Council for Certification Bodies (NACCB). Companies in the United States that want to be certified are not limited to using only RAB-accredited agencies. Any company that wants to be certified can use any certification/registration agency, independent of its home base.

The basic steps involved in certification/registration are as follows:

1. Choose a certification/registration agency.

2. Complete forms and send to agency.

3. Send quality manual to agency.

4. Agency reviews manual and notifies the site of any non-conformances found.

5. Resolve non-conformances.

6. Agency performs an on-site audit.

7. Any minor non-conformances are resolved.

8. Registration is given for three to four years.

9. Within the three- to four-year registration period, compliance review audits are performed periodically.

TABLE 17.2   Functional Areas Required by Each Level of Certification

	Functional area	ISO 9001	ISO 9002	ISO 9003
1.	Management Responsibility	♦	♦	♦
2.	Quality System	♦	♦	♦
3.	Contract Review	♦	♦	♦
4.	Design Control	♦		
5.	Document and Data Control	♦	♦	♦
6.	Purchasing	♦	♦	
7.	Control of Customer-Supplied Product	♦	♦	♦
8.	Product Identification and Traceability	♦	♦	♦
9.	Process Control	♦	♦	
10.	Inspection and Testing	♦	♦	♦
11.	Control of Inspection, Measuring, and Test Equipment	♦	♦	♦
12.	Inspection and Test Status	♦	♦	♦
13.	Control of Nonconforming Product	♦	♦	♦
14.	Corrective and Preventive Action	♦	♦	♦
15.	Handling, Storage, Packaging, Preservation, and Delivery	♦	♦	♦
16.	Control of Quality Records	♦	♦	♦
17.	Internal Quality Audits	♦	♦	♦
18.	Training	♦	♦	♦
19.	Servicing	♦	♦	
20.	Statistical Techniques	♦	♦	♦

10. At the end of the registration period, full audit is repeated for re-registration.

These are just general steps. Once a certification/registration agency has been chosen, a detailed action plan is agreed upon. The main thing to remember is that the site is audited according to its quality manual and not the standards. The standards are just a guideline for preparing the quality manual. ISO 9000 requires that a documented (in the form of a quality manual) system be in place. This documented system describes the manner in which the organization runs itself. The documentation addresses certain key areas of activity, otherwise known as the functional areas of the standards. A strong feature of the ISO standards is that they are flexible in the sense that a company can add additional elements to the manual. If additional elements are added to the manual, they will be audited.

Benefits

Some of the recognized benefits of implementing ISO 9000 include:

1. Reduced scrap and rework, which reduces overall costs

2. Reduced customer complaints, which reduces service call and claims costs

3. Improved customer service

4. Improved work flow

5. Standardized training methods

6. Improved document control, which improves both internal and external communication

7. Improved productivity

8. Increased competitiveness

9. Increased quality awareness

FINAL COMMENTS

The question becomes, "Do we implement TQM or register for ISO 9000?" These two are not independent goals. They are intertwined and complement one another. TQM is a philosophy, and ISO 9000 can be used as a structural framework for implementing a company's TQM philosophy. ISO 9000 needs TQM. ISO certification does not guarantee high-quality products and services, but integration with TQM does. The real benefit of the emergence of ISO 9000 as the international standard is that in order to compete in the international marketplace, top management now must be committed to quality.

EXERCISES

17.1 What is the primary difference between ISO 9001 and ISO 9002 certification?

17.2 What does ISO stand for?

17.3 When was the International Organization for Standardization formed?

17.4 What is the primary objective of the International Organization for Standardization?

17.5 Who are the members of the International Organization for Standardization?

17.6 Which technical committee developed the ISO 9000 standards?

17.7 How many parts are there to the ISO 9000 standards? List them.

17.8 What does the registration process require?

17.9 What is the RAB?

17.10 What does ISO 9000 certification require?

17.11 Is your organization certified to one of the ISO 9000 standards? If so, what are some of the benefits your organization has realized?

17.12 Do you agree that ISO 9000 certification and TQM complement one another? Discuss your answer.

BIBLIOGRAPHY

"ASQC Standards" (pamphlet). ASQC, Milwaukee, undated.

Hoyle, David, *ISO 9000 Quality Systems Handbook.* Butterworth-Heinemann, Oxford, England, 1994.

Hutchins, Greg, *ISO 9000: A Comprehensive Guide to Registration, Audit Guidelines and Successful Certification.* Oliver Wight, Essex Junction, Vt., 1993.

"ISO 9000: The Route to Total Quality Management," *Quality World for the Quality Professional.* March 1994, p. 157(7).

ISO 9000:1994(E) Quality Management Standards Series. Available in the United States from the American National Standards Institute (212) 642-4900.

Sprow, Eugene E., *Building Quality Excellence with ISO 9000.* Society of Manufacturing Engineers, Dearborn, Mich., 1992.

Stratton, John H., "What Is the Registrar Accreditation Board?" *Quality Progress.* January 1992, p. 67(3).

PART V

APPENDICES

APPENDIX A

THE EUROPEAN COMMUNITY: EMERGENCE AND GOVERNING INSTITUTIONS

THE EUROPEAN COMMUNITY

With the increase in international trade, it is important to have an understanding of what the European Community represents. The concept of a united Europe had been around for a long time. In the early 1900s, its primary advocates were philosophers and visionaries. Not until after World War II was the concept put forth by a government official. Jean Monnet, a French businessman and diplomat, was one of the leaders in the movement for European unity. Monnet and Robert Schuman, the French foreign minister, put forth a proposal which urged France, the Federal Republic of Germany, and any other European country that wanted to join them to create a common market for coal and steel. This led to the signing of the Treaty of Paris in 1951, which established the European Coal and Steel Community (ECSC).* Six countries signed the treaty to make up the ECSC: France, the Federal Republic of Germany (West Germany), Italy,

---

* Monnet headed the ECSC from 1953 to 1955. He was also an active supporter of the European Economic Community and of Euratom.

Belgium, Luxembourg, and the Netherlands. The formation of the ECSC meant that the trade barriers in coal and steel between the six member countries were abolished. It also allowed coal and steel workers to work anywhere within the community. This was the initial step in the integration of Europe.

In 1952, the treaty establishing the European Defense Community (EDC) was signed in Paris. This treaty called for the formation of a European army, due in part to the increasing military expansion of the Soviet Union. Two years later, with tension between Eastern and Western Europe lessening, the French Parliament rejected the EDC Treaty. This led to the London Conference, where several countries agreed on a modified Brussels Treaty. The modified treaty was called the Western European Unity Treaty and was signed in 1955. This treaty established the Western European Union (WEU). The Western European Union was made up of Belgium, France, Luxembourg, the Netherlands, the United Kingdom, the Federal Republic of Germany, and Italy.

In 1955, the foreign ministers of the six countries of the ECSC met in Messina and decided to extend the European integration to all branches of the economy. The idea was to create an economic community built around the free movement of workers, goods, and services. This led to the Treaty of Rome being signed by the six countries in 1957. The Treaty of Rome established the economic association of Western European countries. Its purpose was to facilitate:

1. The removal of trade barriers between the member nations

2. The establishment of a single commercial policy toward nonmember countries

3. The eventual coordination of members' transportation systems, agricultural policies, and general economic policies

4. The removal of private and public measures restricting free competition

5. The assurance of the mobility of labor, capital, and entrepreneurship among the members (*Encyclopaedia Britannica,* 1994, Volume 4, p. 606)

This economic association was called the European Economic Community (EEC), also known as the Common Market. The treaty also established the European Atomic Energy Community (Euratom). In 1958, the EEC and Euratom Commissions were set up in Brussels.

In November 1959, the Stockholm Convention was signed, establishing the European Free Trade Association (EFTA). EFTA was organized to remove trade barriers between EFTA members and became effective in May 1960. The primary difference between EFTA and the EEC is that each EFTA member would maintain its own commercial policy toward non-EFTA countries. The original member countries were Austria, Denmark, United Kingdom, Norway, Portugal, Sweden, and Switzerland. Finland became an associate member in 1961 and Iceland a full member in 1970. The founders hoped to eventually merge with the EEC. (After the United Kingdom and Denmark joined the EEC in 1972, the remaining EFTA members negotiated an arrangement with the EEC for mutual tariff removal on all industrial products.)

In 1965, a treaty merging the executives of the ECSC, the EEC, and the European Atomic Energy Community (Euratom) was signed in Brussels. The treaty became effective in 1967. The collective of these three communities became known as the European Community.

In 1968, customs duties in intra-community trade in manufactured goods was abolished (18 months ahead of schedule). Also, the Common External Tariff (CET) was introduced.

In January 1972, the Treaty on the Assession of Denmark, Ireland, Norway, and the United Kingdom was signed in Brussels. Later, in November 1972, Norway's voters rejected membership and Norway withdrew from the community.

In 1979, the European Monetary System was launched. It is based on a system of fixed exchange rates among European currencies which is designed to curb inflation. At the time it was introduced, it did much to stabilize exchange rates, as well as encourage member states to pursue strict economic policies which enabled them to give each other mutual support. Also in 1979, the first direct elections to the European Parliament were held.

In 1981, Greece acceded to the European Community. This brought the number of member states to ten.

In 1984, direct elections to the European Parliament were held for the second time. In 1986, Spain and Portugal joined the European Community. Later in 1986, the Treaty of Rome was amended, and the process of European integration was revitalized by the signing of the Single European Act, which became effective in 1987. This act extended the powers of the European Parliament. Another effect of the act was to bring political cooperation into the system of European Community treaties.

In 1989, the third direct elections to the European Parliament were held. Also, the Berlin Wall collapsed on November 9 of the same year.

In 1990, the agreement establishing the European Bank for Reconstruction and Development was signed. Also, the agreement on the elimination of border checks was signed. On October 3, Germany was officially reunited.

The collapse of the Berlin Wall, the unification of Germany, and the disintegration of the Soviet Union* all transformed the political structure of Europe. The 12 member states thus decided to strengthen their political and monetary ties and negotiated a new treaty, the Treaty on European Union (sometimes referred to as the Maastricht Treaty because it was signed in Maastricht). The treaty was signed on February 7, 1992.

---

* The Union of Soviet Socialist Republics was officially abolished on December 25, 1991.

In summary, the development of the European Community started with the liberalization of trade between member states and related economic policies. Then came the construction of a single border-free market in which people, goods, services, and capital could move freely. The Treaty on European Union launched the move toward political union, economic and monetary union, and the creation of a single currency which will replace the currencies of the member states (scheduled to be introduced in 1999). This treaty also called for the introduction of a common foreign and security policy, which will be followed by a common defense policy.

The integration of Europe has been a long, arduous task, and it is important to remember that the integration is continuing still.

INSTITUTIONS OF THE EUROPEAN COMMUNITY

What sets the European Community apart from other international organizations is its unique institutional structure. By becoming a part of the European Community, the member states agree to relinquish a measure of their sovereignty to independent institutions that represent national and shared interests. Each institution has a specific role in the decision-making process.

Member States

The member states of the European Community are listed here in alphabetical order:

Belgium

Denmark

France

Germany

Greece

Ireland

Italy

Luxembourg

Netherlands

Portugal

Spain

United Kingdom

The 18 EFTA members are:

The 12 member states

Switzerland

Austria

Iceland

Sweden

Norway

Finland

These lists are provided as a reference.

The Council of the European Union

The council is the main decision-making institution. It is made up of ministers from each member state. Meetings are attended by different ministers according to the agenda. For example, agriculture ministers attend meetings when farm prices are to be discussed, and foreign ministers attend meetings when external relation matters are to be discussed. The seat of the council is in Brussels. However, certain meetings take place in Luxembourg. Each member state acts as president of the council on a six-month rotation basis. The rotation is in alphabetical order of the member states (see reference list).

The council has a dual role. First, it adopts the main decisions on community policies on the basis of proposals put forward by the commission. On issues of fundamental importance such as the accession of a new member state, amendments to the treaties, or the launching of a new common policy, decisions require a unanimous decision. In other cases, a qualified majority is required. A qualified majority is 54 out of 76 total votes. (France, Germany, Italy, and the U.K. have ten votes each; Spain has eight votes; Belgium, Greece, the Netherlands, and Portugal have five votes each; Denmark and Ireland have three votes each; and Luxembourg has two votes.) Second, the council is responsible for the intergovernmental cooperation introduced by the Treaty on European Union.

The European Council

The European Council was established in 1974 and is made up of 12 ministers (the ministers are the heads of government of each member state) and the president of the commission. The European Council meets at least twice a year to discuss the important issues being examined by the community. The European Council also deals with current international issues through the European Political Cooperation (EPC), which is a mechanism devised to allow member states to align their diplomatic positions and present a united front. The Treaty on European Union gives the European Council certain operational responsibilities in relation to foreign and security policy and economic and monetary union.

The European Commission

This commission was created when the treaty merging the executives of the ECSC, the EEC, and the European Atomic Energy Community (Euratom) became effective in 1967.

The European Commission has 17 members: two each from France, Germany, Italy, Spain, and the U.K. and one from each of the other European Community countries. Commissioners are appointed by the member states. Under the Treaty on European Union, their term of office increases to five years and their appointment has to be approved by the European Parliament.

The commission acts as the guardian of the treaties. It is an impartial body, which means that the commissioners are required to be completely independent of their national governments. They are supposed to act only in the interests of the community. The commission sees to it that treaty provisions and community decisions are correctly applied. It can initiate infringement proceedings against a member state and may, if necessary, refer matters to the Court of Justice. It can also impose fines on individuals or companies if they breech the community's rules of competition.

The commission acts as the catalyst of the community. It has "the sole right of initiative in the field of community legislation" and is considered to be the community's executive body.

The commission's administrative staff is headquartered primarily in Brussels, with a smaller office in Luxembourg. The staff is made up of approximately 17,000 officials. These officials are divided between 30 directorates-general and similar departments. Each department is responsible for implementing common policies and general administration in a specific area.

The European Parliament

The European Parliament is the only European Community institution whose representatives are elected directly by the people of Europe. It originally had 518 members, but as of the June 1994 elections has 567 members. The breakdown of members is as follows:

Germany	99 members
France	87 members
Italy	87 members
United Kingdom	87 members
Spain	64 members
Netherlands	31 members
Belgium	25 members
Greece	25 members

Portugal	25 members
Denmark	16 members
Ireland	15 members
Luxembourg	6 members

The European Parliament is located in Strasbourg, France. However, committee meetings and some part-sessions are held in Brussels. Its Secretariat-General (3500 officials plus the staff of political groups) is based in Luxembourg.

The European Parliament is made up of political groups organized at the community level. Its main purpose is to provide a democratic forum for debate and to act as a political driving force which generates various initiatives for the development of community policies.

The parliament shares the legislative function with the council, which means that it takes part in drafting directives and regulations and proposing amendments. The Treaty on European Union strengthened the parliament's role by granting it co-decision powers in the areas of free movement of workers, the single market, education, research, the environment, trans-European networks, health, culture, and consumer protection. The treaty also gave the parliament the power to reject the council's common position and halt the legislative process.

The European Parliament also shares budgetary powers with the council. It has the power to adopt or reject a budget (which it has done twice in the past).

Finally, the parliament provides democratic control. This means that it can dismiss the commission by a vote of censure which must be supported by a two-thirds majority of its members. It also comments and votes on the commission's program each year. It monitors the implementation of common policies and the day-to-day management of these policies.

The Court of Justice

The Court of Justice was founded in 1952 and is located in Luxembourg. It is made up of 13 judges who are assisted by 6 advocates-general. They are all appointed by common agreement between the member states for six-year terms. Their independence is beyond doubt. The court has two main functions:

1. To check the laws enacted by the Community institutions for compatibility with the Treaties

2. To give its opinion on the correct interpretation or the validity of Community provisions when requested to do so by a national court (Fontaine, 1992, p. 10)

In other words, it ensures that the treaties and other community policies are interpreted and implemented in accordance with community law. The judgment of the court is binding. In respect to community law, its decisions take precedence over those of national courts. The judgments and interpretations of the court are slowly helping to create a European body of law.

The Court of Auditors

The Court of Auditors was established by treaty in 1975 and is based in Luxembourg. It originally had nine members, but this has been increased to twelve under the Treaty on European Union. Members are appointed by the council after consultation with parliament.

Its primary function is to ensure that all community revenue has been collected, all community expenditures are incurred in "a lawful and regular manner," and that the community's financial affairs are properly managed.

Summary

These institutions direct and govern the European Community. As the Community continues to grow, so do the influence and power of these institutions.

BIBLIOGRAPHY

European Union. Office for Official Publications of the European Communities, Luxembourg, 1992.

Fontaine, Pascal, *Europe in Ten Lessons.* Office for Official Publications of the European Communities, Luxembourg, 1992.

Questions and Answers about the European Community. Office for Official Publications of the European Communities, Luxembourg, 1993.

The New Encyclopaedia Britannica. Encyclopaedia Britannica, Chicago, 1994.

The Institutions of the European Community. Office for Official Publications of the European Communities, Luxembourg, 1993.

APPENDIX **B**

NORMAL DISTRIBUTION TABLE

$$P(x \leq Z_\alpha) = 1 - \alpha$$

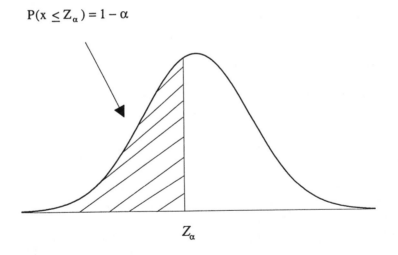

Z_α

Z	0.09	0.08	0.07	0.06	0.05	0.04	0.03	0.02	0.01	0.00
-3.5	0.00017	0.00017	0.00018	0.00019	0.00019	0.00020	0.00021	0.00022	0.00022	0.00023
-3.4	0.00024	0.00025	0.00026	0.00027	0.00028	0.00029	0.00030	0.00031	0.00032	0.00034
-3.3	0.00035	0.00036	0.00038	0.00039	0.00040	0.00042	0.00043	0.00045	0.00047	0.00048
-3.2	0.00050	0.00052	0.00054	0.00056	0.00058	0.00060	0.00062	0.00064	0.00066	0.00069
-3.1	0.00071	0.00074	0.00076	0.00079	0.00082	0.00084	0.00087	0.00090	0.00094	0.00097
-3.0	0.00100	0.00104	0.00107	0.00111	0.00114	0.00118	0.00122	0.00126	0.00131	0.00135
-2.9	0.00139	0.00144	0.00149	0.00154	0.00159	0.00164	0.00169	0.00175	0.00181	0.00187
-2.8	0.00193	0.00199	0.00205	0.00212	0.00219	0.00226	0.00233	0.00240	0.00248	0.00256
-2.7	0.00264	0.00272	0.00280	0.00289	0.00298	0.00307	0.00317	0.00326	0.00336	0.00347
-2.6	0.00357	0.00368	0.00379	0.00391	0.00402	0.00415	0.00427	0.00440	0.00453	0.00466
-2.5	0.00480	0.00494	0.00508	0.00523	0.00539	0.00554	0.00570	0.00587	0.00604	0.00621
-2.4	0.00639	0.00657	0.00676	0.00695	0.00714	0.00734	0.00755	0.00776	0.00798	0.00820
-2.3	0.00842	0.00866	0.00889	0.00914	0.00939	0.00964	0.00990	0.01017	0.01044	0.01072
-2.2	0.01101	0.01130	0.01160	0.01191	0.01222	0.01255	0.01287	0.01321	0.01355	0.01390
-2.1	0.01426	0.01463	0.01500	0.01539	0.01578	0.01618	0.01659	0.01700	0.01743	0.01786
-2.0	0.01831	0.01876	0.01923	0.01970	0.02018	0.02068	0.02118	0.02169	0.02222	0.02275
-1.9	0.02330	0.02385	0.02442	0.02500	0.02559	0.02619	0.02680	0.02743	0.02807	0.02872
-1.8	0.02938	0.03005	0.03074	0.03144	0.03216	0.03288	0.03362	0.03438	0.03515	0.03593
-1.7	0.03673	0.03754	0.03836	0.03920	0.04006	0.04093	0.04182	0.04272	0.04363	0.04457
-1.6	0.04551	0.04648	0.04746	0.04846	0.04947	0.05050	0.05155	0.05262	0.05370	0.05480
-1.5	0.05592	0.05705	0.05821	0.05938	0.06057	0.06178	0.06301	0.06426	0.06552	0.06681
-1.4	0.06811	0.06944	0.07078	0.07215	0.07353	0.07493	0.07636	0.07780	0.07927	0.08076
-1.3	0.08226	0.08379	0.08534	0.08692	0.08851	0.09012	0.09176	0.09342	0.09510	0.09680
-1.2	0.09853	0.10027	0.10204	0.10383	0.10565	0.10749	0.10935	0.11123	0.11314	0.11507
-1.1	0.11702	0.11900	0.12100	0.12302	0.12507	0.12714	0.12924	0.13136	0.13350	0.13567
-1.0	0.13786	0.14007	0.14231	0.14457	0.14686	0.14917	0.15151	0.15386	0.15625	0.15866
-0.9	0.16109	0.16354	0.16602	0.16853	0.17106	0.17361	0.17619	0.17879	0.18141	0.18406
-0.8	0.18673	0.18943	0.19215	0.19489	0.19766	0.20045	0.20327	0.20611	0.20897	0.21186
-0.7	0.21476	0.21770	0.22065	0.22363	0.22663	0.22965	0.23270	0.23576	0.23885	0.24196
-0.6	0.24510	0.24825	0.25143	0.25463	0.25785	0.26109	0.26435	0.26763	0.27093	0.27425
-0.5	0.27760	0.28096	0.28434	0.28774	0.29116	0.29460	0.29806	0.30153	0.30503	0.30854
-0.4	0.31207	0.31561	0.31918	0.32276	0.32636	0.32997	0.33360	0.33724	0.34090	0.34458
-0.3	0.34827	0.35197	0.35569	0.35942	0.36317	0.36693	0.37070	0.37448	0.37828	0.38209
-0.2	0.38591	0.38974	0.39358	0.39743	0.40129	0.40517	0.40905	0.41294	0.41683	0.42074
-0.1	0.42465	0.42858	0.43251	0.43644	0.44038	0.44433	0.44828	0.45224	0.45620	0.46017
0.0	0.46414	0.46812	0.47210	0.47608	0.48006	0.48405	0.48803	0.49202	0.49601	0.50000

z	0.00	0.01	0.02	0.03	0.04	0.05	0.06	0.07	0.08	0.09
0.0	0.50000	0.50399	0.50798	0.51197	0.51595	0.51994	0.52392	0.52790	0.53188	0.53586
0.1	0.53983	0.54380	0.54776	0.55172	0.55567	0.55962	0.56356	0.56749	0.57142	0.57535
0.2	0.57926	0.58317	0.58706	0.59095	0.59483	0.59871	0.60257	0.60642	0.61026	0.61409
0.3	0.61791	0.62172	0.62552	0.62930	0.63307	0.63683	0.64058	0.64431	0.64803	0.65173
0.4	0.65542	0.65910	0.66276	0.66640	0.67003	0.67364	0.67724	0.68082	0.68439	0.68793
0.5	0.69146	0.69497	0.69847	0.70194	0.70540	0.70884	0.71226	0.71566	0.71904	0.72240
0.6	0.72575	0.72907	0.73237	0.73565	0.73891	0.74215	0.74537	0.74857	0.75175	0.75490
0.7	0.75804	0.76115	0.76424	0.76730	0.77035	0.77337	0.77637	0.77935	0.78230	0.78524
0.8	0.78814	0.79103	0.79389	0.79673	0.79955	0.80234	0.80511	0.80785	0.81057	0.81327
0.9	0.81594	0.81859	0.82121	0.82381	0.82639	0.82894	0.83147	0.83398	0.83646	0.83891
1.0	0.84134	0.84375	0.84614	0.84849	0.85083	0.85314	0.85543	0.85769	0.85993	0.86214
1.1	0.86433	0.86650	0.86864	0.87076	0.87286	0.87493	0.87698	0.87900	0.88100	0.88298
1.2	0.88493	0.88686	0.88877	0.89065	0.89251	0.89435	0.89617	0.89796	0.89973	0.90147
1.3	0.90320	0.90490	0.90658	0.90824	0.90988	0.91149	0.91308	0.91466	0.91621	0.91774
1.4	0.91924	0.92073	0.92220	0.92364	0.92507	0.92647	0.92785	0.92922	0.93056	0.93189
1.5	0.93319	0.93448	0.93574	0.93699	0.93822	0.93943	0.94062	0.94179	0.94295	0.94408
1.6	0.94520	0.94630	0.94738	0.94845	0.94950	0.95053	0.95154	0.95254	0.95352	0.95449
1.7	0.95543	0.95637	0.95728	0.95818	0.95907	0.95994	0.96080	0.96164	0.96246	0.96327
1.8	0.96407	0.96485	0.96562	0.96638	0.96712	0.96784	0.96856	0.96926	0.96995	0.97062
1.9	0.97128	0.97193	0.97257	0.97320	0.97381	0.97441	0.97500	0.97558	0.97615	0.97670
2.0	0.97725	0.97778	0.97831	0.97882	0.97932	0.97982	0.98030	0.98077	0.98124	0.98169
2.1	0.98214	0.98257	0.98300	0.98341	0.98382	0.98422	0.98461	0.98500	0.98537	0.98574
2.2	0.98610	0.98645	0.98679	0.98713	0.98745	0.98778	0.98809	0.98840	0.98870	0.98899
2.3	0.98928	0.98956	0.98983	0.99010	0.99036	0.99061	0.99086	0.99111	0.99134	0.99158
2.4	0.99180	0.99202	0.99224	0.99245	0.99266	0.99286	0.99305	0.99324	0.99343	0.99361
2.5	0.99379	0.99396	0.99413	0.99430	0.99446	0.99461	0.99477	0.99492	0.99506	0.99520
2.6	0.99534	0.99547	0.99560	0.99573	0.99585	0.99598	0.99609	0.99621	0.99632	0.99643
2.7	0.99653	0.99664	0.99674	0.99683	0.99693	0.99702	0.99711	0.99720	0.99728	0.99736
2.8	0.99744	0.99752	0.99760	0.99767	0.99744	0.99781	0.99788	0.99795	0.99801	0.99807
2.9	0.99813	0.99819	0.99825	0.99831	0.99836	0.99841	0.99846	0.99851	0.99856	0.99861
3.0	0.99865	0.99869	0.99874	0.99878	0.99882	0.99886	0.99889	0.99893	0.99896	0.99900
3.1	0.99903	0.99906	0.99910	0.99913	0.99916	0.99918	0.99921	0.99924	0.99926	0.99929
3.2	0.99931	0.99934	0.99936	0.99938	0.99940	0.99942	0.99944	0.99946	0.99948	0.99950
3.3	0.99952	0.99953	0.99955	0.99957	0.99958	0.99960	0.99961	0.99962	0.99964	0.99965
3.4	0.99966	0.99968	0.99969	0.99970	0.99971	0.99972	0.99973	0.99974	0.99975	0.99976
3.5	0.99977	0.99978	0.99978	0.99979	0.99980	0.99981	0.99981	0.99982	0.99983	0.99983

APPENDIX C

FACTORS USED TO CONSTRUCT VARIABLES CONTROL CHARTS

	Factors for $\overline{X}$ charts			Factors for R charts					Factors for S charts				Factors for center line		
n	A	A_2	A_3	D_1	D_2	D_3	D_4	d_3	B_3	B_4	B_5	B_6	c_4	d_2	n

$$A_1 = \frac{3}{\sqrt{n}}$$

$$A_2 = \frac{3}{d_2 \sqrt{n}}$$

$$A_3 = \frac{3}{c_4 \sqrt{n}}$$

$$D_1 = d_2 - d_3$$

$$D_2 = d_2 + d_3$$

$$D_3 = 1 - \frac{3d_3}{d_2}$$

$$D_4 = 1 + \frac{3d_3}{d_2}$$

$$B_3 = 1 - \frac{3\sqrt{1 - c_4^2}}{c_4}$$

$$B_4 = 1 + \frac{3\sqrt{1 - c_4^2}}{c_4}$$

$$B_5 = c_4 - 3\sqrt{1 - c_4^2}$$

$$B_6 = c_4 - 3\sqrt{1 - c_4^2}$$

n	Factors for X̄ charts			Factors for R charts					Factors for S charts				Factors for center line		n
	A	A_2	A_3	D_1	D_2	D_3	D_4	d_3	B_3	B_4	B_5	B_6	c_4	d_2	
2	2.121	1.880	2.659	0.000	3.686	0.000	3.267	0.853	0.000	3.267	0.000	2.606	0.7979	1.128	2
3	1.732	1.023	1.954	0.000	4.358	0.000	2.574	0.888	0.000	2.568	0.000	2.276	0.8862	1.693	3
4	1.500	0.729	1.628	0.000	4.698	0.000	2.282	0.880	0.000	2.266	0.000	2.088	0.9213	2.059	4
5	1.342	0.577	1.427	0.000	4.918	0.000	2.114	0.864	0.000	2.089	0.000	1.964	0.9400	2.326	5
6	1.225	0.483	1.287	0.000	5.078	0.000	2.004	0.848	0.030	1.970	0.029	1.874	0.9515	2.534	6
7	1.134	0.419	1.182	0.204	5.204	0.076	1.924	0.833	0.118	1.882	0.113	1.806	0.9594	2.704	7
8	1.061	0.373	1.099	0.388	5.306	0.136	1.864	0.820	0.185	1.815	0.179	1.751	0.9650	2.847	8
9	1.000	0.337	1.032	0.547	5.393	0.184	1.816	0.808	0.239	1.761	0.232	1.707	0.9693	2.970	9
10	0.949	0.308	0.975	0.687	5.469	0.223	1.777	0.797	0.284	1.716	0.276	1.669	0.9727	3.078	10
11	0.905	0.285	0.927	0.811	5.535	0.256	1.744	0.787	0.321	1.679	0.313	1.637	0.9754	3.173	11
12	0.866	0.266	0.886	0.922	5.594	0.283	1.717	0.778	0.354	1.646	0.346	1.610	0.9776	3.258	12

n	Factors for $\overline{X}$ charts			Factors for R charts					Factors for S charts				Factors for center line		n
	A	A_2	A_3	D_1	D_2	D_3	D_4	d_3	B_3	B_4	B_5	B_6	c_4	d_2	
13	0.832	0.249	0.850	1.025	5.647	0.307	1.693	0.770	0.382	1.618	0.374	1.585	0.9794	3.336	13
14	0.802	0.235	0.817	1.118	5.696	0.328	1.672	0.763	0.406	1.594	0.399	1.563	0.9810	3.407	14
15	0.775	0.223	0.789	1.203	5.741	0.347	1.653	0.756	0.428	1.572	0.421	1.544	0.9823	3.472	15
16	0.750	0.212	0.763	1.282	5.782	0.363	1.637	0.750	0.448	1.552	0.440	1.526	0.9835	3.532	16
17	0.728	0.203	0.739	1.356	5.820	0.378	1.622	0.744	0.466	1.534	0.458	1.511	0.9845	3.588	17
18	0.707	0.194	0.718	1.424	5.856	0.391	1.608	0.739	0.482	1.518	0.475	1.496	0.9854	3.640	18
19	0.688	0.187	0.698	1.487	5.891	0.403	1.597	0.734	0.497	1.503	0.490	1.483	0.9862	3.689	19
20	0.671	0.180	0.680	1.549	5.921	0.415	1.585	0.729	0.510	1.490	0.504	1.470	0.9869	3.735	20
21	0.655	0.173	0.663	1.605	5.951	0.425	1.575	0.724	0.523	1.477	0.516	1.459	0.9876	3.778	21
22	0.640	0.167	0.647	1.659	5.979	0.434	1.566	0.720	0.534	1.466	0.528	1.448	0.9882	3.819	22
23	0.626	0.162	0.633	1.710	6.006	0.443	1.557	0.716	0.545	1.455	0.539	1.438	0.9887	3.858	23
24	0.612	0.157	0.619	1.759	6.031	0.451	1.548	0.712	0.555	1.445	0.549	1.429	0.9892	3.895	24
25	0.600	0.153	0.606	1.806	6.056	0.459	1.541	0.708	0.565	1.435	0.559	1.420	0.9896	3.931	25

APPENDIX D

DATA COLLECTION AND PLOTTING FORMS FOR ATTRIBUTES AND VARIABLES CONTROL CHARTS

To ensure that control chart data are easily collected and plotted, many companies have designed data collection and plotting forms. The forms provided here (one for variables control charts and one for attributes control charts) were developed and are copyrighted by Ford Motor Company. (They are reprinted with permission.) The reason for including Ford's version is that these charts provide adequate space (on the back) to document changes that occur in the process while the data are being collected. Remember, it is this process documentation that allows for better and more effective use of control charts.

Other useful features include:

1. Providing all equations that are necessary for calculating the control limits

2. Providing an abbreviated factors table

3. Providing action instructions when a process appears out-of-control

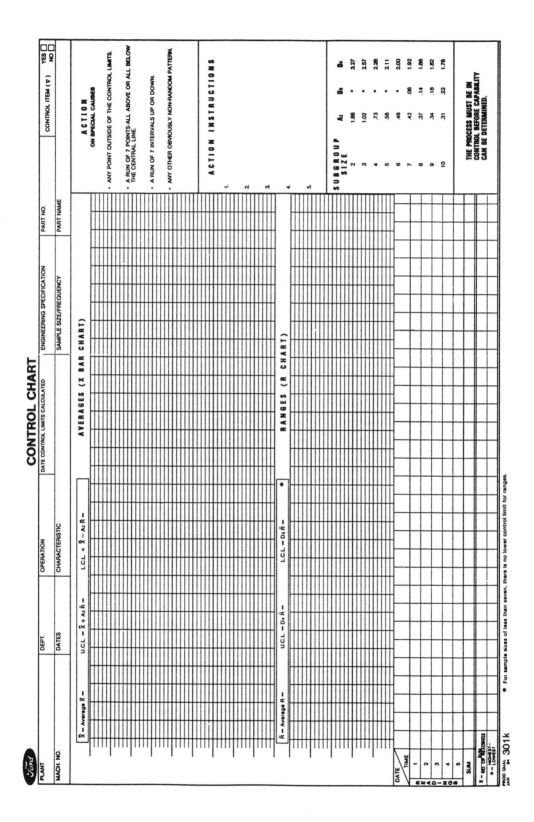

CONTROL CHART

PROCESS LOG SHEET

ANY **CHANGE** IN PEOPLE, MATERIALS, ENVIRONMENT, METHODS OR MACHINES SHOULD BE NOTED. THESE NOTES WILL HELP YOU TO TAKE CORRECTIVE ACTION WHEN SIGNALED BY THE CONTROL CHART.

DATE	TIME	COMMENTS

DATE	TIME	COMMENTS

PROD QUAL 301k (reverse)
APR 83

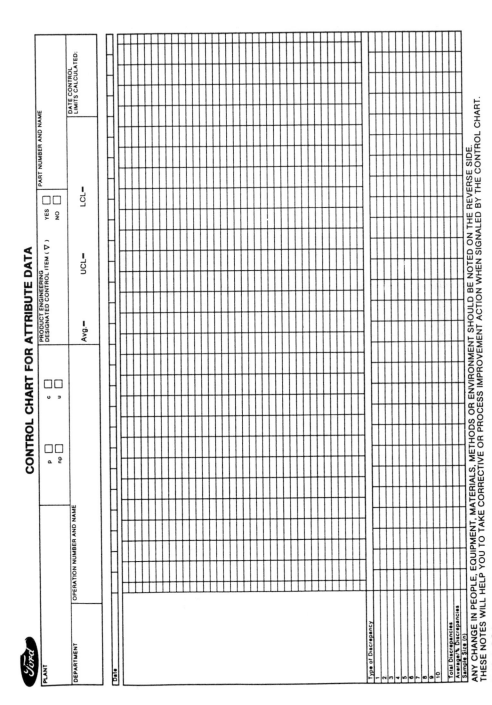

CONTROL CHART FOR ATTRIBUTE DATA

PLANT

PART NUMBER AND NAME

p ☐   c ☐
np ☐   u ☐

PRODUCT ENGINEERING
DESIGNATED CONTROL ITEM (▽)

YES ☐
NO ☐

DATE CONTROL
LIMITS CALCULATED:

DEPARTMENT

OPERATION NUMBER AND NAME

Avg.■   UCL■   LCL■

Date

Type of Discrepancy

1
2
3
4
5
6
7
8
9
10

Total Discrepancies
Average/% Discrepancies
Sample Size (n)

ANY CHANGE IN PEOPLE, EQUIPMENT, MATERIALS, METHODS OR ENVIRONMENT SHOULD BE NOTED ON THE REVERSE SIDE.
THESE NOTES WILL HELP YOU TO TAKE CORRECTIVE OR PROCESS IMPROVEMENT ACTION WHEN SIGNALED BY THE CONTROL CHART.

Prod Qual
Jan 84 **301c**

ATTRIBUTE CONTROL CHART FORMULAS

	Nonconforming Units	Nonconformities
Number	np Chart	c Chart

(Subgroup sizes must be equal.)

$$UCL_{np}, LCL_{np} = n\bar{p} \pm 3\sqrt{n\bar{p}\left(1 - \frac{n\bar{p}}{n}\right)}$$

$$UCL_c, LCL_c = \bar{c} \pm 3\sqrt{\bar{c}}$$

	p Chart	u Chart
Proportion		

(Subgroup sizes need not be equal.)

$$UCL_p, LCL_p = \bar{p} \pm 3\sqrt{\frac{\bar{p}(1-\bar{p})}{\bar{n}}}$$

$$UCL_u, LCL_u = \bar{u} \pm 3\sqrt{\frac{\bar{u}}{\bar{n}}}$$

DATE	TIME	COMMENTS

ACTION
On Special Causes

- Any Point Outside of the Control Limits

- A Run of 7 Points — All Above or All Below the Central Line

- A Run of 7 Intervals Up or Down.

- Any Other Obviously Non-Random Pattern

ACTION INSTRUCTIONS

1.

2.

3.

4.

5.

Prod Qual Jan 84 **301c** (reverse)

INDEX